Affective Spaces

AFFECTIVE SPACES

*The Cultural Politics of
Emotion in China*

SHIH-DIING LIU AND WEI SHI

EDINBURGH
University Press

Edinburgh University Press is one of the leading university presses in the UK. We publish academic books and journals in our selected subject areas across the humanities and social sciences, combining cutting-edge scholarship with high editorial and production values to produce academic works of lasting importance. For more information visit our website: edinburghuniversitypress.com

© Shih-Diing Liu and Wei Shi, 2024, 2025

Edinburgh University Press Ltd
13 Infirmary Street
Edinburgh EH1 1LT

First published in hardback by Edinburgh University Press 2024

Typeset in Sabon LT Pro
by Cheshire Typesetting Ltd, Cuddington

A CIP record for this book is available from the British Library

ISBN 978 1 3995 1826 0 (hardback)
ISBN 978 1 3995 1827 7 (paperback)
ISBN 978 1 3995 1828 4 (webready PDF)
ISBN 978 1 3995 1829 1 (epub)

The right of Shih- Diing Liu and Wei Shi to be identified as the authors of this work has been asserted in accordance with the Copyright, Designs and Patents Act 1988, and the Copyright and Related Rights Regulations 2003 (SI No. 2498).

Contents

Figures

Acknowledgements

This book was conceived between 2004 and 2008 when we came across the work by Chen Yingzhen, Chen Kuang-Hsing, Chantal Mouffe and Yuzo Mizoguchi. The original impetus was a 2008 article on emotional tensions across the Taiwan Strait. Since then, we have cultivated more ideas about this region's affect, emotions and politics. We are very grateful to Dr Ersev Ersoy at Edinburgh University Press for her excellent editorial advice and continual support throughout. Our appreciation to those with whom we have talked about affect and emotion and who offered various kinds of support during the writing of this book, including He Zhaotian, Michael Dutton, Stephen Duncombe, Chris Berry, Huang Yu, Ned Rossiter, Andrea Pia, Hsia Hsiao-Chuan, Anthony Fung and Ning Ying-Bin. Appreciation to Yi Lin, who invited us to give lecture series on affect and emotion at the School of Sociology and Anthropology, Xiamen University. The series generated stimulating discussions about 'feelings and society' from which this book has greatly benefited. We thank the Faculty of Social Sciences at the University of Macau for offering a stable environment in which to work amid the Covid challenge. We also extend our gratitude for the financial support provided by the Institute of Advanced Studies at the University of Macau. Thanks to our doctoral students, who help us stay curious and keep exploring – they have been creative and stimulating company during the years this book took shape. Li Zehua, Huang Anqi, Tan Yan and Wang Yichen offered outstanding assistance in preparing the final manuscript. A special thanks to the editorial team at Edinburgh University Press, especially Beatriz Lopez, Sarah Foyle and Camilla Rockwood, for their assistance and efficiency. Our heartfelt thanks to Yang Jie and the anonymous reviewers, who offered helpful feedback on an earlier draft. Thanks to our family for being around on this emotional journey.

Earlier versions of some chapters have appeared as follows, and we thank publishers for permission to reuse them here:

Shih-Diing Liu (2008), 'Undomesticated Hostilities: The Affective Space of Internet Chat Rooms across the Taiwan Strait', *positions*, 16:2, pp. 435–55 (Duke University Press, www.dukeupress.edu).

Wei Shi (2019), 'Fear as Political Dynamics: Chinese Peasant Workers' Struggle over Social Security', *Inter-Asia Cultural Studies*, 20:1, pp. 19–38 (Taylor and Francis Group, https://doi.org/10.1080/14 649373.2019.1576394).

Wei Shi (2019), '*Ten Years* and the Politics of Fear in Post-Umbrella Hong Kong', *Continuum: Journal of Media & Cultural Studies*, 33:1, pp. 105–18 (Taylor and Francis Group, https://doi.org/10 .1080/10304312.2018.1541164).

Wei Shi and Shih-Diing Liu (2020), 'Pride as Structure of Feeling: *Wolf Warrior II* and the National Subject of the Chinese Dream', *Chinese Journal of Communication*, 13:3, pp. 329–43 (Taylor and Francis Group, https://doi.org/10.1080/17544750.2019.163 5509).

Shih-Diing Liu and Wei Shi (2021), 'Why Is Reconciliation Impossible?', *Made in China Journal*, 6:3, pp. 127–32 (Australian National University Press, http://doi.org/10.22459/MIC.06.03.20 21.15).

Introduction:

Affective spaces in contemporary China

Love happens for a reason in this world. So does hatred.

Mao Zedong

Instead of thinking about politics as a place where we should all get together and try to find the rational solution – this is not what politics is about at all – politics needs to speak to people about their passions in order to mobilize them towards democratic designs.

Chantal Mouffe

THE PEOPLE FOUGHT BACK

Unprecedented protests against Covid restrictions and lockdowns erupted across China in November 2022. Because some young participants held up white sheets of paper to protest censorship, the protests were figuratively named the White Paper Movement, which soon became a symbol of defiance against Xi Jinping's rule and the Communist Party of China (hereafter CPC). Frustration, panic, hopelessness and discontent over excessive and arbitrary lockdowns by the government drove citizens to the street. China's stringent zero-Covid policy, driven by President Xi's zero tolerance for coronavirus, has produced deep emotional pain across the country. The regime has imposed widespread lockdowns nationwide in response to even a handful of positive tests. Since early 2020, strict mass testing, quarantines, surveillance and lockdowns have been implemented, with local governments mandated to act swiftly to curb any outbreaks. With the CPC holding its congress meeting in mid-October 2022, during which President Xi secured a precedent-breaking third term, local authorities imposed stricter Covid measures, placing many cities into partial or complete lockdown.

Political regimes 'need to encourage certain kinds of affect in order to reproduce politically over time' (Mihai 2014: 40). Since he came to power in 2013, Xi 'has been at work building an emboldened security state' (Greitens 2022). Xi has attached the zero-Covid policy to his legacy and framed the CPC's handling of Covid 'as a show of responsibility and stability and leadership in the world' (Kirby 2022). His regime has taken advantage of the pandemic at home and abroad to displace aversive sentiments towards the government's early missteps (Song and Liu 2022). At the beginning of Covid restrictions, citizens saw the government's measures as rational because they successfully kept infections relatively low. However, the initial feelings of triumph and security among the public faded as draconian lockdowns remained in place and continued to disrupt economic and social life. The lockdown measures created profound emotional turmoil and psychological impact as individuals across the country grappled with isolation, confinement and uncertainty. Negative emotions reached a boiling point after Xi was handed a third term as president, but there was no end to his stringent Covid policy. The seemingly perpetual zero-Covid restrictions had resulted in public sacrifice and tragedies of various kinds.

In China, the unnatural death of ordinary people can inflame the public, generate controversy and challenge state legitimacy, especially when the victim constitutes a symbol of injustice. Although the government always downplays deaths for which the state is responsible and prohibits unauthorised mourning, a defiant form of mourning nevertheless exists to express popular discontent (Liu 2019: 40–51). In this process, embodied feelings can be politically activated. The White Paper protests were initially prompted by a deadly fire in Ürümchi in Xinjiang, where residents had been under lockdown for months. People felt compassion for the victims and blamed the zero-Covid measures for the tragedy, leading to demands for an end to the policy. Public sympathy, combined with a growing sense of threat and outrage, immediately triggered candlelight vigils and demonstrations across major cities, unleashing 'an anger over whether China's promise – that its model protected the public – remained true' (Kirby 2022). Anger, on which politics is intensely organised and motivated (Ost 2004; Clarke et al. 2006a), was 'particularly strong among university students, many of whom have had their education severely disrupted and face challenging employment prospects upon graduation amid an economic downturn' (Economist

2

Intelligence 2022). Their anger is 'evidence of perceived injustice, and thus it gives people the impetus to engage in collective action in order to overcome this injustice' (Thompson 2006: 124).

The affective scale of the unpredictable protest caught the state by surprise. Unlike the dispersed, isolated and localised demonstrations of the past, this popular protest was staged across wide geographical locations and directed at central government policy at the national level. With the apparatus of mass censorship temporarily overwhelmed (Economist Intelligence 2022), diverse sectors of society participated in nationwide protests (Karl 2022) that spread across residential compounds and university campuses. These untypical protests, mainly led by the younger generation and involving people from various walks of life, undermined the CPC's authority by reallocating blame and raising doubts about its morality. Moral shocks can mobilise people to join protest actions and propel them to risks (Jasper 2006, 2014). The 'seemingly unthinkable ha[d] happened' as the sporadic protests 'morphed into a more general expression of opposition against the suffocating controls that the [CPC] ha[d] imposed on Chinese society' (Schell 2022). This outright, decentralised civil disobedience was the most extensive nationwide display of dissent in decades, 'arguably of a magnitude unseen in China since the Tiananmen Square protests of 1989' (Schuman 2022). By making the deadly fire and other trage-dies into problems of public morality, the protest was elevated to the most intense show of resistance to the CPC since Xi began his reign. Demands for government accountability, freedom and Xi's resigna-tion were chanted during the unusual outburst of anti-regime senti-ment, revealing a desire to be freed from the regime's tightening grip over all aspects of life. The counter-hegemonic blocs also revealed the limit to the reach of the CPC's power and the impossibility of fully disciplining the unruly bodies of the Chinese population, even under Xi's strongman rule.

The emotional tensions exhibited in these protests provide an opportunity for rethinking the cultural politics of affect and emotion. This rare occurrence was deeply emotional as the protesters sought to articulate 'several simultaneous but as yet uncoordinated social explosions of frustration, anger, anguish, and pent-up pain' (Karl 2022) for popular identity formation (Mouffe 2013). Erupting in circumstances where the CPC's heavy-handed and intrusive controls were framed as a major political achievement, the shared iconog-raphy of the white paper interpellated a new political subject that brought emotions into the public sphere. Through the performative naming of the signifier, these moral emotions, which were avoided in state-promoted narratives, fused as a political response to the excesses that the regime bred.[1] The growing level of discontent and the desire for a return to normal life was a catalyst to cultivate this political community of feeling because of emotion's triggering effect. The popular dissent ignited by the Ürümchi fire reveals the negative shared experiences of physical and emotional disruptions caused by the harsh Covid controls. These fluid and connective experiences are central to the hegemonic construction of a 'people' and a political frontier defining who 'our enemy' is. In this process, the political nodal points 'Ürümchi' and 'zero Covid' became the object of radical emotional investment:

> Diverse individuals connected their horror at the Ürümchi fire to a sense of shared suffering and a collective 'frame' that identified the political authorities as culpable. Lockdowns provided the focus around which multiple grievances coalesced. (Dale 2022)

Given the intensification of state surveillance and repression of civil society under Xi (Fu and Distelhorst 2018), the protests do not seem possible in the first place. The public mourning of the Ürümchi victims entailed a broad emotional resonance and contagion associated with injustice. Diverse emotions, which were condensed around the white paper as a political signifier that produced emptiness, played a central role in activating this popular defiance as frustration and discontent about stringent measures had been building up in urban areas. Since the pandemic outbreak, fear has become a dominant emotion that inadvertently established emotional bonds among the public. While the regime has sought to rule by fear and by confining people to their homes, it has nurtured negative feelings – such as unease, stress, anxiety, insecurity, fatigue, despair and panic – that translated into anti-CPC and anti-Xi Jinping protests. As the protests unfolded, popular feelings of scepticism, grievance and indignation combined and turned towards the authorities and their abuse of power, creating intense political anger that the state could not afford to ignore.[2] The CPC has always been fearful of cross-regional and cross-class protests. Because repression 'may sacrifice regime legitimacy' (Chen 2020: 657), the state does not always suppress those actions demanding policy changes (Yang 2023). After the protest, Xi acknowledged popular frustrations about pandemic controls to defuse the regime-threatening moral outrage. The state announced an abrupt reversal of policies and accelerated the reopening soon after the demonstrations. Some have observed that it was mainly local authorities' fear of punishment that led to the reckless implementation of zero-Covid controls *and* the end of the policy (De Groot 2022). The regime's selective accommodation of protesters' demands demonstrates the power of emotional resonance in creating a political space of constitution of a 'people'. Such a dynamic political process pushed the boundaries of what could be thought and felt within the hegemonic structure of feeling.

In such an antagonistic moment, the CPC's concession to protesters' demands resonates partly with its claim that it is responsive to the public mood (*The Economist* 2023). However, questions of how it engages with public displays of emotion and formulates the mechanism of passionate attachment remain underexplored. The emotional drama unfolding in the recent unrest illuminates the prevailing emotional logic of the broader political context of the geographic region. This book argues that emotions open up new ways of conceiving politics beyond China. Political matters, writes Laclau (2005: 249), 'are always highly charged with emotion' and affect is always required in political processes. Yet how do emotions 'work' to motivate different groupings to engage or disengage politically? How do emotions connect people, position individuals and collectives, and configure the public imagination? What emotions are permissible and who can express them in actual encounters? How do historical effects work on the social body and psyche? Today, everyday emotional dynamics can be felt in the workplace, cyberspace and the historical memories across the Taiwan Strait. Political passions can also be detected in a Chinese state-sponsored art exhibition, in a patriotic or dystopian film, and through virtual chats on social media. These practices, encounters and situations are not only emotionally motivated and charged but also gather enormous affective intensities that unite and divide people, shaping their bodily actions and attitudes towards others. Despite their divergent trajectories, emotions flow and circulate between individuals, groups and territories, articulate identities and fix them within structures of dominance.

Although this geographic region's political formations are laden with many emotions, they are poorly understood. This book seeks to turn emotions manifested in Chinese societies into the focus of critical enquiry. It fills the void by offering an account of how emotions – as driving forces and forms of sociality – intervene in political formation and hold the social body together in specific geohistorical contexts. Rather than treating emotions as merely psychological and individual reactions, we illustrate how they constitute contemporary social and political life and consolidate hegemony in various places across China. Instead of presenting a comprehensive overview of contemporary emotions in China, we are particularly interested in capturing an alternative way of understanding the politics of everyday life through the lens of emotions – including the mobilisation of revolutionary emotions in political movements, the desire of nationalism, the virtual affective space created by antagonistic identity politics, the subaltern body as a surface of emotion work, and the blurring of public–private divides on social media.

IMBRICATION OF AFFECT AND EMOTION

This book uses affect and emotion to understand Chinese politics. It makes its unique contribution by investigating how affect and emotion create a space of politics. Of particular interest for this book are the dynamics of political passions and the contexts from which emotional subjects engage in hegemonic struggles through the creation of various cultural forms.[3] In contemporary lifeworlds, many kinds of affective subjects, relations, sites, situations and strategies are central to formulating forms and spaces of politics. These practices and experiences could produce enormous psychic energy. With emotions becoming more conspicuous in public culture and work as a crucial cultural terrain for the construction of subjectivities (Harding and Pribram 2004, 2009; Grossberg 1988), this book seeks to capture a set of 'cultural feelings' and emotional experiences of social subjects (Huang 2020: 29).

This book takes up affect and emotion as conceptual tools and objects of enquiry. Although the two concepts, sometimes along with passion, are often used interchangeably in the relevant literature, their conceptual differences have received theoretical attention and are disputed between disciplines (Ahmed 2004: 17n7; Massumi 2002).[4] Despite the disagreement on the meanings of the two terms and their relations (Mouffe 2018), affect is typically viewed as instinctive, unconscious, immediate, biological, energetic, excessive and ephemeral, whereas emotion is cognitive, discursive, socially constructed, strategic and long-lasting (Stavrakakis 2007: 108n34; Harding and Pribram 2002; Watkins 2010: 279; Cho 2015: 44–5). Scholars inspired by the work of Brian Massumi and Lawrence Grossberg emphasise that affect as intensity is contentless, unassimilable, undomesticated, unpredictable, autonomous and asignifying because it is outside signifying operations and evades social consciousness. Emotion is theorised as a symbolic and narrative 'capture' of affect and the product of the latter's ideological mediation (Massumi 1996: 220; Grossberg 1992: 79–81).

The conceptual distinctions of affect and emotion refer to emotion's different biological and psychic components and indicate their different functions in political analysis. Affect can explain the *force*, while emotion can describe the *form* of political investment.[5] The emphasis on affect is illuminating in terms of reintroducing the biological into political analysis rather than simply taking it as a byproduct of meaning construction. It helps us make sense of the subtle non-representational dynamism that cannot be conflated with the general notion of emotion. Although we appreciate this distinction, this book does not seek to distinguish these terms as entirely different and mutually exclusive entities. Our purpose is more about understanding affect and emotion as interconnected and overlapping forces that transfix individual and collective bodies than treating them as separate categories. The emphasis on their ontological demarcation is insufficient and sometimes unnecessary when analysing concrete political actions. We wonder if the absolute disjuncture of affect/emotion can fully account for the actual political engagement. The differentiation of affect from emotion could be analytically counterproductive because it closes off the possibilities of their entanglement and mutual influence in actual political processes. The tendency to separate affect (or sensation in Sarah Ahmed's term) and emotion seems too narrow to capture their overlapping and imbrication in political practices. The separation, according to Ahmed,

> creates a distinction between recognition and 'direct' feeling, itself negates how that which is not consciously experienced may itself be mediated by past experiences. I am suggesting here that even seemingly direct responses actually evoke past histories, and that this process bypasses consciousness, through bodily memories. Sensations may not be about conscious recognition and naming, but this does not mean they are 'direct' in the sense of immediate. Further, emotions clearly involve sensations: this analytic distinction between sensation or affect and

emotion risks cutting emotions off from the lived experiences of being and having a body. (Ahmed 2004: 40n4)

Rather than operating independently, affect has to be channelled and mediated to produce emotional effects in the constitution of a specific political being. Affect as a theoretical category could be unanalysable and politically useless if separated from emotional performance (Paasonen et al. 2015: 5). An analysis of particular emotional constructions would not be convincing without acknowledging affect as 'the very essence of investment' (Laclau 2005: 115–16) that involves varying levels of energy (Grossberg 1992) and accumulates bodily memory (Watkins 2010). An economy or field of affect would be unintelligible without scrutinising how ideologies are internalised and naturalised by political regimes (Harding and Pribram 2004: 863). The overemphasis on their differences may fail to explain how particular social and political formations encompass the unmediated and the mediated, the short-lived and the persistent. Our analysis recognises the centrality of affect, emotion and passion[6] to politics without uniformly subscribing to a clear-cut distinction between them. Our purpose is not to deny their analytic distinctions but neither to fall into the dilemma between them. Since our interest lies in dealing with the manifestation of their practical inseparability and interdependence, these concepts are employed interchangeably to refer to the broad spectrum of emotional practices that link the individual to wider political processes (Starvakakis 2007: 184n2). The following sections provide a contextual introduction to how the notion of 'affective space' helps conceptualise their overlapping and interconnection as embodied in various emotional practices that organise political imaginations and motivate struggles.

THE TRANSFORMATION OF AFFECTIVE SPACE FROM MAO TO XI

So what exactly has been missing in most of our analyses, predictions and conclusions? As intellectuals, we overstated the political importance and explanatory force of processes of conscious deliberation and persuasion and we valued them much more than those of unconscious acceptance and obedience. We have generally stressed the content of ideological struggles and ignored the formal aspect of the 'identification–interpellation' loop. And even those of us who managed not to miss the symbolic foundations of hegemony have not always been alert to registering the way these formal foundations rely on the manipulation of emotion, on the mobilisation of transference, on processes of affective attachment and libidinal investment. (Stavrakakis 2007: 180)[7]

If we want to properly understand the way social individuals deploy their emotional desires and fantasies and acquire subjectivities, it is necessary to draw attention to the expressive, visual and inter-active forms of 'affective communication' (Grossberg 1997a: 156) and examine their functions for antagonistic constructions. How do popular culture and media offer a site of political intervention to construct us–them distinctions? Where are the spaces for the subject to cultivate affective bonds? How is private concern articulated with public events in ways not anticipated by authorities? How do cultural imaginations inform hegemonic discourses and offer sources of emotional conflict? We share Grossberg's view that 'the terrain of commercial popular culture is the primary space where affective relationships are articulated; and the consumer industries increasingly appeal not only to ideological consensus, but to the contemporary structures of affective needs and investments' (1992: 85). By taking culture into account, this book grasps the performative role of emotions in negotiating hegemonic relations. The affective component of politics produces a shared intensity predicated on libidinal energy permeating across geopolitical entities and the social body. Emotion's potential to spill over and create political effects makes hegemonic struggle possible.

Informed by such spatial thinking, this book formulates the concept of 'affective space' to outline the particular trajectories that constitute affective politics in contemporary China. The concept describes a distinct conception of affect as a spatial effect and a motivating force of identity formation in China, in contrast to the currently dominant, oversimplified way of thinking about China as a top-down political regime and authoritarianism. The construction of popular identity and a 'people' depends crucially on not only the linguistic production of meaning but the mobilisation of ideological affect and political passion in the psychological domains, which are interwoven in actual articulatory, signifying practices:

Affect is not something which exists on its own, independently of language ... 'discursive or hegemonic formations' ... would be unintelligible without the affective component. (This is a further proof ... of the inanity of dismissing emotional populist attachments in the name of an uncontaminable rationality.) So we can conclude that any social whole results from an indissociable articulation between signifying and affective dimensions. (Laclau 2005: 111)

In contemporary China, there are many different ways through which affects are deployed and performed as political resources.[8] We coin the notion of affective space precisely to address the one-sided account of China and to capture the complexity of historical moments. Compared to other explanations of political practices in terms of rational interests and opportunities, the affective space addresses the psychic dimension of political practices and the role that emotion plays in motivating the struggle for subjectivation (Bargetzs 2015: 588). In short, the concept helps distinguish the actually existing political processes from common Western assumptions about China. Attending to the concept allows us to understand social and geopolitical changes in contemporary China through the lens of cultural and psychological dispositions (Huang 2020: 25).

What, then, constitutes an affective space? What has affect got to do with space? The mutual configuration of affect and space in contemporary China can be identified by the following features and dispositions. First, *the affective space is an overdetermination of state politics, emotional governance and geopolitical transformations.* In response to specific political situations and needs, the resourceful and powerful state often deploys a wide range of emotional discourses, practices, institutions and techniques to construct political subjectivity, creating a pervasive, tremendous affective power in everyday life. In the affective space, the state actively produces, manages and mobilises emotions 'to construct a new popular vision of the nation and a new national popular' (Grossberg 2007: 198). Political regimes 'produce and regulate the subject through the constitution, organization and management of emotions' (Harding and Pribram 2002: 421) as routine practices. Here, emotions can be viewed as 'strategic formations' that encompass discourses, institutions and technologies (ibid. 413). If ideological affect is about 'how emotion governs people's conduct' (Harding and Pribram 2004: 880), in the post-1949 context, the consistent mobilisation of love for the leader and the ruling party, as well as hatred of enemies (both internal and external), provides a solid emotional basis for directing people's conduct, which is a key component of the party's hegemonic project.

10

Attention to the state's emotional project allows us to address the question of 'how subjects become *invested* in particular structures' (Ahmed 2004: 12) and why some sensations are cultivated. Through affective investment and its fixity, ideologies are internalised and naturalised (Grossberg 1992).[9] In Laclau's theorising, investment plays a central role in collective identification and mobilisation (Mihai 2014: 34), which 'requires a radical investment – that is, one that is not determinable a priori – and engagement in signifying games' (Laclau 2005: 71). For Mouffe:

> What is at stake in politics is the construction of political identities; this always entails an affective dimension, what Freud calls a libidinal investment. . . . This libidinal energy is malleable and can be oriented in multiple directions, producing different affects. The point is that it is important to realize that different forms of politics can foster different affective libidinal attachments. This helps us to refute the essentialist view that attributes given affects to specific social agents. (Mouffe 2018)

It is precisely the 'malleability' of affect that makes the state's emotional governance possible. The affective space is thus opened up by such investment and offers a key site for its sustained psychological operation: it is where subjects and others are invested in social and political norms (Ahmed 2004: 56; Demertzis 2013). Meanwhile, the space also affords a reverse operation – affective *disinvestment* – defined by 'attempts to weaken if not eliminate people's concern with particular sorts of issues and activities' (Grossberg 2007: 182). Geopolitical changes such as shifts in national strength and the transfer of sovereignty can initiate new emotional energies, dynamics and objects of investment, transforming the affective space's intensity and trajectory. Such psychic transformation is often crystallised in political arrangement, institutional regularity and cultural imaginaries, which seek to consolidate a link between individuals and national rejuvenation or produce alternative affective attachments.

The malleability of emotion leads to the second characteristic of the affective space: *it is created by an economy of situational emotional practices and passionate attachments performed by social subjects.* By economy, we mean the volume of emotional intensity and energy produced by the distribution of affect across social spaces and between bodies (Ahmed 2004: 45). The affective space, as an effect of the movement and circulation of emotions that create sociality (ibid. 8, 14), configures emotions as fluid, intersubjective processes

11

simultaneously part of the constitution of individuals and collectives (Harding and Pribram 2009: 15). Public displays of grief constitute a unique sensational moment of this kind. Such practices bring strangers together, articulate their relationships and hold the social body together. More crucially, they offer the individual a way of narrating personal experiences and desires that blurs the public–private divide and negotiate the hegemonic relation between state and society. This implies that the affective space is neither inherently consensual nor oppositional. Only if we recognise the economic nature of the affective space can we come to terms with various emotional practices in different situations.

The affective space consists of multiple emotional encounters and interactions animated by different beliefs, desires and life forms. It allows us to understand the interaction between culture and politics. The agents performing emotional practices are diverse across the contradictory terrain of the affective space, including the state. Despite its dominance in creating an economy of context-appropriate emotions, the state's emotional education does not go 'all the way down' to produce a perfectly transparent subject (Mihai 2014: 38). Instead, due to the irreducible antagonism in the split self, there are always politically inappropriate emotions and unpredictable passions that are oriented in different directions and thus do not entirely conform to state-led socialisation. This leads to contradictory economies in everyday life. For Grossberg (1997a: 159), affective economy can 'empower' difference, open up hegemonic and potentially disruptive moments and produce unintended consequences (Harding and Pribram 2009: 30) in the political scene. The affective space accommodates a wide range of libidinal subjects, elements, struggles and relationships that the state fails to absorb. These passionate attachments may be private and hidden from view or ambivalent and ironic in terms of their relations with the state, but they do offer a crucial site for articulating forms of collective dissent. Protest actions, for example, create an embodied, localised economy of anxiety, anger, frustration, fear and vulnerability felt by the participants, who turn physical settings into temporary sites of affective struggle 'that is being fought with affectively constituted tactics, for affectively defined stakes' (Grossberg 2007: 178). In this sense, the body in protest serves as a 'surface' of emotion work by evoking a constellation of feelings and creating affective impact.

12

Third, *the affective space is saturated with cultural imaginaries and emotional memories, often creating tension and conflict.* One of the reasons why the political landscape in this geopolitical area is emotionally tense is because of the coexistence of multiple structures of feeling among different subjects who, as invested with divergent cultural imaginaries and historical sentiments, consolidate their political boundaries (Yang 2014: 6) against perceived 'others'. The concept of the structure of feeling, initially formulated by Raymond Williams, refers to:

> complexes of emotional and related behaviors, operating at particular historical moments and sites, which participate in the processes of constituting and reproducing individual subjectivities, subcultural identities, and social communities. Structures of feeling as processes of mediation between the individual and the social occur in the context of socially organized affective economies imbued with power relations working towards the production and reproduction of various cultural practices. (Harding & Pribram 2004: 882)

Different emotional structures of feeling, as a product of broader cultural forces and historical processes, play out in political processes and give rise to entrenched tensions and conflicts. Structures of feeling produce 'sticky' emotions such as nationalist or nativist passions and inform contrastive cultural imaginations about us–them relations. The notion helps us detect how emotional subjectivities are reciprocally constituted (Harding and Pribram 2009).

The us–them distinction – which is fuelled by the libidinal instinct of aggressiveness (Mouffe 2013: 799) – is central to collective identity formation. The cultural imaginary refers to 'a result of the encounter between colonialism and local historical and cultural resources . . . [it] refers to an operating space within a social formation, in which the imaginary perception of the Other and self-understanding are articulated' (Chen 2010: 111). The cultural imaginary is accumulated over time and becomes a site of political tension. Through hegemonic articulation, the cultural imaginary can produce enormous psychic energy and reinforce the logic of othering by turning nationalism and nativism into hostility. This othering process requires establishing a 'frontier' and a 'friend/enemy' type of antagonistic division charged with passions and desires (Mouffe 1993). The antagonism between 'us' and 'them' is present in many kinds of social relations – as manifested in intergroup conflicts – and is irreducible:

The concept of antagonism is central because it postulates the existence of a radical negativity that impedes the totalization of society and forecloses the possibility of society beyond division and power. . . . To assert the ineradicability of antagonism requires acknowledging the impossibility of reaching a final ground, and instead recognizing the dimension of undecidability and of contingence that pervades every order. (Mouffe 2018)

Historical experiences such as colonialism, nationalism and nativism can produce antagonistic emotions and memories about selves and others. These emotionally charged memories work as a means of distinction and tighten existing boundaries. The obsession with these historical and cultural forces often leads to the attachment of signs to particular objects (Ahmed 2004) while producing mechanisms of exclusion (Bargetz 2015: 592) as a form of affective economy.

The notion of affective space precisely captures the complex and multifaceted nature of affective politics in China. It offers a novel approach to nationalist and nativist politics. The affective space, full of historical intensities and energy, shapes the political terrain through which various emotional subjects represent and perform themselves. It is not a singular space in an empirical sense but instead disseminated into and entwined with different social fields and hegemonic struggles in everyday life. It houses a range of widely felt, commonly shared emotions. Rather than limited to a set of ideologies, practices and institutions, it has a tendency and potentiality to cross the physical boundary, extending beyond any single locale, event or community by constituting a shared space of experience. It is amorphous and ever-shifting. As a platform and intervening entity facilitating identification processes, the affective space is a medium bridging subject and object, private and public, self and other. In this space, there is no strict separation between emotion and reason. By revealing the configuration of affective bonds, the concept of affective space illuminates the shifting disposition and distribution of passions that involve complex moral sensibilities, judgements and embodied practices central to the organisation of people's affective lives.

However, the affective space in contemporary China is a subject that has yet to be sufficiently studied (Yang 2014; Lee 2007). Understanding the radical potential of the affective space in channelling the ever-present emotions in identity construction is key to our enquiry. It entails a larger contextual question of how they are deployed and performed as political resources. This requires a register of major shifts in the transformation of the affective space. In what follows, we examine historically specific configurations of affective spaces that are identified by their relations with the state as an affective regime, their affinity with nationalist and nativist sentiments, and their mediation of lived experiences of displacement and rupture. How the transformation of collective emotional states plays out into the affective space needs to be historicised. How has China become a 'desiring nation-state' (Rofel 2007: 29)? We investigate the historical operation of the affective space, far from smooth and coherent but full of internal contradictions and struggles.

The 'total' affective space during the Mao era

The affective space during the Mao era was predominantly shaped by Maoist politicisation and its revolutionary structure of feeling. Since its inception, the CPC has put extensive effort into formulating emotional mobilisation tactics and psychoanalytical practices (Javed 2019: 260) for revolutionary action. 'Chinese history', writes Sorace (2019: 151), 'is replete with examples of the Communist Party asserting its control over people's affective lives.' After 1949, the affective space was defined by the state engineering of emotions (Liu 2010: 333) to create 'a new worldview and a new way of organising social relationships' (Lee 2019: 23). Affective investment has always been central to the communist creation of a new socialist, selfless individual. During the land reform, for example, the Communists stirred up emotions by encouraging 'public expressions of anger, fear, and shame' (Perry 2002: 112). Mao Zedong himself addressed the importance of harnessing emotional energy to revolutionary ends. The charismatic leader's name was symbolised as an object of love and identification, invested with 'the capacity of representing an absent fullness' (Sabsay 2020: 819). The love for Mao,[10] which stuck people together and was crucial to the formation of revolutionary identity, enforced a particular political ideal onto the affective space, translated his radical visions into concrete actions and energised popular participation (Perry 2002). The emphasis on ideology and culture can be seen as an attempt to enlarge the affective space and its political intensity dominated by the emerging total political state.

The affective space during this period was characterised by a synthesis of the total political state and society. The 'blurring of the lines between what would conventionally be termed state and civil society', claims Dutton (2008: 105), 'was not just a feature of the Maoist campaigns but of this politicized society generally'. For the party-state, emotion was not the private realm of the individual but a crucial mechanism for shaping a collective revolutionary body. During high socialism, the individual's private life was almost completely colonised by this all-consuming affective regime (Lee 2014: 9). The total state, concerned with generating popular enthusiasm for a new socialist subject, turned everyday language, bodies, family, schools, work units and government programmes into an all-encompassing affective regime. This process enabled the regime to exert 'affective sovereignty', meaning that 'the party-state claims sovereign jurisdiction over people's emotional life and that the party-state's sovereignty is revitalized through its extraction of affective energy' (Sorace 2019: 150). This regime 'channeled affective energy from the individual to the party organization, binding them together in the process' (ibid. 152). As a result, 'the sovereignty of the individual self' was severely undermined and its emotions were suppressed (Brown 2018: 1728).

The cultivation of socialist personhood was predominantly configured by the affective regime's manufacturing of antagonistic contradictions among the people, especially when capitalists and landlords had been eliminated and the revolution reached an impasse. Maoism 'attempted a Cultural Revolution as a means to develop machines of intensification' (Dutton 2019: 84). The identification and naming of 'class enemies' and the formulation of the friend/enemy distinction became crucial to the continuation of the revolution. The party-led popular indignation was 'organized around an intensification of the friend/enemy distinction' (Dutton 2008: 105). Mittler (2012: 347) indicates that the Mao era's class feelings were stimulated by name-calling – for example, 'revisionist', 'capitalist', 'slave-holder' and 'landlord' – through which the sense of class solidarity was consolidated. The affective space was imbued with a morally charged distinction between good and bad political subjects and the demonisation of class enemies (Liu 2010). Through the creation of the terrain of binary politics, the Maoist class struggle produced what Lee (2019: 28) calls 'tribal feelings' and resorted to a racialist logic:

> Like all things Maoist, class feeling needs to be grasped dialectically. On the one hand, it is comradely love for brothers and sisters from

one's class. It is a horizontal, fraternal feeling that extends equally to all members of the proletariat, but finds its most intense and sublime expression in the love for the supreme leader, Mao Zedong. On the other hand, it is hatred and resentment for the class enemy, usually belonging to the former propertied classes. (Lee 2019: 23)

The Maoist discourse sustained the emotional intensity of the affective space by associating the designated enemies with injury and 'us' with victimhood,[11] defining them as the source of failure to fulfil the revolutionary ideal. During the Cultural Revolution, 'emotion became the guiding force behind Chinese politics. Everyday life became a theatre' (Brown 2018: 4294). In the socialist affective community, individuals were constructed as 'a crusader with a mission, burning with rage and hatred against all enemies of the people' (Lee 2019: 25–6). The intensely emotional experiences of resentment created by these political movements were deeply felt and are still remembered by many who lived through the revolutionary era.

Mao once said, 'Love happens for a reason in this world. So does hatred.' To elicit politically appropriate emotions such as anger, rage, hate, revenge, sympathy and fear among ordinary people, the affective regime carried out extensive emotion work by creating various kinds of pedagogic situations in the form of big-character posters, mass meetings and campaign struggles, broadcasts, exhibits, schooling, drama performance, high-spirited genres of music and film, and everyday rituals. These pedagogic practices penetrated the social space for the construction of 'oppressed class subjects', where people 'showed great indignation in struggle meetings, cried during the ritual of speaking bitterness, sank into deep guilt and despair while writing confessions, experienced moments of ecstasy during the Great Leap Forward' (Liu 2010: 330). Moreover, pedagogic practices such as 'speaking bitterness' and accusation sessions were routinely organised at individual and group levels to raise emotions.[12] These practices aimed to configure 'a new structure of feeling' (Lee 2019: 23). However, the class struggle reached an impasse when the Maoist affective space was shrinking. When the revolutionary passion was increasingly exhausted and met with a growing sense of frustration and grievance, the regime struggled to channel the affective flow and sustain its ecstasy, leading to the dismantling of the revolutionary structure of feeling and the subsequent transformation of people's affective lives across the nation.

THE FRACTURING OF THE AFFECTIVE SPACE
SINCE DENG'S REFORM

The shrinkage of the Maoist affective space would entail a breakdown of the revolutionary emotional spectacle and a radical reconfiguration of how the emotional community was organised in the coming decades. The excessive political enmity and revolutionary zeal previously deemed essential to Maoist politicisation were increasingly delegitimised and demoralised as negative affect destructive to China's development. Since Mao's death, the socialist state 'has worked diligently to neutralize Mao's legacy and remove the people from the scene of politics' (Sorace 2019: 154). Revolutionary fervour was cooled off. A new form of emotional subjectivity was demanded in the face of the exhausted and frustrated society. There was a drive towards normalcy and a desperate 'disengagement from Mao's revolutionary utopia' (Zhang X. 2001: 324), leading to a new mode of emotional governance and a remaking of the self under Deng Xiaoping's reform policies, as Brown (2018: 1805) observes:

> In most accounts, reform and opening up from 1978 is seen as having impacts which were largely economic. What is less attended to is the very profound impact the changes from this period had on the psychology of the nation. Ideas, processes and a whole world-view were allowed space that subverted the selflessness and self-sacrifice in service of the CPC and elite leadership around Mao which had reached their peak in the Cultural Revolution.

When the Cultural Revolution ended, the political fantasy that had once elevated some class subjects over others was broken, replaced by the collective trauma of failing to live up to the revolutionary ideal incarnated by Mao. Despite the diminution of political intensity, public emotion remains the legitimating basis for a new social order. To motivate people's sense of hope and optimism, Deng's state would need to downplay the revolutionary sentiment while extracting different kinds of affective surplus and redistributing them differently for its legitimation. It began rebuilding the affective regime by reconstructing people's desires and inventing new emotional subjects and political-affective assemblages. Refocusing on economic development became the strategy of legitimation through which to accomplish this task:

By the mid-1970s, Chinese people were exhausted by the psycho-drama they had been unwittingly recruited into. The endless campaigns and the ups and downs of elite politics of the time, with one week's hero being the next week's arch villain, necessitated the need for a quieter era, one where the onus was on simply getting on with things, reconstructing the country, and living more quietly. No wonder that, for all its dryness, the elite leaders' neutral language of mechanical outputs and business was welcomed. (Brown 2018: 3772–6)

Deng's economic experiments, argues Rofel (2007: 7), 'initiated the process of creating "desiring China". Economic reform eventually entailed a rejection of collective enterprise, the gradual promotion of a market economy, and the steady move toward privatization.' The new regime would turn China into a desiring nation-state and produce numerous desiring individuals. At the heart of Deng's new modernisation project lay complex renegotiations of class, social and national identities against the restructuring of economic and political power.

The transition to the reform era highlighted a fundamental transformation of emotional dynamics concerning what to feel and how to feel (Huang 2020: 25) and its modes of affective distraction (Sorace 2019: 151). Since Deng's reform experiments, the previously 'total' affective space has been split up and saturated with multiple desires and desiring subjects that traverse the post-Mao landscape with their aspirations, dreams, hopes and frustrations. To appease the widespread discontent of the destructive consequence of class struggle, the new affective regime encouraged the active pursuit of individual self-interest and the discovery of new fields in the lifeworld, which satisfied the emotional and material needs previously suppressed during the Mao era. These tendencies would give rise to an array of fractured and dispersed affective spaces laden with different hopes *and* contradictions.

THE SUBALTERN AFFECTIVE SPACE

One consequence of Deng's economic reform has been the invention of a new labour subject who experiences radical marketisation and displacement as China is transformed into a world factory. High-speed growth has inspired dreams of success among rural youths and opened up distinct affective spaces of the subaltern class. The market economy and privatisation demand cheap labour supply from rural

19

areas, triggering a massive flow of rural migrants to the cities who desire to make a better living and a better future for their families. This new labour subject, whose rural body is individualised and disciplined for capitalist production, not only constitutes a core workforce for China's robust economic development but formulates a new form of emotional subjectivity radically different from that of the Mao era when state-sector workers were the 'masters of the country' and the leaders of the revolution (Pun 2005: 12). Their subaltern experiences are profoundly registered in emotional terms and cause physical insecurities.

This subaltern affective space is cultivated by the migratory experiences of hardships, suffering and grievances of their working lives on the move. Migration is 'an inherently uncertain process shaped by hopes and dreams, as well as feelings of fear and anxiety' (Pun and Qiu 2020: 620). These floating populations, many of whom are female, leaving their rural hometowns and exposed to market risk and uncertainty, have to cope with poor working conditions, exploitative exclusions and dispossession generated by market and state forces in post-Mao China. Their employment status is highly insecure and precarious: employers frequently violate labour contracts; market conditions are becoming more uncertain; their labouring bodies are vulnerable to the abusive production regime. Dislocated and uprooted from their traditional social networks, migrant workers are seen as second-class citizens by the urban government and are deprived of the right to reside in the city (Friedman 2014; Pun et al. 2010; Standing 2017). They are recognised as strangers and potential sources of disturbance who threaten to disgrace the city. Despite the desire to survive on the margin of the city, their aspirations are incessantly frustrated by unpleasant experiences of economic and social deprivation (Chan and Selden 2014). Suffering from heightened work pressure while lacking social protection, their transient and displaced working lives have entailed emotional upheavals and created 'feelings of being doubly subordinated by the market and the state' (Lee 2007: 200).

Bearing the stigma of being 'rural' (Zheng 2003: 151; Zhang L. 2001), migrant workers' emotional experiences are intensely conflictual and contested. Their emotional lives must cope with various kinds of discrimination and harassment (Goodman 2014) generated by social inequality. As strangers in the city, they face existential insecurity. Their subjectivity is marked by a mixture of acute emotional experiences of subordination associated with rural–urban disparities, disposability and the exploitative production regime (Lee and Friedman 2009). These emotional experiences include hope, loneliness, uncertainty, confusion, anxiety, depression, despair, injustice, insecurity, desperation, trauma, loss, anger, pain and powerlessness (Zheng 2012; Pun and Lu 2010; Becker 2014; Pun 2016; Pun and Qiu 2020).[13] As temporary sojourners, they 'experience spatial estrangement and alienation physically, emotionally, and spiritually. Given this, it is not surprising that nostalgia and homesickness for the native village have become such commonly expressed subaltern sentiments' (Sun 2014: 99). All these negative feelings circulate across their bodies and produce a culture of fear.

Fear, as an unpleasant form of intensity involving 'anticipation of a future injury' (Ahmed 2004: 47), is a dominant emotion in the subaltern affective space of contemporary China. Migrant workers' fear is displayed in different ways, including the fear of unemployment and the lack of social security; fear of exclusion; fear of sanctions and state repression; fear for the future; and fear about life chances. The sense of fear, as a negative apprehension of the future (Demertzis 2013), often bubbles into resentment and blame, causing uncontrollable bodily symptoms and traumatic effects.[14]

THE RISE OF AFFECTIVE PUBLICS

In removing many of the Maoist restrictions on self-expression, Deng's affective regime also unleashed a variety of emotions and produced numerous desiring individuals whose private concerns and personal experiences reshaped the ways emotional communities are formulated and the form of public engagement. The reform state has opened up more social spaces to explore different identities, producing citizens with wide-ranging aspirations and needs (Rofel 2007). With the radical reconfiguration of people's affective lives, the desiring individuals have sought multiple spaces to perform their emotional agency (Brown 2018). Although the state has continued to legitimise its rule by constructing positive feelings (Yang 2014), the shifting contexts provide individuals with more resources and opportunities to achieve emotional fulfilment. The post-Mao social conditions make possible the active pursuit of emotional experiences and self-expression. Emotionally charged conversations and interactions occur across different terrains of daily social spaces, blurring the private–public and personal–political divides. Public issues such as nationalism and public health crises are increasingly framed in personalised language and discourse. With the diffusion of digital communication, personal and emotional narratives can give rise to numerous issue-based 'affective publics' and produce temporary sites of contention that often contest state-approved structures of feeling. Through such practices, people use public events to reinterpret their lives and identities, where private experiences are interwoven with public concerns in ways not anticipated by authorities.

In China, the Internet constitutes a crucial site for popular affective investment and the formulation of emotional support, producing myriad sentiments about daily life situations and self-positioning. Social media, in particular, is widely deployed by individuals for the production, expression and dissemination of passions. Social media brings together individuals connected by common feelings. The emotional outpouring of personal experiences of social displacement and contradiction that are not in line with state narratives is often seen as a potential threat to regime legitimacy. The Chinese affective publics, enabled by networked media platforms, are characterised by social togetherness and solidarity (Papacharissi 2015). The unexpected public display of moral emotions such as sympathy, anger, sorrow and fear often generates a moment of dissent and political crisis, posing a challenge to state power.[15] Emotional antagonism and subtle critique often come into play in this process. Public outpourings of grief over shared loss and vulnerability, which call into question what and who is worthy of grief, open up debates about state accountability, problematise the official distribution of emotion and produce antagonistic intensity.[16] A politically subversive affective space is opened up when 'those who have been designated as ungrievable are grieved, and when their loss is not only felt as a loss, but becomes a symbol of the injustice of loss' (Ahmed 2004: 191–2). Through articulating a collective desire to speak out about the traumatic aspects of daily life, public mourning can translate grief into more politicised sentiments towards authorities and engender contentious actions. Such emotional practices are contagious and grow exponentially into massive affective flows, allowing public expression of the self in ways that often turn intimate narratives into a site of political statements without appearing overtly political. This ambivalence helps bypass state repression and disturbs the state's distribution of emotions.

THE INTENSIFICATION OF NATIONALIST FEELINGS

Although post-Mao China has focused its political energy mainly on economic development, nationalism, 'the leitmotif underlying twentieth-century Chinese politics' (Fewsmith 2008: 103), has remained one of the main emotional forces for the creation of the affective space. Nationalism is emotional because it cultivates 'a feeling of connection, belonging, and attachment to the collective body of the nation as well as detachment from those outside of or threatening the nation' (Militz and Schurr 2016: 55). Chinese nationalism is connected to moral sensibilities such as pride and shame. The formation of contemporary Chinese nationalism coincided with the invasion of Western power (Wong and Zheng 2000), which generated a shameful memory of national weakness and the ambitions to pursue autonomy, wealth and modernity. National humiliation and its resultant sense of insecurity 'is a key part of modern Chinese subjectivity' (Callahan 2004: 206). The lasting desire to make China 'strong and prosperous' and to join the club of great powers, as vividly expressed by such slogans as 'Backwardness incurs beatings by others' (*luohou jiuyao aida* 落后就要挨打) and 'Surpass Britain and catch up with the US' (*chaoying ganmei* 超英赶美), have always been a driving force of national development since the Maoist era (Chen 2016). It makes nationalism a dominant structure of feeling and the most powerful tool for constructing political subjectivity.

Building a powerful country that would never fall victim to foreign oppression and restoring China to its former status have always been the mission of all Chinese leaders (Brown 2018; Wang 2012). Since the Mao era, the party-state's channelling of affective flow has always involved formulating specific forms and narratives of nationalism as the basis of regime legitimacy (Dimitrov 2013). China's traumatic historical experiences of foreign oppression and national humiliation have been widely deployed to mobilise popular support. The Maoist regime, for example, emphasised the suffering of Chinese people during the twentieth century and sought to combine its nationalist visions with developmental goals to become a *daguo* (an important nation on the world scene 大国) (Song and Sigley 2000: 56). The deep-seated desire for the modern would continue to inscribe the nation as a love object (Ahmed 2004: 134) and produce ambivalent feelings about the national self.

The Deng regime's reconfiguration of its relationship with the outside world reshaped the contours of Chinese nationalism as it participated in the global reordering. In the wake of the chaos of the Cultural Revolution, the party had to fill the ideological void. 'The fundamental task of the Party-state since 1978', writes Guo (2004: 43), was 'modernization that primarily aims at national strength and national revival'. Paradoxically, the public mood, particularly that of college students and cultural elites, was predominantly pro-Western (Song and Sigley 2000: 62; Rosen 2010). While the West was 'regarded as [a] model for China to follow' (Wong and Zheng 2000: 325), the intensification of globalisation also caused 'insecurity and raises the question of identity' (Moisi 2009: 261). In such new geopolitical circumstances, China had to remake its identity to participate in the globalising process, to which nationalism can be seen as a response and resistance (Cheek 2006: 139; Wang X. 2003: 184; Hall 1996). During this period, nationalism was invested in the project of economic development:

> In the 1980s, China had adopted a cosmopolitan orientation, linking domestic reform with opening to the outside world. This did not mean that China was not nationalistic in this period, but rather that its nationalism was directed toward economic development and a critique of traditional socialism which impeded that development. (Fewsmith 2008: 103)

That is to say, on the surface Deng's reform was purely economic, depoliticising and obsessed with the West, the regime's desire to make China an economic *daguo* was imbued with the nationalist aspiration to revive its glory:

> 'Invigorating China' (*zhenxing zhonghua*) was probably the most popular political slogan in China in the 1980s. . . . 'Invigorating China' thus became Deng Xiaoping's favorite slogan and the mission statement for the CCP in this period of redefining its identity. After Jiang Zemin came into power, he used the word 'rejuvenation' (*fuxing*) to replace 'invigoration' (*zhenxing*). The new catch phrase was 'the great rejuvenation of the Chinese nation' (*zhonghua minzu de weida fuxing*) . . . the term rejuvenation refers to the psychological power contained in the concept of China's rise to its former superior world status. (Wang 2012: 2696–711)

The Tiananmen incident in 1989 was an intensely emotional event that redirected the affective flow of popular sentiment, with which the party had to find ways to regain popular support. In the wake of the event, Western sanctions 'were interpreted in official propaganda as anti-China. . . . The Communist regime repositioned itself as the representative of China's national interest and the defender of Chinese national pride' (Perry 2013: 8). As a result, the 1990s was marked by a resurgence of anti-Western nationalism encouraged by the party. The uncritical attitude towards the West was replaced by the pursuit of national interest (Rosen 2010). Popular publications and discourses critical of the West mushroomed (Wang H. 2003: 94–5; Zhang X. 2001). The collapse of the Soviet Union raised insecurities for the Chinese regime and provided a basis for the rise of anti-Western nationalism (Saich 2004: 93). Multiple factors pushed the rising tide of nationalism: the Taiwan Strait crisis in 1995–6, the handover of Hong Kong in 1997, and the bombing of the Chinese Embassy in Belgrade in 1999 allowed the state to engage with the public in a more emotional way (Wong and Zheng 2000; Guo 2004; Hughes 2006). The Jiang Zemin leadership then took advantage of the upsurge of nationalism to replace socialism as China's new ideology (Wang 2012: 2543–5).

The entry into the World Trade Organization can be seen as a turning point from which China's relationship with the world has become more complicated, mixing old desires and new emotional conflicts (Fewsmith 2008: 221). The dream and hope of regaining China's status and of standing on an equal footing with the West, observes Rofel (2007: 12), 'have motivated much of China's actions in the post-Cold War world'. Compared with Jiang, Hu Jintao, an advocate of China's 'peaceful rise', was even more enthusiastic about national rejuvenation and reunification with Taiwan (Wang 2012). His leadership actively promoted traditional culture and referred to the 'great revival of the Chinse nation' (Perry 2013: 6). Citizens were allowed to engage in nationalist protests. During his term, 'people's sense of security, identity, and emotional pride [was] linked to an idea of being Chinese' (Brown 2018: 2377). The history textbook controversy with Japan in 2005 and the boycott of Western products before the Beijing Olympic Games in 2008 further consolidated the nationalist energy. Despite concerted efforts to portray the party as the champion of the Chinese nation, capable of saving the country from past humiliations, the regime has found it increasingly difficult to control the outburst of nationalist sentiment against perceived enemies in Taiwan, Hong Kong, Japan and the West (Tismaneanu 2013).

The affective space opened up by nationalism has been further expanded since Xi Jinping came to power in 2013. Under his leadership, the growth of national wealth and strength has brought profound changes in how China feels about itself and the world, giving rise to a new emotional structure of feeling (Huang 2020). The Xi regime has created a new way of feeling the nation by advocating the utopian theme of the Chinese Dream, a political desire combining Xi's vision of China's future with emotions of pride, hope and aspiration for a better life:

> What is distinctive in the leadership of Xi Jinping is his double departure from the previous periods of political projects in China: first, the departure from Maoist China in which national slogans emphasized revolutionary sentiments and socialist spirits upholding the principle of equality and participation to liberate the working class and peasantry; and second, the deviation from Deng's regime which highlighted 'rationality' and 'practicality' to cultivate educated and technocratic elites in order to rebuild the modernization project in the reform period. (Pun and Qiu 2020: 623)

Compared to the former leadership, the Xi regime has successfully fused Maoist emotional dynamics with Deng's developmental vision. As a result, the nationalist feeling under Xi has become more positive, assertive and optimistic about China's national achievement, with Maoist surpass-speak being 'rejuvenated as a guide for the future' (Callahan 2019: 276). The new affective regime aims to energise and recruit nationalist emotions by cultivating a triumphalist sense of China's technological advancement and global influence, as well as maintaining 'loyalty to the party' (Pun and Qiu 2020: 624). Such affective investment has profoundly reshaped China's self-perception and the view of the world as China continues to grow into a great power on the world stage, creating not only an economy of desire and excitement but widespread sentiments of uneasiness, anxiety and fear within the region.

THE AFFECTIVE SPACE OF IDENTITY STRUGGLE

The affective space configured by the Xi regime and its disposition of nationalist passions has disseminated into broader geopolitical entities beyond mainland China. Paradoxically, the desire to make China a strong nation has caused tremendous insecurities and engendered antagonistic feelings. Instead of sharing in China's sense of success, pride and security, neighbouring regions and countries, despite their internal divisions, have increasingly dealt with their 'lack of enjoyment' by attributing it to China's national revival. The utopian fantasy of the Chinese Dream has entailed an unpredictable impact on the cultivation of the affective space.

What happened in Hong Kong in the past decades can shed light on this ongoing emotional tension. In the modern Chinese national imaginary, Hong Kong has always been an emotional symbol of colonial trauma and humiliation. The desire to reclaim the territory as part of China had run deep. The 'Hong Kong question' was one of modern China's most important national reunification concerns (Ren 2010: 28). Hong Kong's return was regarded as a critical moment of national salvation and a righteous ending to national shame originating from China's encounter with Western powers, which resulted in its loss of the Taiwan, Hong Kong and Macao territories (Brown 2018: 711–16). The termination of colonial rule coincided with the rise of China on the world scene. Although the Chinese government praised Hong Kong's return to the motherland as a renewal of national pride, it has not been the triumph of nationalism within the territory. The people of Hong Kong played a marginal role in the Sino-British negotiations, setting in motion a growing sense of crisis and a new affective struggle over identity and an unknown future (Abbas 1997; Ma 2018: 36). Among the various emotional reactions to the uncertainty of Hong Kong's prospects, worry and fear ran deep:

> Hidden fears of communist rule cropped up again and again in the course of negotiations over Hong Kong's future; indeed, the initial general reaction to China's insistence on resuming Hong Kong's sovereignty was one of fear. (Mathews et al. 2008: 43)

Hong Kong has a distinct identity and structure of feeling shaped by its colonial experiences. Although most of Hong Kong's population is ethnic Chinese, they are culturally different from mainlanders and have psychologically distanced themselves from mainlanders. With the reconfiguration of sovereignty, Hong Kong people had to remake their identities to participate in the 're-nationalization' process (Erni 2001). However, learning to become a nation is a contradictory and ambivalent emotional experience marked by uneasiness, frustration, expectation and disappointment. It also involves feelings of emotional displacement. In addition to the differences between 'capitalist' Hong Kong and 'socialist' China, both entities have divergent historical experiences that make the project of national reunification particularly challenging. Most Hong Kong people are immigrants fleeing political chaos in China and their descendants. Their cultural imaginary is 'bound by colonial identifications on the one hand and the nation-state on the other' (ibid. 398). Rather than characterising its colonial history as oppressive and shameful, Hong Kong's cultural imaginary has been predominantly pro-Western, while mainland China was seen as uncivilised and backward. Regarding political values, the idea of 'national identity' has always been ambiguous and accompanied by such negative emotions as suspicion, distrust and antagonism towards China (Mathews et al. 2008). Many locals were reluctant to return to China, preferring to 'identify themselves according to an image of the modern free world with which they associate the British, and they perceive China as a nation of backward, erratic, and violent politics' (Ng 2009: 31–2). During the handover, there was a strong sense of political powerlessness and dissatisfaction; the public mood was uncertain, restless and anxious (Mathews et al. 2008: 51). Despite Beijing's attempts to elicit optimistic feelings of excitement and pride, some have observed that the handover 'exacerbated Hong Kong people's conflicting emotions of love for and fear of the Chinese state' (Lo and Pang 2007: 351). The handover profoundly reconfigured how people perceived the local and the motherland emotionally. Despite official efforts to mobilise popular support, China's robust economic growth and national strength, as well as the resulting emotions of aspiration and hope, gave rise to mixed feelings among Hong Kong people. The handover also created intense experiences of identity displacement and rupture among local populations, stimulating a collective search for a more definite identity and reshaping people's affective lives in the postcolonial era.

Hong Kong's post-handover sequence of renationalisation has been marked by an intensification of emotional strain and conflict with mainland China, as unfulfilled political demands for universal suffrage are increasingly interwoven with identity and cultural issues (Law 2018). Politically, there have been growing concerns about Beijing's political control and the Hong Kong government's performance. Culturally, people are getting more anxious about losing their own distinct identity and way of life in the face of the growing interdependence of Hong Kong and the mainland. The co-presence of the state's recruitment of nationalism and Hong Kong's emerging interest in the local as a love object has created a site of cultural and political tension and contestation. Government initiatives to strengthen patriotism have been met with solid opposition (Cooper and Lam 2018). Since 2003, there has been growing discontent and enmity towards the Hong Kong and Beijing authorities and a rising consciousness of the need to preserve and defend local culture. Populist feelings of resentment, insecurity, depression and fear have converged into a new wave of nativism saturated with 'vengeful passion' against perceived 'others' (Ip 2017: 169). This surge of nativism, which draws a line of exclusion in identity politics, is resistant to state-sponsored political energy. The year 2008 was a turning point in the radicalisation of nativist emotions, which attempted 'to enforce real and imagined boundaries with China in urban spaces and the political scene' (Wang C. 2017: xii). When Xi came to power in 2013, nationalism was already losing its appeal among Hong Kong's younger generation, who had increasingly seen the Communist Party and mainlanders as the cause of Hong Kong's problems (Ma 2018: 48). Anti-China sentiments have fed the everyday affective politics of blame and stimulated the desire for Hong Kong independence, giving rise to emotional encounters with mainland tourists, shoppers, pregnant women, immigrants, parallel traders and students who are perceived as 'taking our city from us'. With the intensification of emotional antagonism, more and more nativist demands are made in the name of love (Huang 2020: 31). As a result of the cumulative effects of a series of affective disturbances, 'China' has been further established as a source of threat and a sign of injury. The affective experiences generated by these ongoing emotional confrontations have rendered the reconciliation between Hong Kong and mainland China difficult, if not impossible.

THE CHAPTERS

This book explores how affect and emotion create new ways of understanding Chinese politics from Mao Zedong to Xi Jinping. Reflecting our interest in the political formation under the CPC's affective regime, it focuses mainly on contemporary case studies, especially after 1949. The book is arranged into six chapters, each presenting original research in the form of a case study. What connects these studies is the substantive theme of affective struggle as part and parcel of the shifting conceptions of the political self in contemporary China. This book puts forward innovative analyses of Chinese state power and authority, nationalism and subaltern politics through the lens of emotion. It focuses on the *doing* of emotions and how everyday emotional practices contribute to political formation. We suggest that China's public cultural arenas – particularly the museum, film and cyberspace – are central to creating an affective space. Much of the work of bringing into existence an emotional subject takes place through engagements with public culture. Our analysis weaves together extensive research by drawing on public spectacles, events and narratives (of which affect is a constitutive aspect) deployed to invent emotional subjects and communities in specific historical and cultural processes.

The book presents a logical connection between the top-down and bottom-up perspectives.[17] Part I, 'Affective Investment through Art and Cinema', mainly focuses on cultural representations and their underlying structures of feeling. Part II, 'Body, Social Media, Affective Struggle', explores the affective spaces created by subaltern political expressions and social media participation. Part I features top-down emotional production. It deals with how political affects are produced and mediated by the Maoist artwork of the 1960s and contemporary political films advocating Chinese nationalism and Hong Kong nativism. The three chapters focus on affective regimes that produce political emotions in specific geopolitical contexts.

Chapter 1, 'Emotional sculptures', concerns the manifestations of the Communist Party's affective sovereignty. It investigates how emotions are motivated and articulated as part of a process of class struggle. It deals with the production and manipulation of revolutionary identities through the staging of psychodramas during the Mao era. How do we understand the revolutionary excess unleashed during political movements? How does the Maoist party-state elicit negative emotions? What emotional techniques and mechanisms are deployed in moments of political crisis? This chapter seeks to answer these questions by paying attention to the party-state's emotional practices. Its primary focus is on how the deployment and forms of sculptures housed in a landlord manor near Chengdu, *Shouzu Yuan* (收租院), became the most sensational socialist icon leading to the Cultural Revolution. We investigate the emotional politics formulated by this state-promoted artwork, particularly how it reinvents the political fantasy of class enemies by appealing to the aesthetic realm of sculpture. Our analysis draws upon an assortment of state-sponsored cultural practices and investigates how revolutionary sentiment is unleashed to create a new political person. This case provides an instance of how the political regime produces the subject through the organisation of emotions.

The following two chapters deal with manifestations of Chinese nationalism. Chapter 2, 'Enjoy the nation', focuses on the emotional energy of national pride articulated in the film *Wolf Warrior II* (*Zhan lang* 战狼) within the shifting geohistorical context of the Chinese Dream. The chapter contextualises how emotional subjects are shaped by and mediated through state-sanctioned media representations. Focusing on the psychic terrain articulated by the film, we analyse it as a surface of affective investment where nationalist feelings are activated to foreground the present emotional structures of feeling. We consider the shifting formation of Chinese nationalism and the psychic domains that produce a new desiring subject and motivate a sense of dignity. The chapter elucidates the affective politics of pride by comparing the films produced during the eras of Mao and Deng. We propose that the emerging national subjectivity of pride is an affective transformation and reinvention of previous nationalist fantasies in the new geopolitical context. The chapter illustrates how the Chinese Dream, through the operation of fantasy and enjoyment, is activated by empowering the insulted and outraged subject and by reordering the power hierarchy.

How are specific emotional trajectories formed and how do they operate as part of the broader nationalist context? In Chapter 3, 'The future as an injury', we consider the emotional impact of Chinese nationalism by focusing on the controversial political film *Ten Years*. We are interested in how specific emotions trigger imaginations about Hong Kong and China. This chapter investigates how the film articulates negative emotions such as frustration, depression, anger and hate against mainland China in the post-Umbrella Movement era. How is the collective sense of displacement felt by the people of Hong Kong articulated with competing public moods? Through the portrait of ordinary people's emotional experience of displacement and hardship in the face of Chinese encroachment into Hong Kong, *Ten Years* evokes a politics of fear as part of Hong Kong's rising nativism. China, as an affective signifier, is represented as a source of threat and danger, destroying Hong Kong people's way of life, culture and autonomy. We propose that the construction of

31

the injured subject is an emotional response to its being a historical object of nationalist desire and presents political dilemmas for the territory's future.

Part II, 'Body, Social Media, Affective Struggle', illustrates how bottom-up emotional struggles create affective spaces. It concerns embodied and online practices for creating affective spaces in China. The three chapters explore how ordinary people utilise their bodies and cyberspace to do politics. In addition to the emotional mediation of art and film, the body is also a crucial site for transmitting affects in China. Chapter 4, 'The body in fear', considers the emotional experience of subaltern groups by analysing an instance of factory occupation at a UNIQLO subcontractor in Shenzhen. Based on a fieldwork investigation conducted in 2015, the chapter focuses on the embodied struggle for social security staged by a group of peasant workers, exploring how their fears for the future are triggered and how their sense of insecurity turns them into a political force and reconfigures their emotional subjectivity in the face of extreme risk. Fear, alongside other emotions such as outrage, despair and hope, opens up possibilities for subaltern political practices during economic restructuring. The study traces the trajectory of their actions, specifically considering how embodied feelings become a site of struggle. We examine how fear binds peasant workers with company management and the state in their co-production of emotional subjectivity. The political subject formation in contemporary China occurs through bodily feelings, where the body is deployed as a medium of affective struggle.

Cyberspace is a place where nationalist energy proliferates and diffuses across borders. Chapter 5, 'Affective publics' encounter', continues to trace the manifestation of nationalist subjectivity by drawing upon heated political conversations among Taiwanese and mainland Chinese participants in online chat rooms. This chapter starts with a critique of the Habermasian conception of a rational public sphere. It demonstrates how these online chatroom users, who belong to different political regimes across the Taiwan Strait, engage with historical memories in their emotional encounters that are imbued with the imbrication of trauma, power and desire. In bringing their different historical experiences marked by divisive nationalist imaginaries into the dialogic zone, the participants create a shared, contestatory and fluid affective space of cybercommunication where shame and resentment constitute a central element of popular political expression. In this case, we can see how national-ism operates at the level of individuals and produces antagonism, division and conflict.

Chapter 6, 'The wailing wall', examines how personal narratives have prompted a temporary structure of feeling by investigating public displays of grief and sorrow – an old way of expressing dis-content and dissent in Chinese culture. This chapter focuses on the affective space created by the public mourning of Li Wenliang, a whistleblower who became known for raising awareness of early Covid-19 inflections in Wuhan. Having tried to warn about the coronavirus outbreak, Li was investigated for allegedly spreading rumours. His death sparked widespread sentiments. The study draws evidence from this emotional event to explore how the mourn-ing subject engages in this affective space to register a multitude of personal experiences that run counter to the state-promoted master narrative of fighting the pandemic. The research, which takes mes-sages posted online in response to Li's final blog entry as the focus of analysis, illustrates the complex emotional states that are intricately woven into the texture of daily life. Mourning as a public display of emotions involves specific power relations. Why do netizens share their most intimate feelings, concerns and experiences with strangers, and how can we understand the cultural and political implications of such mourning? This chapter analyses how blogging practices articulate contradictory experiences and emotional trajec-tories and how these emotions register netizens' self-concerns, lived experiences and emotional positions. We are particularly interested in how an affective public is formulated via the collective outpour-ing of sentiment. The study examines how social media engage-ment politicises the object of grief and creates a personal politics of mourning.

NOTES

1. On the shifting and mixed emotions towards Xi's zero-Covid policy and the White Paper protest, see Xiao (2022); Skopeliti (2022); Wang (2022); Karl (2022); Che and Chien (2022); Hessler (2022); and Schuman (2022).
2. On the primary role of emotion in motivating collective action in China, see Bondes and Schucher (2014); Ji (2016); and Tong (2015).
3. Mouffe (2013: 91–3) argues that 'the cultural terrain occupies a stra-tegic position because the production of affects plays an increasingly

important role . . . this terrain should constitute a crucial site of inter-vention for counter-hegemonic practices'.

4. For a review of the reconsideration of affect as opposed to emotion in cultural theory and cultural studies, see Harding and Pribram (2009: 16–17); Hemmings (2005: 548–9).

5. This point is inspired by the distinction between the force and form of affective investment in Laclau (2005). Unlike Massumi and Grossberg, Laclau argues that affect is not external to signification but 'an internal component of signification' (Glynos and Stavrakakis 2010: 235).

6. Mouffe (2018; Hackl 2014) distinguishes between passions and emo-tions, arguing that 'emotions are usually attached to individuals' while the term 'passion' can better 'underline the dimension of conflict' and 'suggest a confrontation between collective political identities'.

7. Stavrakakis's *The Lacanian Left* (2007) is a thought-provoking work that provides a sound theoretical source to formulate the main argu-ment of this book. We benefit from his brilliantly crafted critique of rationalist bias in the study of politics. His take on the crucial role of emotion in politics and the neglect of affect in the social sciences and humanities motivates us to fill the gap by examining the psychic dimen-sion that remains unaddressed in Chinese politics. Informed by his views about antagonism, our book speaks to the 'silences' in the field and addresses a more affective understanding of Chinese politics. The acute awareness of the political function of enjoyment will be further pursued in the following chapters.

8. The study of political emotions in China is not an entirely new field, as more scholars have explored the issue from various perspectives. Our review of the Chinese-language literature shows a growing interest in the intersection of emotions, protest and social media in recent years, so much so that some scholars call it an 'emotional turn' in Chinese studies. Yuan (2021: 69) offers an overview of the Chinese scholarship on social and political emotions through the lens of constructionism and emotional practice. He argues that emotions operate according to different socio-political logics in different 'fields'. The study of public emotions in China cannot be reduced to its social structures; instead, emotions are dynamic, interactive and situational (ibid. 58). He also addresses the function of emotional expression in evoking emotional experiences in China's new media spaces.

9. Perry's (2002: 11) critique of the absence of emotion in the scholarship of Chinese communism deserves a lengthy quote: 'Previous explana-tions of the Chinese Communist revolution have highlighted (variously) the role of ideology, organization, and/or social structure . . . Building upon pre-existing traditions of popular protest and political culture, the Communists systematized 'emotion work' as part of a conscious strat-

egy of psychological engineering. Attention to the emotional dimensions of mass mobilization was a key ingredient in the Communists' revolutionary victory . . . patterns of emotion work developed during the wartime years lived on in the People's Republic of China, shaping a succession of state-sponsored mass campaigns under Mao. Even in post-Mao China, this legacy continues to exert a powerful influence over the attitudes and actions of state authorities and ordinary citizens alike.'

10. Guo (2020: 47) indicates that during the Mao era, love became a political language at the expense of individual expressions, because 'valuing any aspects of private life, or personal or sexual relationships were considered bourgeois, and anything bourgeois was considered antagonistic in a socialist society . . . love as a spontaneous expression of individual emotions was heavily regulated during that time'.

11. For the personalisation of victimisation and its production of indignation, see Liu (2010).

12. Participants would articulate their accusations and share their experiences of suffering during these discussions as a technique of emotional mobilisation. This was a typical emotional practice deployed by the party to translate the revolutionary discourse into personal narratives and to exert peer pressure. These highly organised rituals constructed 'the old order as oppressive, inherently violent, and immoral by recalling instances of social antagonism between individuals who occupy very different positions within hierarchies of power in Chinese society' (Javed 2019: 258).

13. Some literary-minded young migrant workers have recorded these emotional experiences in the poem (Sun 2014).

14. Widespread fear, despair and discontent manifest in the recent mass exodus of Foxconn workers in Zhengzhou, the capital of Henan province and the iPhone manufacturing hub. Local authorities locked down one of its most populated districts in early October 2022. Foxconn, which hires about 300,000 workers in the city, has also placed restrictions on its assembly plants to comply with policies. The company has sought to maintain operations by implementing closed-loop measures locking workers inside the factory compound to minimise the outbreak's disruption to its peak production season. Under the bubble-like arrangement, indoor dining was closed. Workers' lives were restricted to the dorms and assembly plants (Shushangdemiaowu 2022; Koetse 2022). Nevertheless, closed-loop production has operated at the cost of deteriorating living conditions. The tightening of physical restrictions has triggered widespread bodily and emotional distress among the employees. Workers complained about the company's prioritising of production over safety and lack of food and medication amid worries

of infection spread (Li 2022; Deng 2022). The management chaos led to tens of thousands of workers escaping the facility. Since 29 October 2022, striking scenes of Foxconn workers trekking across fields laden with personal belongings and making their way down highways on foot have provoked a national outcry. In the next few days, dramatic photos and videos of escaping workers climbing over fences to flee the world's largest iPhone assembly site went viral in cyberspace. Amid censorship, Chinese social media were charged with shock, sorrow, sympathy and anger. People are confused about the contrast between the government's propaganda and the on-site information widely shared online. The lack of verified sources amplified uncertainty and insecurity. For a discussion of the accumulation of Foxconn workers' anger, see Karl (2022).

15. As zero Covid morphed into a contest between the state and society (Schuman 2022), social media served as a temporary site for facilitating horizontal affective connections on a global scale (Karl 2022). The reverberation of negative emotions created a fluid, dissensual affective space for outpouring criticism and personal experiences on platforms like WeChat and Weibo, eroding the state's popular approval for its measures without explicitly blaming central authorities. Such emotional practices were central to the proliferation of the White Paper struggle.

16. Power differentials result in different ways of distributing emotions. We draw on Ranciere's notion of the 'distribution of the sensible' and reframe it as the 'distribution of emotions' (Bargetz 2015: 580). This reconceptualisation allows us to not only capture the affective intensity of subaltern political subjects but also bring to light the governing through emotions. It is also through the distribution of emotions that the management of emotional states (Harding and Pribram 2002) becomes possible. Yet emotion is not simply an instrument of power. The distribution of emotions also 'builds upon the idea of equality among people' (Bargetz 2015: 592). Experiences of subordination or unfair treatment can stimulate the struggle for different distributions of emotions that have the potential to challenge the predominant order (Goodwin et al. 2001). The most common way is to trigger a moment of political dispute or formulate affective solidarity for those whose emotions are politically excluded (see Part II of this book).

17. A relational perspective is useful to bridge the two perspectives. Most emotions result from outcomes of social relations and interactions (Barbalet 2002). Emotion is relational in the sense that it always motivates relations among individuals as well as between individuals and social forces (Harding and Pribram 2004: 873). Emotion obtains meaning only in the reciprocal context of relations and interactions

(Burkitt 2002: 153; Barbalet 2002: 4). It always involves '(re)actions or relations of "towardness" or "awayness"' in relation to different objects (Ahmed 2004: 8). Such a relational view allows us to understand top-down and bottom-up productions of emotions as manifestations of different relations, reactions and interactions involved in political processes and struggles. The top-down and bottom-up perspectives can also be articulated by reference to the notion of the distribution of emotions. The following case study analysis demonstrates how emotions are distributed in different ways and produced by different agents.

PART I

Affective Investment through Art and Cinema

CHAPTER ONE

Emotional sculptures

On a sweltering afternoon in the summer of 2019, we visited the manor house of a former wealthy landlord, Liu Wencai (1887–1949), in Anren Town, Dayi County, 50km west of Chengdu (see Figure 1.1). The house, now a nationally ranked cultural relic, used to be a revolutionary museum and the display site of a 118-metre-long set of 114 life-sized clay figures made for class education (*jieji jiaoyu* 阶级教育)

Figure 1.1 Liu Wencai's manor house. Author photo, 26 July 2019.

41

purposes during the mid-1960s. The statues, designed for the specific location of the manor, consist of a set of dramatic scenes to narrate a story of class oppression in the 'old feudalistic society' before the communist Liberation. The sculpture series, which bears the title *Rent Collection Courtyard* (hereafter *Shouzu Yuan*), showcases how poor, starving tenant farmers were oppressed by Liu Wencai and reveals the exploitative process of rent extraction. The work highlights such pathetic figures as helpless elderly people, mothers and children to illustrate the cruel treatment of the Liu family. Overall, the sculptural scene is saturated with feelings of suffering, misery and horror under the exploitative landlord class. This politically inspired artwork did create a lasting emotional impact on us as viewers: we were startled by not only the vividness of the figures and the power of the visual form of storytelling, but the intensity of the political project that motivated the artistic production.

Many other visitors have had a similar viewing experience. The artwork also created a powerful emotional appeal across China in the 1960s and 1970s. A tour guide told us that in the old days, visitors would hit or spit at the statues to vent their anger. In terms of artistic achievement, *Shouzu Yuan*, which gives 'a social afterlife to things of the "old society"' (Ho and Li 2016: 6), is probably the most influential sculpture series that 'marked another heyday for art creation in the PRC' in the Mao era (Zheng 2008: 22; Erickson 2010: 126). When completed and opened to the public in 1965, it was 'an immediate success' and widely praised by the media, scholars and artists (Wu 2013: 146). During the Cultural Revolution (1966–76), the sculptures were 'hailed as an "artistic atom bomb", with replicas on display in major Chinese cities and copies sent abroad' (Ho and Li 2016: 4). It is 'one of the most iconic and most enduring exhibitions' in China (ibid. 6). At its peak, the exhibition attracted tens of thousands of viewers daily, receiving tens of millions of visitors in the Mao era. During the most heated years of Maoist movements, this artwork evoked intense emotions among its viewers. After it was first put on display, the public 'responded to the exhibit with hyperbolic enthusiasm, praising it as the supreme achievement of socialist art that was nourished by folk traditions and sublimated by communist ideology' (Lee 2014: 228).

Our visit to the manor – which used to be 'the arch symbol of the landlord class in the 1960s and 70s' (ibid. 198) – has prompted us to reconsider how such artistic practice could offer a strategic space where affective investment is made possible. In retrospect, the sculptural installation is a good illustration of the CPC's ambition to create a new political–cultural form to refashion the new socialist subject prior to the Cultural Revolution. It also represents the Maoist regime's purpose of achieving a 'unity between political theme and artistic form' (Galikowski 1998: 124). We are interested in understanding how the political use of art – as a form of propaganda – contributed to the work of emotion during the Mao era. If *Shouzu Yuan* is an artistic initiative taken by the socialist state, how is this cultural form articulated and invested by Maoist passionate politics? What political imaginary does it invent, and what psychological operations does it encourage? What roles do art and emotions play in Maoist cultural practices, and how do they constitute the kind of political subject favourable to the affective regime? How do they 'legitimize the regime and encourage participation in political movements?' (Ho 2018: 14). These are the main questions addressed in this chapter.

Propaganda plays a central role in post-1949 Chinese political culture. Yet propaganda needs to touch people's hearts and minds by evoking their emotional identifications and establishing attachments. How to move the mass audience in emotionally charged ways has always been crucial to the CPC's legitimacy to rule. Since its inception, the party has been known for its skilful manipulation of cultural symbols and rituals for political mobilisation. However, past scholarship on the CPC's politics has paid insufficient attention to the cultural and emotional dimension of mass mobilisation, particularly how 'the Communists systematised "emotion work" as part of a conscious strategy of psychological engineering' (Perry 2002: 111). The negligence of the centrality of culture and emotion to the organisation of state power has led to an inability to understand 'the complicated processes of manufacturing, disseminating, encountering, receiving, and appropriating the government's cultural forms' (Hung 2011: 5). If *Shouzu Yuan* serves as a model 'for shaping the postures, emotions, and spirit of its audiences' (Ho and Li 2016: 22) during the Mao era, the question of *how* it works to mobilise collective identity emotionally (Mouffe 2013) and frame public sentiments should not be overlooked. In the case of *Shouzu Yuan*, it is about cultivating passionate subjects that can join state-led political campaigns. This is why a cultural analysis is needed in order to examine 'how the Party systematically utilized culture as a propaganda tool' (Hung 2011: 5) and 'understand the power of the Cultural Revolution experience' (Clark 2008: 4). Hung (2011: 7), among others, calls for closer analytic attention to 'visual images, especially the regime's use of pictorials to manipulate public opinion'. Exhibitions and museums, which replaced traditional ritual spaces and became indispensable tools for class education from 1949 (Ho and Li 2016: 6), offer a crucial space for the visual articulation of public emotions. *Shouzu Yuan* did play a critical pedagogic role in this political sequence, yet its cultural meaning as a socialist emotional icon remains under-studied. We argue that propaganda requires complex and creative emotion work that must be closely scrutinised.

A cultural studies analysis of emotion focuses mainly on how emotions operate in constructing power relations and subjectivities in specific historic-political contexts (Harding and Pribram 2004: 864). Emotion is a constituent in the production of power through which identities become fixed within structures of dominance. It is 'the means by which social and cultural formations affect us' (Harding and Pribram 2009: 13). In this sense, emotion works like a technique or mechanism facilitating the constitution of political subjects. How, one may ask, does Maoist political formation affect people's social psyche through the work of emotion? What are specific moral sentiments permitted to express and experience? As a government-initiated political–cultural form (Hung 2011: 5) and precursor of the Cultural Revolution, *Shouzu Yuan* serves as a critical emotional organiser for exercising social and political control. We suggest that it offers a site for rethinking 'how emotions are constituted, experienced and managed . . . [as well as] the techniques and contexts in and through which the emotional subject is produced' (Harding and Pribram 2002: 407). Rather than taking *Shouzu Yuan* as a finished product of top-down propaganda, we see it as embodying a set of complex cultural practices that are deployed to reconfigure the popular imaginary and transform the structure of feeling of that period. The sculpture series, in short, symbolises the aestheticisation of politics as part of a broader discourse of class oppression and emancipation.

This chapter aims to investigate the affective investment engineered by the state-promoted artwork, particularly how it reinvents the political fantasy of class enemies by appealing to the aesthetic realm of sculpture. We take *Shouzu Yuan* as an emotionally charged visual text shaped by – while also shaping – Maoist passions. Our analysis begins with how Maoism gave rise to a distinctive style of ritualistic aesthetics as the engine of class struggle on a national level. Then we explore the artistic processes, practices and dispositions through which the class enemy was invested with emotional meanings. Through such analysis, we identify anger and hate – constituted mainly through the perception and feeling of threatening Others – as the two primary emotions that the Maoist state aestheticised as a means of organising the revolutionary community. We argue that the Maoist politics of purity proceeded primarily through the production and mobilisation of these two negative emotions among the populace. Anger and hate, we argue, offer a means through which individuals can recognise and constitute themselves as revolutionary subjects.

The Maoist intensities

Racialising class

Shouzu Yuan was initiated in the context of radical Maoist politicisation, which was characterised by an intensification of class struggle and incessant purges of reactionary class enemies. The Chinese Communists defined landlords as a class as early as 1922 (Wu 2013: 132). From 1949, class labels continued to be used to determine one's political status, even after the socialist transformation of industry and agriculture. Mao's 1962 affirmation that classes persisted and the 'bourgeois capitalist class' still sought to restore its power in socialist China paved the way for such campaigns as Four Cleanups and Socialist Education in the name of reversing 'ideological erosion' (Lee 2014: 198; Galikowski 1998: 120; Ho 2018: 143–4). In launching the two political movements that are widely seen as a precursor to the Cultural Revolution, Mao warned against 'the remnants of "feudalism" who hankered for "a change of sky" (*biantian*) and the new bourgeois elements bred by an entrenched bureaucracy' (Lee 2014: 197). Without class struggle, according to an official document in 1963, 'the landlords, the rich peasants, the counter-revolutionaries, the bad elements and the devils (*niugui sheshen*) would all come out; our comrades would do nothing about it, and many people would even resort to collusion without distinguishing friend from foe, and thereby allow the enemy to erode and invade, to divide and dissolve, to abduct and penetrate' (cited from Lee 2014: 197). By placing the class issue on the ideological agenda, Mao urged party members to 'raise our vigilance and properly educate our youth as well as the cadres, the masses, and the middle and basic level cadres' (cited from Ho 2018: 143). By the end of 1962, several provinces – including Sichuan, where *Shouzu Yuan* is located – started taking measures to reeducate the public with Mao's class ideology, which would lead to widespread condemnation and attacks on those labelled as 'revisionists' and 'enemies' across the country. Ironically, the labelling and purging of class enemies occurred in a context where landlords and capitalists had already been eliminated.

For Perry (2002: 122), most such struggle campaigns involved 'the manufacturing of subjectively defined class enemies', which were used to identify Mao's antagonists. The 'excessive political enmity' (Dutton 2008: 103) that unfolded during that period was partly a response to the crisis generated by the devastating catastrophe of the Great Leap Forward, causing widespread famine and death. The insecure regime had to 'address the loss of faith that lay behind peasant indifference and even unrest' (Clark 2008: 22). The Socialist Education Movement, for example, 'targeted particular kinds of cadre corruption – unclean work styles – while also attributing the reemergence of individual farming in the wake of the Great Leap to the erosion of socialism' (Ho 2018: 143). On the surface, the movement targeted local officials, and it was precisely through such rectification campaigns that Mao alluded to the threat of emerging enemies from within the party leadership (notably Liu Shaoqi, the then-second powerful leader of the CPC). With politics being reduced to the doctrine of class singularity, the definition and criteria for class identity as a moral-political category were expanded, and Mao's exhortation 'Never forget class struggle' served as a means of suppressing opposition and reconsolidating state power.[1] As a response to perceived internal threats, the political function of class labels was to forge an 'imagined alliance' between old and new class enemies (Ho 2018: 143) and define them as a problem for the 'purity' of a socialist nation. As such, threatening and unwanted Others must be identified, blamed and eliminated from the social body. Such an exclusive form of class politics works through *othering* and the moral logic of good vs evil. The logic 'works to create a distinction between those who are "under threat" and those who threaten' (Ahmed 2004: 72). It is characterised by an 'obsession with purity' and 'a principle of exclusion' (Lee 2014: 207, 202):

Class racism was the internal supplement of communist nationalism, not its ugly antithesis. In racializing social classes, it supplied a fictive ethnic basis for the socialist nation. Its mechanisms of exclusion and denigration resembled those of the more common strand of racism accompanied by biological theories. (Lee 2014: 236)

The essentialising of class identity, which evokes tribal feelings and resorts to a racialist logic (Lee 2019: 28), dictates whose bodies and lives belong to the people-nation and should be maintained while reducing those classified as unpeople to subhuman states. Mao's political project, to borrow Badiou's (2006: 215) description of Nazi fascism, was to create 'a completely imaginary "new man", by means of the very real eradication of all those who are alleged to represent the "old man", which is once again completely imaginary'. In *Shouzu Yuan*, the figure of Liu Wencai was meant to symbolise this 'old man'.

Producing enmity

'Identifying enemies and mobilizing emotions against those enemies', writes Ost (2005: 23), 'is the way that political leaders get citizens to do what these political leaders want them to do . . . to use Carl Schmitt's language, getting citizens to accept *your* friend-enemy dichotomy.' The reinvention of the Maoist friend/enemy distinction would not have been possible without mass mobilisation in consciousness and feeling. Mao was preoccupied with the function of ideology and culture in revolution (Žižek 2007: 7; Perry 2002: 121), believing that class struggle 'was fundamentally a battle for the correct ideologies and ultimate transformation of Chinese culture' (Hung 2011: 2). One crucial mechanism of Maoist mobilisation was 'cultivating beliefs through propagating revolutionary discourses' (Liu 2010: 329). Dutton (2008: 100) indicates that Maoist revolutionary campaigns 'are based on enmity produced and harnessed by an affective community that defines itself in terms of what it is not'. The campaign-style politics, which was carried out by all-pervasive propaganda apparatuses and systems of control, aimed at motivating the masses to follow along the Maoist line and sustaining the emotional intensity. The successive Socialist Education campaigns were mounted to construct ideological narratives of class oppression for cadres and the masses, and 'engage in comparing the past and the present, arouse "class feeling" (*jieji ganqing*), and stimulate consciousness' (Ho 2018: 144). Through the 'recreation and repetition of the ruling regime's master narrative' (Hung 2011: 6), the propaganda state could manipulate the interpretation of modern Chinese history and 'create new facts' (Ost 2004: 231). Its psychological manipulation had to rely on 'eliciting appropriate emotions' (Liu 2010: 330) and the formulation of specific 'communities of feeling' (Berezin 2002: 43) for revolutionary causes.

Emotions such as anger, hate and a sense of victimhood play a central role in the production of political belief. They work by attributing the injury of subordination to some targets. The heightened class rhetoric during the 1950s and 1960s defined what ought to be the masses' primary object of emotional investment and loyalty. Scholars observe that the CPC-led land reform focused on 'the catalytic role of fear, grief, rage and revenge in energising the course of popular participation. Appeals to sentiments of fairness (*gongping*) also figured centrally in the process' (Perry 2002: 115). It was through formulating a 'socialist grammar of emotion' (Lee 2019: 23) that moral sentiments were incorporated into state governance and became its strategic resources. As Dutton (2008: 104) writes:

> what Maoism offered, through endless life and death campaign struggles, was a reification of the binary form of political understanding that then came to form and forge the template of a very particular mentality of government. That, in turn, was designed to 'touch people to their very souls' and produce an ontology of (revolutionary) life. This was then structured into the considerations of government and the structures of the state.

The party had strategically employed various emotion-raising techniques and psychological mechanisms to direct political conduct and build a sense of solidarity against the 'constitutive outside' (Mouffe 1993: 141). The name-calling of 'capitalist roader', 'landlord' and 'revisionist' is to 'stimulate hate and fear and at the same time to create "empty signifiers" into which people could project whatever they wished' (Mittler 2012: 374). Slogans such as 'Don't forget class bitterness! Remember blood-and-tears hatred!' and 'Down with the evil tyrant landlord, a blood debt must be repaid in blood' were created to instigate moral indignation and constitute a victimised subject. Sustained by the friend/enemy distinction, the dualism of good vs evil marks the boundaries of morality (Ost 2004: 239), defining who does not have the right to life.

Recalling/speaking bitterness as an emotional technique

In order to arouse negative emotions against perceived enemies, the CPC deployed dramatic propaganda techniques and ritualistic practices as strategic resources that created distinctive patterns of revolutionary mobilisation under Mao. Rituals are 'formalized manifestations of emotion' (Berezin 2002: 44) and 'collective means of emotional communication, ways of formalizing shared feelings . . . Rituals possess sensuous, aesthetic qualities, drawing people into collective performances where bodies are meaningfully active together' (Barker 2001: 188). The repetition of ritual participation, through which political beliefs are born (Žižek 1994), could consolidate a sense of solidarity and blur the boundary between self and nation-state (Berezin 2002: 44, 84). One foremost mechanism of Maoist emotional production is encouraging public expressions of emotions (Perry 2002: 112), such as pain and anger entailed by suffering through various ritualistic forms of popular participation, notably accusation (*kongsu* 控诉), struggle (*douzheng* 斗争) and speaking bitterness (*suku* 诉苦) meetings. The dramatisation of pain characterises these rituals. *Suku* is 'the public expression of an individual's woes with the intent to cultivate sympathy toward the speaker and outrage against those who caused his or her suffering' (Javed 2019: 257). Combining traditional cultural forms of storytelling and the perspective of the injured, these emotional practices 'used individual instances of landlord malfeasance to elicit outrage and establish hostility towards landlords as a group' (ibid. 258–9). The emotional energy of such rituals was generated by the authentic voice of *kuzhu* (the aggrieved 苦主) against their alleged oppressors and often involved a high degree of bodily engagement: participants (usually villagers, peasants or workers) spoke about their tales of past hardship, cruelty and injustice of the evil old society before audiences, who often 'showed great indignation in struggle meetings, cried during the ritual of speaking bitterness' (Liu 2010: 330). In some meetings, the audiences 'ate "bitterness meals" and inspected artefacts that accompanied such narratives: a begging gourd, a ragged blanket, and even scars on the storytellers' bodies' (Ho and Li 2016: 11).

As a public performance that relates class ideology to people's lived experiences, *suku* and its similar practice 'recalling (past) bitterness and reflecting on (present) sweetness' (*yiku sitian* 忆苦思甜) were widely deployed during the land reform and Socialist Education campaigns. The CPC's preoccupation with *suku* and *yiku sitian* 'illustrates its utility as a tool of ingroup consolidation for mobilising outrage and violence ... [and] shows how the Party used it to ... forge a violent hatred of internal "class enemies" ... these stories were designed to conform to generic narratives of suffering that could trigger the righteous indignation of soldiers before battle' (ibid. 259).

Exhibiting bitterness

Shouzu Yuan can be seen as a different propaganda genre of recalling bitterness that is based on a more visually powerful pattern of emotional mobilisation. It incorporates the ethics of expressing bitterness publicly but harnesses its emotional energy to another level and scale. The design of *Shouzu Yuan* was intended to create a new form of *suku* as a means of distracting public attention from the consequence of the Great Leap campaigns:

> The Landlord Manor Museum presented a microcosm of the 'old society', in which viewers were exhorted to imagine innumerable Liu Wencais and victims, and in mothers represented by Luo Erniang or a clay figure, their own. It became especially important to 'speak bitterness' about the pre-Liberation past following the Great Leap Forward and the worst man-made famine in history. Between 1957 and 1961, in the surrounding Dayi county, official estimates show that the population decreased by 65,170 people, or almost one in five. .... Grain production had fallen by half, so that the new society had produced its own orphans. .... In the wake of famine and all over China, the impetus to depict the 'old society' in all of its evils intensified. (Ho and Li 2016: 11)

Compared to the performative rituals of *suku* and *yiku sitian*, which are largely confined to small-group meetings and a limited number of local participants, *Shouzu Yuan* creates a different way of condemning the past and instigating class feelings. First, it focuses on a historicised archetype and tells the pitiful story of pre-1949 peasants through the mythical symbolisation of Liu Wencai as a figure of the old oppressive society. By reconstructing the scenes of Liu's rent extraction from peasants, this work renders him a master symbol of the exploitative class and an object of revolutionary investment (see Figure 1.2). As such, Liu's tale provided a 'script' for the broader articulation of class politics across the country. Second, *Shouzu Yuan*

Figure 1.2 The heavy load of rent grain is a symbol of the exploitative class. From Foreign Languages Press (1968), *Rent collection courtyard*.

tells the story visually. Before they took power, the Communists already 'understood that if they wanted to draw the widest popular support, they would have to rely on vehicles other than scripts and writings, especially in a land with high illiteracy' (Hung 2011: 13). One of the means was 'the manipulation of visual images for propaganda purposes' (ibid. 4). *Shouzu Yuan* turns the personalised narratives of suffering into visual storytelling that could be more appealing to a broader public. Third, it raises class emotions by showcasing the natural setting and artefacts of local peasants and the landlord class, which encourages 'visitors to recall their own bitterness' (Ho 2018: 16). The exhibition of Liu's possessions and the extraction tools, as part of an emerging socialist 'exhibitionary culture' at that time, offers 'living teaching materials' (ibid. 149) for class education purposes.

Exhibitions on class struggle were ubiquitous during the Socialist Education campaigns, while *Shouzu Yuan* was probably the most spectacular and famous one. The sculpture series is a unique genre of public display 'mounted by all units, from the village to the city, from the school to the factory' (ibid. 139). Informed by Mao's insistence on the importance of popular involvement in the revolution, the installation stirred up passion by way of a different kind of emotional engagement:

> Intended for the masses, such exhibitions were didactic and visits were ritualistic; the *jiezhan* [class education exhibition] was deemed a classroom for class education. Involving the masses in curation, incorporating the familiar routine of *yiku sitian*, and using objects as lessons, the class education exhibition fulfilled the requirement that propaganda be 'living'. Like the omnipresent history displays that sprang up during the Great Leap Forward, the genre was intensely local. (Ho 2018: 141–2)

By combining traditional storytelling and drama techniques, *Shouzu Yuan* represents a participatory form of propaganda involving not only historical narratives, curation and personal accounts but also the participation of docents and visitors (ibid. 13) in the collective production of class feelings. Altogether these factors turn the exhibition into a 'classroom'. But Ho and Li (2016: 13–14) argue that *Shouzu Yuan* works more like a temple for the regime 'to redirect grievances toward scapegoats in the wake of its catastrophe, and to convince the population that the Communist state was still their one and only savior'.

Shouzu Yuan as a political text

Sculpture as a vehicle of political emotions

Art and emotion are 'inextricably linked' (Hjort and Laver 1997: 3). In the context of Maoist China, the CPC was characterised by skilful manipulation of artwork to turn emotions into art and evoke an emotional response in the viewers. The party knows that history is best told visually (Wu 2013: 132) without requiring the audience to wrestle with complex ideas. By reducing complex political ideas to visually expressive symbols, the artwork compels politically correct emotions by telling a story quickly and dramatically. It enables the regime to showcase different class sentiments and sustain the class struggle.

Sculptures uniquely capture emotion with a focus on the human body (Robinson 2005: 284). Heavily laden with emotions, *Shouzu Yuan* exhibits feelings of political tension and conveys the emotional aura of the figures intended by the state. By combining bodily gestures, facial features and expressive scenes of landlord exploitation, the sculpture creates an 'empathetic simulation' (Hjort and Laver 1997: 4) of the fictional characters' emotional states by weaving their postures, action tendencies and behaviours into a coherent narrative: 'While the individual statues were in the socialist realist, public-hero mould, the idea of a whole suite of statues in one place narrating a story was a new concept' (Clark 2008: 205–6).

State-led collaboration

Art during the Mao era expressed the CPC's political will. With the CPC's monopoly on history writing (Hung 2011: 14), the artistic team was concerned with showcasing official interpretations of history by 'condensing the entire story of the "old society" into the story of Liu Wencai' (Wu 2013: 147). It needed to make an emotional scene and script the revolutionary sentiments desired by the authorities. *Shouzu Yuan* is the product of 'a state-controlled network of cultural production, distribution, education, museumification, and of its foreign propaganda' (ibid. 159). The state played a leading role in orchestrating the creation of the exhibition:

> Between August and September of 1958, the central government's Ministry of Culture convened two conferences on antiquities and museums in Zhengzhou and Hefei; the resolution passed in the conferences called for campaigns of 'establishing museums in every county' and 'establishing an exhibit room in every village'. The Bureau of Culture of Sichuan Province, in its own directive, decided that because the big landlord Liu Wencai of Dayi County was very prominent in exploiting and oppressing peasants, his manor should be preserved and transformed into a museum. In October of that year, the Party Committee of Dayi announced the formation of a preparatory committee to construct the museum. (Wu 2013: 140–1)

In 1959, Liu Wencai's manor house was converted into an exhibition space for the first time as a response to the call of the Ministry of Culture to create museums across the country. Before the definitive 1965 version, the exhibition had undergone several rounds of revision since the Great Leap Forward, featuring Liu's material artefacts and smaller sets of clay figures on a similar theme (Erickson 2010: 124–6). To make the display more engaging, during the heightened climate of the Socialist Education campaign, some local officials came up with the idea of recreating scenes of peasants' payment of rent (Lee 2014: 219). The cultural bureaucrats mobilised local folk artists, schoolteachers and opera actors and also formulated investigative teams to collect materials and interview former tenants of Liu Wencai (Wu 2013: 146–7). According to investigative journalist Xiaoshu, during the planning stage of the creation:

> The Sichuan Provincial Culture Bureau laid down the principles of artistic creation: the sculptures should represent the miserable life of the peasants, but also their unyielding rebellion; they should demonstrate the viciousness and cruelty of landlords, but also their fears and vulnerabilities; class struggle in the old society should be the thematic keynote. (Wu 2013: 146–7)

In order to accomplish the project before the National Day celebration, the authorities asked a group of teachers and students at the Department of Sculpture, Sichuan Academy of Art, for assistance.[2] The professional artists and craftsmen started brainstorming collectively to maximise the political impact of the sculptures. After the state approved the fourth draft, the artists completed the work just in time for National Day.

Socialist realism with Chinese characteristics

The curators and artists used the dramatic techniques, cultural materials and symbols available to them. Two visual strategies were employed to increase the emotional appeal of the statues. First, to increase the story's authenticity and make visual storytelling more credible and persuasive, the exhibition is established in the residence of Liu Wencai. It relies heavily on real-life artefacts as object lessons. *Shouzu Yuan* features the original house and other personal possessions as proof of Liu Wencai's class status and luxurious lifestyle before the Liberation. As Ho (2018: 17) writes, 'objects offered a tangible authenticity that allowed possessions also to become proof'. However, the goal of *Shouzu Yuan* is not to tell an empirical truth, but a 'higher, ideological Truth' (Lee 2014: 220).[3] These objects include instruments allegedly used by Liu to exploit and torture the poor, such as an abacus, a winnowing machine designed to extract grain, knives, and the notorious water dungeon –all supplemented with emotional narratives of bitterness. Meanwhile, the museum also features humble, everyday objects of rural life, such as pecks, ropes and wheelbarrows with life-sized clay figures. These ordinary

Figure 1.3 The installation draws inspiration from a wide range of folk elements. Author photo, 26 July 2019.

things serve as props of the drama of old society to offer historical testimony and aura; they 'had a powerful impact on the children's imagination, sharpening their antennae for class enemies who might lurk in their everyday lives' (Ho and Li 2016: 12). The visual spectacle also allows for a comparison of the material lives of the rich and the poor, which is indispensable to the arousal of class feeling.

The second strategy is to draw inspiration from a wide range of foreign and folk elements for a socialist-realist visual production with Chinese characteristics (see Figure 1.3). As Lee (2014: 229) indicates, the popularity of the sculptural installations

> may also have had something to do with the sculptures' European flavor that was sanitized by their subject matter. . . . For all the talk about the successful deployment of the 'national form' (*minzu xingshi*), the sculptured figures were chiefly praised for their quality of verisimilitude – vivid, lifelike, expressive – the hallmark of the classical European sculpturing tradition. Anecdotes abounded about the audience's proclivity to

mistake the sculptures as 'real'. One old lady is said to have tried to strike at a ferocious looking lackey with her cane and had to be reminded that it was made of mere clay.

The sculptors, especially those trained in Soviet-style Western sculpture, recreated the pre-1949 figures of rent collection by paying close attention to the faces and the proper proportions of the statues: 'The Western sculpturing tradition places a far greater emphasis on the face, eye, and hand – body parts that are considered most expressive of human personality and emotions' (Lee 2014: 230; see Figure 1.4). During the sculpting process, the artisans also resorted to folk art traditions and exploited the cultural resources available in local cir-

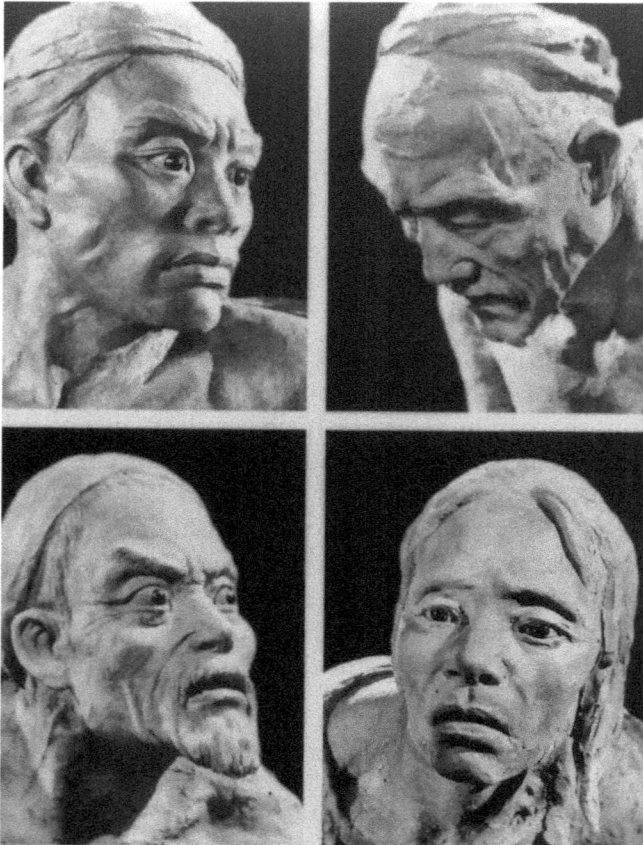

Figure 1.4 The highlight of facial expression. Author photo, 26 July 2019.

cumstances. This practice 'fulfilled the Party's aim to utilize folk art in presenting new revolutionary content' (Galikowski 1998: 124). To make the artwork accessible to the masses, they sought help from peasants and 'went to markets to observe rural customs . . . [and] visited local temples to study folk sculpturing art . . . a group of Sichuan opera actors were recruited to model the various scenarios' (Lee 2014: 220). Rather than following conventional sculpting rules, the sculptors

> critically adopted the traditional techniques of making clay figures loved by the common folk in China. . . . The use of black glass for eyes and the treatment of some of the drapery also come from this tradition. On the other hand, they critically took over some of the modern carving techniques that give these figures a greater realism than the ancient clay figures. Their experience serves as an example for other artists in making the past serve the present, making what is foreign serve China. (Erickson 2010: 128–9)

During political campaigns, the CPC often deployed a rich repertoire of native folk tales and art forms to 'evoke familiar images' and to assert a distinct Chinese identity (Hung 2011: 179; Croizier 2008: 62). Under the guidance of a local propaganda official named Ma Li, the sculptors modelled such religious sculptures as Dazu rock carving and city god temples to depict the old feudal society as *hell*, where 'Liu Wencai reigned over it as a king, surrounded by toadies like the ox- and horse-headed demons of the underworld' (Ho and Li 2016: 16). In order to highlight the evilness of Liu, for example, the sculptors added long nails to the hands of his lackeys to make them look like demons' claws (ibid.; see Figure 1.5). Through such visual representation, the abstract concept of class enemy is articulated with and translated into the traditional form of demonology (ter Haar 1996) that could move ordinary people and stir their negative feelings.

Politics of purification and the invention of moral emotions

The ideal socialist subject is 'a crusader with a mission, burning with rage and hatred against all enemies of the people. . . . In his/her eyes, across the friend/enemy (*diwo*) line there can only be a demon, vermin, or malignant tumour, not a vulnerable human being' (Lee 2019: 25–6). In order to sustain the affective intensity required for

Figure 1.5 A scene depicting the old feudal society. The lackey's figures are created like 'demons' claws'. Author photo, 26 July 2019.

subsequent campaigns, *Shouzu Yuan* was carefully designed to construct the image of the evil landlord and was meant to be read by the viewer as a historical drama. This emotion work was carried out by repetitive state-orchestrated storytelling, collaborative visualisation and the creation of archetypes (Wu 2013: 159). The party-state plays a crucial role in turning the working class into a revolutionary subject and 'purifying' the masses (Hallward 2003: 36). It does so by articulating the political identity with a 'pure' people and inciting class hatred. Since the 1920s, the Communists have developed this politics of purification by using real stories to make *typical* characters (Clark 2008: 141; Ho and Li 2016: 18). The truth claim of revolutionary discourse is grounded in the typicality of the characters invented by socialist-realist dramas.

Shouzu Yuan is inspired by the fantasy of political purity and promotes citizens' sentiments of indignation and hate of the enemies within. The fantasy animates the sculptors to frame some objects and characters as hateful. Hate 'involves a feeling of "againstness" that is always . . . intentional' (Ahmed 2004: 49). The script of traditional opera inspired the statues to elicit the moral emotions of anger and hatred: 'There must be hatred within bitterness, evil within cunning, hatred within sadness, and enlightenment within revenge 苦中有恨, 奸中有恶, 悲中有恨, 仇中有悟' (Ho and Li 2016: 18–19). To achieve this goal, the sculptural display has to construct hate figures and insert them into a coherent emotional narrative that could represent the 'truthful' process of the feudal landlord's exploitation and turn audiences into indignant subjects. The manifestation of moral emotions relies on the stereotyping of a set of dramatic characters and the *personification* of key figures in a good or bad light:

> The landlord – perhaps the most important cultural icon of villainy and victimization – dominated the Mao-era imagination of society before 1949. Beginning in the late 1940s, party- and state-sponsored historiography fiction, film, and art portrayed landlords as a class that inflicted suffering, pain, and trauma on the peasants, and individual landlords became the personification of the 'evil old society'. . . . The names of these landlords, as archetypes, pervaded the political vocabulary . . . (Wu 2013: 131)

The moral emotions projected onto the landlord, to borrow Appadurai's (2009: 235) words, 'set boundaries and mark off the dynamics of the we'. The party-led emotion work is organised around an intensification of the friend/enemy distinction (Dutton 2008: 105): the establishment of 'we as victims' and the class enemy (villain) as an indispensable supplement serves to maintain the level of intensity necessary for revolutionary mobilisation. Enemies 'forge bonds of solidarity and intensify feelings of community – us against them' (Berezin 2002: 44). Through the emphasis on suffering, *Shouzu Yuan*'s emotion work generates political enmity towards the villain who violates moral norms and causes 'our' pain – this immoral Other is a source of insecurity and fear, and 'someone to blame, someone or something to be angry at' (Ost 2004: 241). He is the source of threat to 'our' identity and existence and thus needs to be exterminated. 'Anger, enmity, fear and indignation', writes Berezin (2002: 38), 'are different forms of reaction to threat . . . [they] articulate with the feeling of pain . . . [and] may excite hate.' Political parties and authorities play a crucial role in mobilising anger (Ost 2004: 239), which 'affect what feelings we are able to express and how . . .

and against whom we are able to express our anger' (Ost 2005: 21). It functions as a technology of state governance.

Some landlord archetypes have also become an object of artistic intervention as political movements unfolded in the 1960s. In an analysis of the relationship between art and emotion, Robinson (2005: 266, 268) argues that certain 'emotion causes the artist to choose – whether consciously or unconsciously – certain shapes, sounds, images, and so on, so as to produce a finished work that will be expressive of the emotion', and 'if a work of art is an expression of emotion, the emotion expressed is exhibited or manifested in the character of the work'. The form of theatre, an indispensable element in the CPC's mobilisation (Perry 2002: 113), played a central role in creating these symbolic characters. The artistic team invited opera actors and actresses to imitate the characters. It formulated the characters' emotional states by juxtaposing individual stories that could seduce audiences into the vivid portrayal of traditional theatrical character types of victims and villains (Figure 1.6). These stereotypical characters work to stir up audiences' compassion, outrage and hate by playing out moral dramas of right and wrong and by creating blame for the villains:

> The images produced were both simple and vivid, and easily appreciated by ordinary people. . . . *Its content unfolds as it would in a picture-story book. Thus, the group of people are presented in a simple, straightforward way, with clear and obvious patterns . . . a series of characters and stage sets, like actors on a stage who have been fixed (in place) following continuous rehearsals and corrections by the Director.* (Galikowski 1998: 125; original italics)

The entire set of 114 clay figures is arranged in several emotional episodes presented in sequence like the pictorial frames of a comic book. Historically, cartoons and *lianhuanhua* (连环画) are popular cultural forms commonly used by the Chinese Communists to demonise their enemies:

> Cartoonists often produced direct, simple, and easily recognizable images that make this art form ideally suited for conveying a compelling viewpoint. Artistically, the cartoonists' technique of distortion and exaggeration, coupled with their ability to make complex subjects appear simple and to the point, succeed in making a sharp, sometimes shocking, impression on their viewers. (Hung 2011: 156)

60

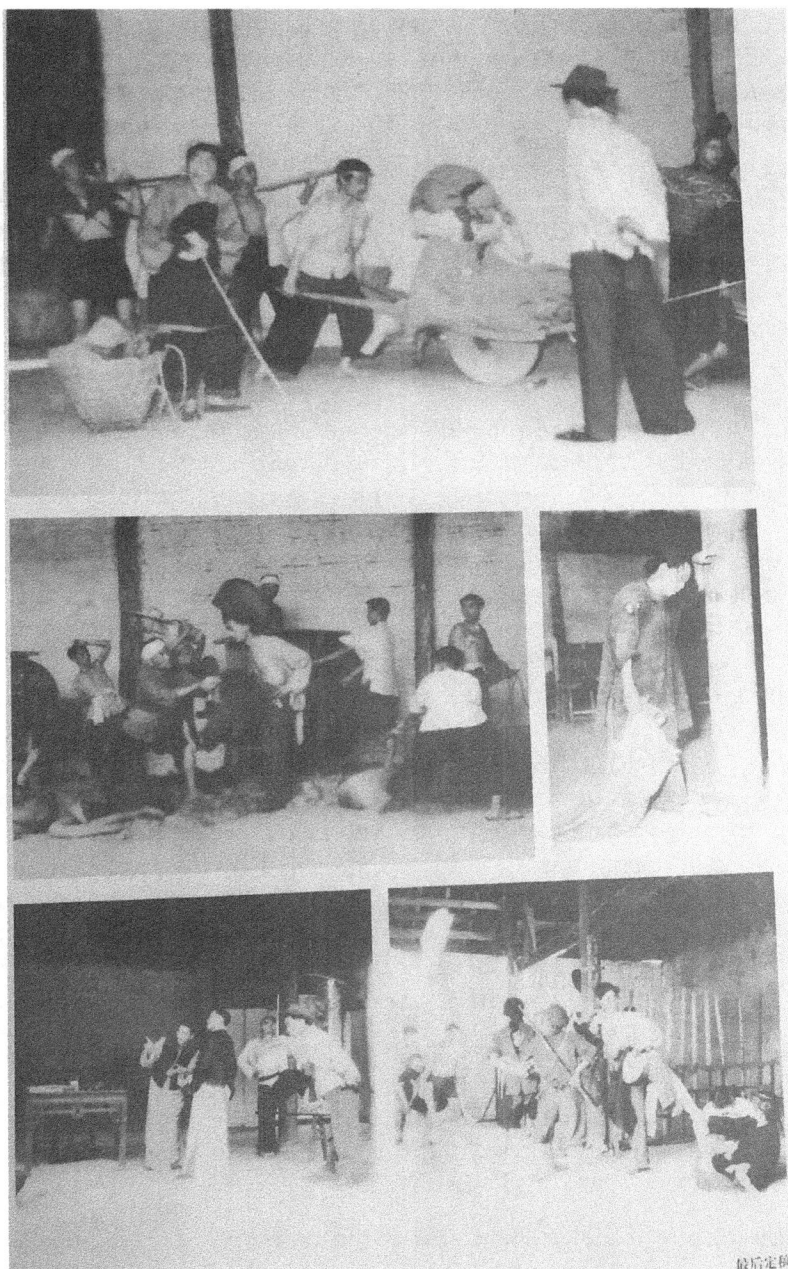

最后定稿

Figure 1.6 The artistic team invited opera actors and actresses to imitate the characters. Author photo, 26 July 2019.

In addition to the helpless, starving peasant figures, the negative characters include Liu's accountant and bodyguards, who force the peasants to pay rent. What is worthy of note is the presence of Liu – usually, he would not show up during the rent collection process. He is intentionally 'made to be present so that the class contradiction can be personified and anchored' (Lee 2014: 228). Personification is one of the main techniques of the CPC's emotion work, which 'refers to the technique of mobilizing people to translate the national discourse into personal stories . . . revolutionary discourse, after being translated into personal stories, could better connect to ordinary people' (Liu 2010: 334). This method allows the masses to identify concrete and specific enemies.

In this microcosm of the old society, the miserable life of peasants is visualised as originating from the exploitative relationship of rent payment. The opening section, 'Delivering Rents', features a group of peasants bringing their grain into the house. The rent grain will be a fetishised object as the drama unfolds. The scene highlights their sense of exhaustion, bitterness and sorrow by focusing on the heavy load of the grain, their postures and facial expressions of pain. In order to arouse viewers' sympathy for the victims, the installation deliberately features elderly people, mothers and children who are portrayed as suffering in the old cannibalistic society (Figure 1.7).

The poor are depicted as dehumanised. There is a hopeless mother with an infant on her back and her little son crying for food (Figure 1.8); an old widow leaning on a cane brings along a hen to make up the insufficient rent; a blind old man, led by his granddaughter, carries a heavy bag of grain on his back that almost crushes him. Evoking sympathy towards those suffering, as a technique frequently deployed by the CPC for its revolutionary cause, serves to consolidate solidarity among people:

> Sympathy is a powerful method for building ingroup solidarity: empathising with another's pain triggers the same affective responses in an individual as if he or she were the recipient of pain . . . it was seeing one's own suffering reflected in the stories told by others that forged this collective bond among villagers. (Javed 2019: 258)

Following the scene of bitterness is the cruel treatment of peasants by Liu's lackeys, who examine and measure the grain with physical coercion. To borrow the phrase from Ahmed (2004: 44), these characters signify the 'danger of impurity' and threaten to violate the

Figure 1.7 A statue depicting the exhausting, miserable life of women. From Foreign Languages Press (1968), *Rent collection courtyard.*

pure bodies of the masses. These images are designed to elicit such emotions as anger and horror by featuring the ruthlessness of the exploitative system. Anger is associated with injustice and can motivate political action (Clarke et al. 2006a: 66). However, anger is 'not the automatic response to misrecognition, nor is it intuitively guided towards the source of injustice. It all depends crucially upon the way in which the experience is framed' (Thompson and Hoggett 2012: 11). Some statues are invested with anger and revenge (Figure 1.9).

63

Figure 1.8 A mother in despair. Author photo, 26 July 2019.

The feelings of pain also get converted into hate for class enemies who cause 'our' pain. The images of rent payment and cruel treatment are intended to offer '"evidence" of the very antagonism it affects' (Ahmed 2004: 52). The obsession with counting (Ho and Li 2016: 13) and the instruments of rent payment presented in these scenes are meant to visualise how 'an economic relationship morphs into a moral and political relationship' (Lee 2014: 234). The curation focuses on the counting procedure, including inspection, winnowing and measuring (*guo dou* 过斗) of the grain. It highlights the method of landlord exploitation through the winnowing machine (*feng gu ji* 风谷机), which is spun hard by a lackey to eliminate much grain as chaff that is neither counted nor returned. Then the grain is measured with specially made pecks that, along with the winnower, symbolise the wickedness of Liu Wencai: the big peck (*da dou* 大斗) is larger than the standard ones and used for receiving grain from peasants while the small peck (*xiao dou* 小斗) for loaning grain out to peasants. These tricks are why the peasants can never pay off the rent (Figure 1.10). The visualisation of the process serves to pave the way for the construction of a phantasm of an enemy:

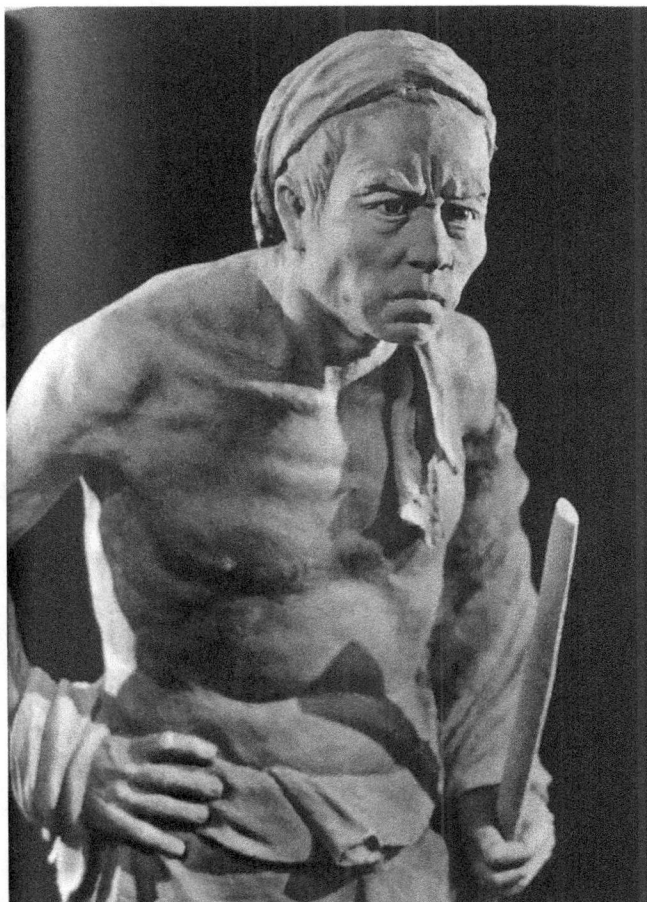

Figure 1.9 Statue of an angry peasant. From Foreign Languages Press (1968), *Rent collection courtyard.*

> What the rent grain revealed and concealed at the same time was the reification of the landlord as the objective enemy, or the enemy within that must be exposed, excluded, and exterminated. . . . When the grain was whittled down next to nothing, the socialist subject was born. (Lee 2014: 235–6)

There are also images of physical abuse: one scene portrays an old man being kicked to the ground by Liu's lackey and a young man being whipped because he tries to take home some of the grain that is blown out of the winnower. The scene of a lackey sitting in a chair

Figure 1.10 A scene capturing the use of the pecks and the winnower. From Foreign Languages Press (1968), *Rent collection courtyard*.

and dispassionately surveying a group of terrified peasants who are unable to pay their rent serves to stir anger and hate (Figure 1.11 and Figure 1.12).

The sensational narrative guide states that some peasants must make up for rent shortfalls by selling their children. One image shows an old peasant's son being forced by a Kuomingtang soldier and a gangster as a mortgage to the army. In this dramatic scene of the severing of peasant family bonds, the local tyrant Liu Wencai is present and instructs his accountant to make the mortgage contract. The scene creates an economy of hate by featuring the landlord-Other, whose proximity is imagined as threatening the object of love (Figure 1.13).

Through the staging of these tableaux, the oppressive instruments and measures are 'transformed into an object lesson in exchange value, measuring not only grain but also blood and tears' (Ho and Li 2016: 13). The emotional drama, as it reaches an ecstatic state of purity, 'sutures individual peasants into the collective by inscribing contingent, heterogeneous grievances and miseries with overarching ideological significance and absorbing them into a grand narrative of injustice and redemption' (Lee 2019: 25–6). Lee argues that what *Shouzu Yuan* showcases is a kind of 'ritual cannibalism' carried out by the less than human:

> The peasants did not just farm Liu's land; they offered up themselves, flesh and bones, to his rapacious appetite. The tenant farming system was the fulcrum of the cannibalistic 'feudal' society and would go on perpetuating itself unless the to-be-eaten rose up in rebellion and revolution, which is emphatically portrayed in the final group of sculptures. . . . The landlord class might look human, but they were 'wolves and jackals' (*chailang*) at heart. (Lee 2014: 235–6)

The moral construction of Liu Wencai as a sexual pervert who drinks fresh human milk further heightens the wickedness of the landlord class. In *Shouzu Yuan*, a scene titled 'Milking' depicts a peasant woman squeezing a cup of her breastmilk for Liu (see Figure 1.14). At work is a victimisation discourse associated with breastfeeding peasant women, notably Luo Erniang, as part of a larger moralisation strategy employed by the CPC to demonise class enemies since the Kuomintang era (Wu 2013: 149). The statue's act of pumping milk serves as a symbol of female suffering in the old society: Luo is one of those mothers separated from their children and forced to

Figure 1.11 Lackey's physical abuse. From Foreign Languages Press (1968), *Rent collection courtyard.*

Figure 1.12 A lackey surveys a group of terrified peasants. From Foreign Languages Press (1968), *Rent collection courtyard.*

Figure 1.13 An old peasant's son is forced to join the Kuomintang army. From Foreign Languages Press (1968), *Rent collection courtyard.*

Figure 1.14 A peasant woman squeezes a cup of breast milk for Liu Wencai. Author photo, 26 July 2019.

feed Liu with their milk every day because they fail to pay rent, which leads to the death of many infants according to the propaganda book circulated during the 1960s (Lee 2014: 226–7). Sensational stories about Liu's biting of her nipple and his attempt to rape her – as repeatedly told by Luo during various speaking bitterness sessions – were crucial for the mass mobilisation of indignation and revenge during that time.

The best-known tale of suffering has been told by a female victim named Leng Yueying since the 1960s. Leng accuses Liu of imprisoning her and other peasants in the secret 'water dungeon', a basement room inside the manor allegedly filled with water and converted to a torture instrument outfitted with spiked iron cages. Claiming herself to be the only survivor of the torture room, Leng spoke at numerous speaking bitterness meetings about her experience of being locked up and abused by the Liu family because of the failure to pay rent. Her story was widely published by influential magazines and school

71

textbooks and became the key material for history lessons (Wu 2013: 143). Leng's oral testimony, however, has been questioned for decades and finally she 'admitted that everything she said had been prepared by the Dayi County's Party Committee' (ibid. 145).[4] Under official instruction, the water dungeon was turned into an opium storage room to reflect its original utility in the late 1980s and put on display. The Leng incident has raised more doubts about the truthfulness of Liu's alleged atrocities, which are seen by some scholars as purely politically motivated and 'fabricated to cover up the post–Great Leap famine that killed tens of millions in China – and millions in Sichuan alone – between 1959 and 1961' (Ho and Li 2016: 5). The class politics of purification that inspires these sensational stories

> invented a phantasmagoric imaginary of the class enemy that powerfully elicited the aesthetic-affective experience of horror and abjection. It was a quasi-hallucinatory imaginary because the pseudo-ethnic grouping called 'class enemy' was little more than an empty signifier designating more an ideological fantasy than a socioeconomic reality. (Lee 2014: 236)

Despite the intensity unleashed by the sculptures, *Shouzu Yuan* would not have been so emotionally powerful without creating a larger emotional economy that makes Liu a ubiquitous free-floating signifier (Lee 2014: 239). 'Villainous landlords', writes Wu (2013: 132), 'were prominent in visual media.' In addition to the museum exhibits, literary magazines and school textbooks, the circulation of landlord-related class feelings relies on a vast network of disseminating propaganda that involves replica displays, printed texts, pamphlets, comic books, songs, ballets, photographs, picture albums, operas, films, puppet shows, international exhibitions, radio broadcasts and media organs (Erickson 2010: 124–6; Galikowski 1998: 123; Ho 2018: 14; Ho and Li 2016: 12; Wu 2013; Lee 2014: 228–9; Wu 2013: 132). These forms of propaganda relay the same narrative structure and offer visual details of the alleged crimes (Andrews 2010: 31) that produce an emotional spillover effect. Beijing TV Station produced a documentary film that was later disseminated for nationwide screening. The film features Mao Zedong's remarks on class struggle, Leng Yueying, Liu Wencai's extravagant lifestyle and the various crimes he commits, and the good life of the peasants in Sichuan under the leadership of the CPC.[5] In addition to the voice-over using emotional tones and narratives to enhance viewers' feelings, the documentary calls Liu a 'four-in-one' (landlord, warlord, bureaucrat and bandit). As a result, 'all of the imaginable evils of the exploitative class – from locking up and beating people, forcing rent payment, separating families, drinking human milk, and sexual harassment to its connection with the nationalist government, warlords, and secret societies – were "concentrated" in the figure of Liu Wencai' (Wu 2013: 151–2). Li is turned into a common threat by sticking different figures of hate together. It is through the personification of revolutionary discourse and the emotion work of phantasm that absolute evil is brought into being.

CONCLUSION

This chapter analyses how the operation of the Maoist regime relies on the capture of political intensity – in particular, how strategic and selective representation of emotions matters for state politics. Through the analysis of an exemplary piece of work that embodies 'all the aspects of a work of art advocated by the Party' (Galikowski 1998: 125), we demonstrate the emotional possibilities of Chinese socialist-realist art and the inevitably entangled nature of the political and the cultural, as well as the visualisation of the friend/enemy distinction as a revolutionary mentality of government (Dutton 2008: 99). Through closely examining *Shouzu Yuan*'s productive context, innovations and the emotional drama it created, we illustrate how emotional mobilisation played a central role in the symbolic production of revolutionary identities and purification of the revolutionary body politic during the Mao era. We employ emotion as an analytical lens to generate new understandings of Chinese revolutionary politics.

The manufacturing and stimulation of class anger and hate, as carried out by state-controlled networks of cultural production, served the need to demonise class enemies and politicise affective communities. This was made possible by the creative combination of Mao's radical aspirations and the aesthetic sensibility of artists and cultural bureaucrats. It is through reimagining the past that the bitterness and horrors of the old society are invested. *Shouzu Yuan*'s emotional fixing of landlord otherness, informed by Mao's interpretation of class struggle, is achieved through the phantasmagoria of class racism. The politically racialised mode of differentiation distinguishes between those who are under threat and those who threaten

(Ahmed 2004: 72) and visualises the villains to blame.

If our analysis of *Shouzu Yuan* illustrates how the CPC's affective regime produces political emotions during the Mao era, it is logical to ask what happens now. After four decades of the Cultural Revolution, some Maoist affective residues have continued to play out and mix with new elements of emotional governance. If emotions are manifestations of specific relational contexts, how does Xi Jinping's regime redistribute emotions and reformulate the affective space in the twenty-first century? How does it construct an affective community by stimulating certain popular feelings and enabling the persistence of identification with the regime? How does popular cultural production reveal the impact of Maoism on the emotional subject of our time? Through a close analysis of the film *Wolf Warrior II*, the next chapter seeks to address these questions by turning to a more contemporary form of emotional hegemony in China, looking closely and directly at the political intervention of cinematic representation in the shifting geopolitical context of global order.

Notes

1. According to Chiu (2008: 4–7): 'Mao mounted a purge of senior party officials with whom he was locked in a struggle for political control. His excuse was the need for change within the party, which he asserted had become complacent and decadent.' Žižek (2007: 26) calls this process 'Maoist permanent self-revolutionizing, the permanent struggle against the ossification of state structures.'
2. During that time, not only were teachers and students urged to 'learn from the masses' and devote themselves to social practices, but writers and artists were asked to learn the language of the masses and 'work in a language readily comprehensible to the masses while simultaneously raising standards' (Erickson 2010: 128–9).
3. In fact, the emphasis on Liu Wencai's lifestyle was questioned by local cultural bureaucrats because of the possibility that it might arouse envy in the viewer, rather than hatred. This is why later versions focused more on the monstrous image of the landlord.
4. Leng's case demonstrates how *suku* is not entirely spontaneous but highly scripted:

> The Party did not simply find those who were aggrieved to serve as accusers, they actively guided them to understand their suffering and trained them to deliver their stories in the most effective way possible. ... The ways in which cadres coached 'accusers' to speak bitterness resembled

acting lessons . . . speaking bitterness participants received a great deal of instruction on how to deliver their tragic stories. . . . Cadres treated accusers like actors playing before an audience. (Javed 2019: 261)

5. The video is available at <https://www.youtube.com/watch?v=LAu06w QlZMM>. Source: quikr fuzes (uploader), Title: 【收租院】1966 年 中国经典怀旧纪录片 Chinese classical HD. Date: 2018/1/30.

CHAPTER TWO

Enjoy the nation

Although constructing a sentimental subject is central to the coherence of a modern national community, this affective dimension is insufficiently acknowledged. The nation, which operates as a central register in people's everyday lives, is configured in the transmission of affects (Wang C. 2017: ix). In other words, there exists a crucial relation between emotions and national belonging (Antonsich and Skey 2020: 580). In contemporary China, the construction of the nation as an affective community (Hutchinson 2016; Berezin 2002) that fuels specific identification processes (Stavrakakis 2007: 165) has always been crucial to producing affective space. Since 1949, the Chinese party-state has been actively deploying soft power instruments to consolidate its emotional hegemony (Brown 2018). To create specific ways of feeling and manage the emotional states of the social body under specific historical conditions, political regimes internalise ideological affects by investing in the nation as a love object (Ahmed 2004: 134; Yuan 2021). In the past two decades, the regime has deployed a wide range of cultural narratives and spectacles to address public feelings of pride and nationalism as a means of emotional governance (Ren 2010: xv; Pun and Qiu 2020: 623).

Placing Chinese nationalism at the centre of our analysis, this chapter deals with the embodiment of affective space during the Xi Jinping era by situating the film *Wolf Warrior II* within the geohistorical context of the Chinese Dream, an emotional project advocated by Xi. In Chinese history, nationalist passions have informed the development of popular culture and created a repertoire of cultural imaginaries. The film is an essential site of affective investment for recruiting nationalist subjectivities. As a symbolic terrain for the everyday reproduction of the nation, it channels and mediates emotional effects through symbols and representations. Among the

Chinese films produced in recent years, *Wolf Warrior II*, released in 2017, has created a miracle that most domestic movies could not match. It has stimulated extensive commentary and achieved enormous success. It is also the first and only Chinese film to have been included in the top 100 box office successes worldwide. The movie, which depicts China as an emerging superpower, receives general praise and arouses a strong feeling of confidence, dignity and pride among Chinese audiences. It is an excellent example to illustrate the proliferation of affective space during the Xi era. In terms of film productions, the film arguably marks the 'maturity' of Chinese action films compared to Hollywood blockbusters. As some critics have noted, it blends the Hollywood-style superhero genre with war, military and action elements and creates political passions. It 'has the traces or elements of many genre films of the US, yet they are fully mixed within the context of China' (Chen 2017). Moreover, the film's success also indicates the combination of a commercial operation and the promotion of nationalism through state-approved 'main melody movies' (*zhu xuanlv dianying* 主旋律电影). Some film critics have pointed out that the film 'has far-reaching implications for making the main melody movies more robust' and helping China's movies enter the global market (Zeng 2017). Because almost everything in the emotional formula of typical Hollywood movies is included, the film evokes a set of historical feelings through which an affective space is created.

As a strategic formation, the Chinese Dream offers utopian possibilities by provoking new feelings of national connection and new ways of distributing political emotions. We are interested in how the film redistributes the feelings of the Chinese Dream by inspiring forms of love, hate and hope. By representing cases of overseas Chinese emergency evacuations in Libya and Yemen in recent years, *Wolf Warrior II* tells the story of an ex-soldier, Leng Feng, who conducts special missions to protect Chinese nationals, medical aid workers and civilians from local rioters and arms dealers in Africa. The following scenes serve to strengthen the nationalist feeling of the Chinese: Leng proudly exclaims, 'I am Chinese' to the rebels; China's national flag becomes a special permit of passage amid chaos; the Chinese People's Liberation Army (PLA) plays an active role in the mass evacuation; and a Chinese passport is displayed.

The film's success 'ignites not only the audience's enthusiasm but also the pride of national belonging when China becomes the world's second-largest economy and an emerging superpower in the world' (*Economic Times Review* 2017). The emotional energy of the film has also triggered extensive debate. Some commentaries claim that it signals the coming of age of the Beijing Consensus, while others relate its expression of Chinese self-confidence to arrogance and contempt (Liu 2017; Xiang 2017). The film's director, Wu Jing (who also plays the lead role of Leng Feng) has said, 'the film is not my achievement. It is an outbreak of patriotic emotions of all the Chinese people. . . . The patriotism of Chinese people has just been evoked. What I did is only to take a matchstick to light it' (Chu 2017). In the specific geopolitical context of cultural self-confidence (*wenhua zixin* 文化自信) and self-confidence in the 'path' of Chinese socialism (*daolu zixin* 道路自信), emphasised by the Xi regime (*People's Daily* 2016), the charm of Chinese heroes is regarded as 'the emotional appeal of Chinese core values' (Shi et al. 2017), which kindles 'a Chinese Dream for the nation's rejuvenation and prosperity' (Bai 2017). This chapter investigates how the affective space associated with the Chinese Dream is opened up by the psychological dispositions of the film, as well as its underlying emotional structure of feeling.

Cinematic affective articulation

This chapter explores how the nationalist passions manifested in *Wolf Warrior II* contribute to the construction of affective space. During the Xi era, nationalism is the regime's most potent legitimating resource. We conceptualise the film as an emotional practice that organises nationalist enjoyment. As a 'cognitive affect', nationalism enjoys emotional legitimacy and triggers deep sentiments about the differences between self and other (Wang C. 2017: viii–ix). Nationalism legitimises specific affects and can mobilise 'the human desire for identity and to promise an encounter with (national) enjoyment' (Stavrakakis 2007: 205). As a powerful binding force, nationalism, which results from the historical experience of interacting with foreign others, is the critical affective element in the film that allows for the projection of imaginary others. If nationalism is 'very much a matter of one's self-view, of one's estimation of oneself and one's place in the world' (Kedourie 1993: 141), the study of Chinese nationalism should attend to what emotions *do* to the collective psyche. The state-sponsored film attempts to reconstruct Chinese nationalist sentiment by reimagining international encounters. According to

Mouffe (2013: 779–80), 'A collective identity, a "we", is the result of a passionate affective investment that creates a strong identification among the members of a community.' *Wolf Warrior II*'s phenomenal success concerns how certain emotions configure cultural imaginaries about us–them relations, thus providing a psychic terrain through which national identities become fixed and sticky.

Recognising the state's role in extracting nationalist affective surplus, we suggest that questions of how to make specific emotions 'stick' to Xi's political project and formulate affective discursivity cannot be addressed simply in terms of top-down political indoctrination. Instead, state politics is more than just propaganda. The nationalisation of society 'has to be integrated into a more elementary process of fixing the affects of love and hate and the representation of the self' (Lee 2007: 309). The conventional constructionist perspective cannot explain why and under what circumstances the nation becomes a desirable object of identification and why its antagonism persists (Stavrakakis 2007: 189–94). We suggest that nationalist attachments are not merely products of strategic investment and manipulation. The authoritarian regime must capture the affective intensity of national myths and historical experiences of geopolitical transformation for legitimation. China's emotional response to the outside world is driven by multiple historical *forces* that produce durable, ineradicable nationalist aspirations. To produce enormous psychic energy, the dramatic techniques deployed by authorities must effectively tap into popular sentiments (Cheek 2006: 118). Nationalism 'works through people's hearts, nerves and gut. It is an expression of culture through the body' (Jusdanis 2001: 31). In other words, the affective regime has to identify, intensify and organise the emotional economy of *enjoyment* that allows for 'the persistence of socio-political forms of identifications' (Mouffe 2005: 27).

Regarding the methodological approach, the mediated affective space of Chinese nationalism is at the centre of our analysis. The film is not only a product of Xi's affective regime but a 'capture' of its nationalist enjoyment and the emotional effects of historical processes. Rather than seeing it simply as a state-approved script, we analyse it as an affective plane of representation where historical antagonism arises, persists and reproduces emotional effects. The film also provides a fantasmatic site of political intervention. The cinematic representation of the cultural text allows us to detect how emotional subjects are invested in particular historical structures and

79

why some passions are prioritised. National identities 'are formed and transformed within and in relation to *representation* . . . a nation is not only a political entity but something which produces meaning – a *system of cultural representation*' (Hall 1996: 612). We hope to illustrate how contradictory feelings of desire and humiliation are played out in imaginary global relations by focusing on how the film represents specific emotions.

Chen (2010) offers an insightful methodological source for studying cinematic affective articulations. His research focuses mainly on the psychological domains of emotional feelings and psychic desires expressed in public discourse and media representation. He argues that a critical cultural study 'works best when it brings sentiment to the forefront, making it a source of thought and analysis' (ibid. xvi). In analyses of two Taiwanese films, he conceptualises the historically rooted 'emotional structures of sentiment' shaped by historical forces such as colonialism and the Cold War, constituting deep-seated emotional attachments to specific identities. In doing so, he contextualises local conditions of sentiment saturated with emotional memories and unconscious desires, which often entail antagonistic forms of nationalism or nativism in which the imaginary perception of self and other are formulated. His research illustrates how the film presents emotional spectacles embedded in the logic of identification and offers a site for a sustained psychological operation where popular feeling finds an expression. The conceptualisation of emotional structure is also useful to understand 'the internal mechanisms of the psychoanalytic space' (ibid. 73) and what Stavrakakis (2007: 164) calls the 'depth' of emotional attachment. Chen's analysis of the nationalist desire for the modern also enables us to pay attention to how the affective investment in Chinese nationalism is oriented and mediated through cinematic representation. His analysis prompts us to address the intricacies of nationalist attachment and the psychological forces at work.

Inspired by Chen's reconceptualisation of identity politics in emotional terms, our analysis focuses on how the structural effects and lived experiences of Chinese modernity have shaped the psychological forces and emotional mechanisms of Chinese nationalism, which are played out in the film. We contextualise the film as articulating a surface of affective investment and drawing a 'psychological map of the nationalist imaginary' (Chen 2010: 49) in the shifting context of global order. In treating nationalism as relational and embedded in broader global power politics, we situate the film text in the specific geohistorical milieu of the pain and shame suffered in modern Chinese history.

EMOTIONAL EFFECTS OF WESTERN AGGRESSION

The dynamics of passion emanating from the film evoke China's emotionally charged history. If identity is historically defined (Hall 1996), then Chinese nationalism is primarily constituted by stories about the traumatic past. It is 'shaped by interactions with the West and evolving narratives of the national past' (Gries 2004: 20). The film explicitly contrasts the pride of the present with the shame of the semi-colonial past of Western aggression. Pride is often associated with other emotions such as pain, shame, harm, injury and depression (Scheff 1990, 1994, 1997; Britt and Heise 2000; Kleres 2005; Jasper 2006). Shame, among other emotions, can produce an emotional dynamism that allows it to be sublimated into pride. As Munt and Smyth (1998: 4) note, '[P]ride is dependent on shame; pride is predicated on the denial of its own ostracized corollary, shame.' According to Ahmed (2004: 109), 'shame and pride have a similar affective role in judging the success or failure of subjects to live up to ideals, though they make different judgments'. Shame can bind the suffering of individuals and unify the nation as an affective community (Ahmed 2004: 108; Berezin 2002). From the overthrow of the Qing Dynasty in 1911, which led to the establishment of the Republic of China, to the establishment of the People's Republic of China in 1949, shame has been a component of the broad nation-building process (Xu 2018). Cleansing national humiliation (*xishua guochi* 洗刷国耻) has become a driving force of modernisation since the Maoist era.

Historical memories of suffering and victimisation associated with foreign invasion have fuelled China's long quest for survival and configured the psychic realm of the Chinese. Modern Chinese history can be considered a 'history of pain' (Berry 2008). The pain and shame experienced by China in the past two centuries of encounters with the West – such as the Opium War, the first Sino-Japanese War, the invasion of the Eight-Nation Alliance, and the War of Resistance against Japanese Aggression in the first half of the twentieth century – run throughout its modern national consciousness. The nation's weakness is deeply rooted in how the Chinese imagine their 'Century of Humiliation' at the hands of foreign powers. This historical experience also shows how power hierarchies result in specific ways of distributing emotions.

Experiences of subordination or unfair treatment can stimulate the struggle for different distributions of emotions (Goodwin et al. 2001; Clarke et al. 2006b). Traumatic experience has made the mission of creating a prosperous, strong nation an integral part of the regime's claim for legitimacy. The act of intrusion and spatial transgression has produced a tremendous emotional effect on the Chinese psyche (Wang 2012). Defeat by the West has created sticky emotions, including insecurity, anxiety, desire, resentment, fear and hate, and resulted in a superiority/inferiority complex about the West (Song and Sigley 2000: 61). The West, which has loomed large in China's popular imaginary since the twentieth century, has rendered its subjectivity contradictory and incoherent. On the one hand, the West represents a menacing and evil Other, an enemy of excessive enjoyment who deprives China of its desire and dignity (Stavrakakis 2007: 199). It is an anticipation of a future injury and a sign of disturbance that constantly threatens to prevent the Chinese nation from satisfying desire fully and living up to its ideal (Ahmed 2004: 47, 132; Lee 2014: 16). As a result, humiliation is frequently mobilised by domestic political forces to 'draw ethical boundaries between self and other, between domestic and foreign' (Callahan 2004: 203). Meanwhile, the ghost-like figure of the West embodies modernity and positive things that are more advanced and civilised. It constitutes China's model for the future. The historical encounter with imperialism has fixed the West as a complex emotional symbol of injury, theft, loss and admiration, giving rise to contrastive pro- and anti-Western imaginaries around which China's national attachments are organised.

Here, the distribution of libidinal dynamics in media representation is crucial to positing the national ideal. A critical emotional mechanism in this psychic process is the production of fantasy, which 'operates through narratives of loss and the possibility of recovering fullness, and more importantly, [is] also an experience of jealousy, desire and hatred' (Palacios 2020: 796). As a constitutive outside, the West is hated because it is fantasised as stealing 'our' enjoyment; it is desired because it represents the ideal of a modern nation. If the rendering of the nation as an object of identification 'relies on the ability of nationalist discourse to provide a convincing explanation for the lack of total enjoyment' (Stavrakakis 2007: 204–5), how does film, as a means of organising and materialising enjoyment, reimagine the global power hierarchy and create fantasies of threat, theft, lack and the recovery of stolen enjoyment? What kinds of imaginarised promises and ideals are offered by the cinematic narratives of the nation, and how do they transform the ways such fantasies are projected? Addressing these questions helps reveal the implications of Xi's affective regime.

SCREENING NATIONAL FANTASIES

Since 1949, film has played a central role in dealing with the lack of national enjoyment. The cinematic production of shame and pride has been transfixed by political ideologies that project fantasies and ideality onto certain bodies and objects. These political films formulate an affective space where the imaginarised enjoyment promised in fantasy is articulated. Considering such films as manifestations of fantasmatic political projects, we suggest that their signifying operations illustrate shifting emotional structures of feeling configured by different national fantasies of fullness and affective dynamics.

Regarding the reconstruction of the national ideal, 'saving the nation from foreign invasion' has always been a common and recurring theme of contemporary Chinese films. These films recount foreign invaders' theft of national enjoyment, expressing perceptions about China's imaginarised interaction with the outside world. Such emotional preoccupation with the loss of enjoyment is reflected in the protagonists' repeated efforts to overcome historical suffering and shame. For example, *Wolf Warrior II* restores the lost enjoyment of Chinese pride by portraying the Chinese as capable, intelligent and resilient subjects. Such a positive construction seeks to deliver the fullness of the fantasmatic promise of the Chinese Dream as a national ideal. Symbolising the aspiration to modernity, Leng Feng is highly skilled in martial arts and adept at using advanced military technologies. This image of the modernised subject is also represented by other Chinese figures in the film: the Chinese develop antivirus technology (Dr Chen), operate transnational factories, and engage in global business (Zhuo Yifan). The film's display of technological power is driven by the notion that 'past humiliations can be repeated if China remains technologically backward' (Guo 2004: 34). Throughout the film, high-tech knowledge, professional skills and military strength constitute the main characteristics of the modern Chinese subject of the twenty-first century.

This mode of affective investment in national myths is radically different from the past. Under the Maoist total state, China was portrayed as a victim of Western aggression and the myth of national destiny was aimed at animating revolutionary desire. The revolutionary affect provided a source for the emancipation of all oppressed people. The founding of New China signified that the Chinese people overthrew the oppressive 'three big mountains' (*san zuo dashan* 三座大山) – imperialism, feudalism and bureaucratic capitalism – thereby completing the historical mission in which 'the Chinese people have stood up since then'. In this context, the national subject referred to workers and peasants with a strong class and anti-imperialist sentiment. In Maoist narratives of loss, they were motivated by shame and oppression to overthrow the 'three big mountains', thus gaining the pride of 'being their own masters'. In such affective dynamics, the West and Japan were imagined as the source of injury and bad feelings, posing a danger to the national body. Nationalist affects were embedded in the politics of exclusion. China was fantasised as the victim of foreign bullying, and the political boundaries against perceived enemies were clear-cut. The common use of such derogatory appellations as *guizi* (鬼子, devils) to scorn foreigners reflected the political logic of othering under the Maoist regime.

In the movies of that time, there was a celebration of national victimhood and insecurity where the Chinese people suffered from the double oppression of the domestic ruling class and imperialism. There was the relegation of the West into signs of pain and shame that failed 'our' national ideals – overcoming the humiliation of the past served as a vital component of revolutionary pride. Such narratives worked through the fantasmatic projection of national enemies. For example, *The Naval Battle of 1894* (*Jiawu feng yun* 甲午风云, 1962), based on the Sino-Japanese War of 1894, depicted the Qing government as incapable and weak in the face of the Japanese navy. The regime's inability to satisfy the desire to restore national pride fuelled popular discontent that the government had paid vast sums of money and ceded land in exchange for temporary security. The resulting shame was not tolerated by soldiers or civilians, represented by the protagonist Deng Shichang, who forced the government to fight back to maintain national dignity. The film deliberately attributed China's defeat to the greed and cruelty of the Japanese imperialists as well as to the incompetence of the Qing government. As a result, in the final battle, Deng Shichang, who realised that, 'If you want to fight Japan, you cannot rely on the imperial government,' ordered his soldiers to seek support from local people. The national subject is laden with a tragic sense of victimhood and revolutionary consciousness. National solidarity was achieved by eliminating the evil Other who blocked the economy of the national ideal. The revolutionary body was imaginatively bound together by those who tried to destroy the nation. The founding of New China marked the 'victory of the people', who became the new masters of the nation. If nationalism is a 'byproduct of colonialism' (Chen 2010: 91), emotional pride was motivated and animated by the film's display of the collective overcoming of the shame caused by colonialism.

However, the revolutionary and proletarian subject formation in Mao's era – animated by an instinct of aggressiveness – was disrupted after Deng Xiaoping came to power in the late 1970s. The pain inflicted by the chaos of the Cultural Revolution and the ensuing political crisis resulted in a dramatic turn in the national narrative of loss during the postrevolutionary period. The energy of class struggle was neutralised and redirected towards material construction. Economic reform and modernisation aimed at national strength were highlighted as solutions leading to national strength and prosperity. It was also assumed that China would restore national pride only through economic development – not class struggle. Yet the Deng regime had to offer new fantasies to recover national fullness. A new national ideal and dialectics of enjoyment were in demand. Although the shameful past remained unforgettable, the suffering of the Cultural Revolution prompted people to attribute China's failure to its cultural tradition, which hindered China from becoming a powerful nation (Gan 2006). This perception resulted in an intricate renegotiation of the relationship between the Chinese self and foreign others. Meanwhile, the affective antagonism of Mao's era was displaced by a binary opposition consisting of the civilised, modern West and the backward, unmodern China. Despite growing affection for the West, the new affective articulation under Deng was imbued with the old aspiration to revive the lost national glory. The affective residue was a deep-seated ambition to 'surpass Britain and catch up with the US' (*chaoying ganmei*) and make China a wealthy and robust *daguo* (great nation) on the world scene.

During the 1980s, as an emotional signifier, the West performed an ambivalent role in refashioning national fantasies of loss. Public feeling towards the West became more complicated and ambiguous.

Although the desire to surpass the West remained intense, the logic of othering no longer turned nationalism into absolute hostility. Contrary to Maoist fantasies that attributed the lack of enjoyment to the presence of an external enemy which was stealing it, the West now served more as 'a system of reference, an object from which to learn, a point of measurement, a goal to catch up with, an intimate enemy' (Chen 2010: 216). Hatred and resentment for the class enemy evaporated. Nationalism was channelled towards material development and a critique of Maoist politics. With the Maoist us–them distinction shaken, the West was no longer imagined as an absolute threat but, instead, as a model to be admired and emulated. Popular sentiment turned pro-Western at the beginning of Deng's reform regime: 'the Chinese regarded the West as a symbol of comfortable material life, spirit of initiative, rational institutional arrangements, and advanced technologies' (Wong and Zheng 2000: 325). The new middle classes aspired to live a Western lifestyle (Moisi 2009: 725). The West worked as a contradictory site of affirmation and competition. The lost national enjoyment vis-à-vis the West primarily operated through rechannelling the affective flow towards the foreigner as a figure of modernity, who 'as stranger only reappeared on Chinese soil in the post-Mao period' (Lee 2014: 16).

Under the new dialectics of enjoyment, the national subject was imagined as inferior to and needing to learn from the West to recover national fullness. Revolutionary politics was abandoned entirely. The West was no longer fantasised as predatory and violent. One example is *Black Cannon Incident* (*Heipao shijian* 黑炮事件, 1986). In this film, the protagonist Zhao Shuxin is not a member of the revolutionary worker-peasant class but an intellectual who shoulders the task of modernising the country. Compared with his Western partner, the German engineering expert Hansen, who represents a figure of progress and technological advancement, Zhao is an anxious subject aspiring to catch up with and seek recognition from the West. The teacher–student relationship is a proper metaphor (Gries 2004: 33) to capture his emotional state, whose lack of enjoyment is driven by rigid socialist bureaucracy, the exclusion and distrust of intellectuals inherited from the Mao era, the suppression of individual freedom, and the Chinese tradition which privileged the state over the individual (Dai 2000). The West is regarded not as equal but as superior in terms of technological, material and intellectual strength. The film reflects a broader desire to use Western modernity to reform China.

This uncritical attitude towards the West was intensified in a series of movies produced in the mid-1990s, such as *Lover's Grief over the Yellow River* (*Huanghe jue lian* 黄河绝恋, 1996), *A Time to Remember* (*Hong se lian ren* 红色恋人, 1998) and *Red River Valley* (*Hong he gu* 红河谷, 1998). These films share an obsession with white, male Western figures (e.g. the British soldier in *Red River Valley*, the American pilot in *Lover's Grief over the Yellow River*, and the American doctor in *A Time to Remember*). By contrast, China is represented (usually by a female character) as a voiceless, deficient and incomplete subject that is 'othered and defamiliarized' (Zhang 2014: 13), lacking the ability and autonomy to speak for itself. In stark contrast to the Maoist spectacle, these films demonstrate that affective energy is highly malleable and can produce contradictory, incoherent and inconsistent fantasies of national ideal and fullness under different geopolitical circumstances. This process has given rise to mixed emotions regarding the national self.

THE FANTASY OF THE INDIVIDUAL HERO

Wolf Warrior II is the product of a specific affective regime. It inherits some of the affective residues of the Deng regime, which opened up more space for cultivating individual subjectivity and desires. Deng's reform encouraged the active pursuit of individual self-interest, previously eliminated during the Mao era. It forged a sense of individualism by redirecting the affective flow of dissatisfaction towards the lack of personal freedom and enjoyment under Mao. The remaking of the self during the Deng era contributed to the expansion of the space and psychological power of the individual.

Leng Feng has impressed domestic audiences because of his firm and unruly personality. In the film, the old victimisation complex is replaced by a more positive self-image of the individual. Unlike traditional revolutionary heroes who serve as moral-political models, Leng is an individualistic heroic figure. Compared to the conventional characters of selfless individuals during the Mao era, Leng has his private life, emotions and romantic love. If love 'became a political language at the expense of individual expressions' (Guo 2020: 47) during the Mao era, Leng's emotional expression is much more individualised and undisciplined, always causing him trouble. However, his private passions and desires are not portrayed as opposed to the myth of national destiny but offer a driving force for the latter. By linking individuals with national rejuvenation, the fantasy of personal heroism is subsequently animated by the rescue of the Chinese and Africans. Here, Leng's image embodies individualistic pursuit and self-sacrificing love for the nation. According to one commentary, 'in the past, patriotism meant no room for individual values. This movie is different, as it satisfies the audience's worship for superheroes and a strong national consciousness together' (Yin 2017). Another commentary observes that the film configures 'a new relationship between individuals and the nation, and this new identity is reconfigured by the shared interests between individuals and the nation in the context of market economy' (Zhang 2017). *Wolf Warrior II* can be seen as a Chinese version of *Rambo* that features an individual whose heroic acts yield loyalty to, and sacrifice for, the cause of the nation. In the film, Leng's intimate, personal emotional relationships, including his relationship with his fiancée, are quickly overwhelmed by a keen patriotic love and loyalty. As the story unfolds, his individualised pursuit is invested in the mission to save the Chinese nationals. His subsequent acts embody the bolstering of China's strength. It is not the revolutionary ideal but the rising national power status that produces imaginarised promises.

The film channels nationalist energy from the individual. Its director, Wu Jing, has said that it expresses the heroic spirit of defending the nation (Lin 2017). In a scene where Leng confronts his rival Big Daddy, the leader of a group of European mercenaries, the latter places a knife on Leng's neck and tears off his armband. A close-up shows the image of a Chinese national flag with the words, 'I'm fighting for China', through which the individual act is identified with the recuperation of national enjoyment. The individualised pursuit runs through the whole film, in which all Chinese expatriates go to Africa for their own sake, but eventually, they all join Leng Feng to save the Chinese people (the only exception is the profiteer Qian Bida, who cares only for his own interests). They are ultimately united by a fraternal feeling, translated into the synthesis of the nation's bigger self (*dawo* 大我) and the smaller self (*xiaowo* 小我) of the individual, who is cosmopolitan in orientation. Meanwhile, the positing of the individualised ideal also relies on fantasies of state power. As some commentaries have indicated, an individual hero without the support of the state is not a 'true' hero, and the glorification of an individual hero is not enough to represent the film's ethos. According to Zhou (2017), 'There is still another level of support behind individual heroes, namely, the prosperity of the country and its rising power in the world.'

In this sense, 'the heroic story of the film is not a personal narrative, but a national narrative. The heroic act of Leng Feng becomes the self-narration and construction of the image of China' (Wu Q. 2017). Throughout the film, his heroic images are consistently invested with the meaning of national pride, which is signified, for example, by a spectacular scene involving a naval fleet, a symbol of national wealth and military strength (*fuguo qiangbing* 富国强兵). The display of military facilities implies a desire to recover national fullness and achieve Deng's modernisation goals. The sense of technical rationality also represents an imaginary solution to the lost ideal of an autonomous and assertive China. The film ends with an extreme close-up of a Chinese passport with the subtitle, 'When you encounter any dangers overseas, don't give up and remember that there is a powerful motherland behind you.' As a result of the rearticulation of national feelings, Leng becomes 'the metaphor of the era of the rise of China and the collective expression of the Chinese Dream' (Chen 2017). He represents the one who gets back the lost enjoyment and restores the dignity of the formerly wounded nation. If Maoist politics fuels a 'defensive' nationalism marked by rejection of any activity that might threaten 'our' enjoyment (Moisi 2009: 637), Leng represents a 'positive' nationalism that inscribes the lack of enjoyment with optimism and confidence.

A NEW DIALECTIC OF ENJOYMENT

The nationalist vision of *Wolf Warrior II* is a continuation of broad historical trajectories. Before the film's release, the new dialectic of enjoyment had taken shape in the ideological sphere. Shifts in national strength had generated new emotional energies and dynamics. During the Hu Jintao administration (2003–13), economic success was a primary source of national pride (Dimitrov 2013: 309). Hu's projects reinforced the stronger nationalist sentiment that had been intensified during the last few years of Jiang Zemin's administration (1993–2003). Hu made multiple references to the 'great rejuvenation of the Chinese nation', which acknowledged the continuity of the nation's past greatness and the regime's mission to recover China's lost dignity. The regime also reorganised people's national enjoyment by promoting Chinese culture and tradition. His affective investment has resulted in a new breed of anti-West patriots.

Since the late Jiang era, there has been a transformation in the intensity of nationalism. The beginning of China's twenty-first century was marked by a series of historical films that attempted to rewrite history, such as *Hero* (*Ying xiong* 英雄, 2002), *The Promise* (*Wu ji* 无极, 2005), *Curse of the Golden Flower* (*Man cheng jin dai huang jin jia* 满城尽带黄金甲, 2006) and *Red Cliff* (*Chi bi* 赤壁, 2008). Rewriting history had become a key strategy for reorganising national enjoyment. These spectacular productions displayed both China's glorious past and its rejuvenation in the present. For example, in *Hero*, the most controversial figure is Wu Yan, whose mission is to assassinate Qin Shi Huang and rescue people from his tyranny. He attempts to approach the emperor but gives up when he can accomplish the mission and instead chooses to sacrifice himself. Moreover, Qin Shi Huang is portrayed as a self-willed, dedicated ruler who unifies and strengthens the country, and his dictatorship and brutality are downplayed. The plot is 'very much in line with the political ideas and needs of those in power in China' (Lu 2007). Glorifying the past became a mechanism for formulating new affective attachments: China's historical past and tradition were no longer seen as backward feudalism and obstacles to its modernisation but were reinvented as a means to *justify* and *legitimise* China's current regime. The shifting projection of national fantasies was manifested in *The Rise of the Great Powers* (*Da guo jue qi* 大国崛起, 2006), *The Road to Rejuvenation* (*Fuxing zhi lu* 复兴之路, 2007) and a series of state-sponsored TV documentaries. In these works, the Chinese nation-state 'emerged as a "modern subject" with a long history and tradition that has gradually realized modernization after undergoing long-time traumatization and shame in modern history' (Zhang 2014: 18). During this period, China increasingly viewed itself as a great power on the world stage.

After Xi Jinping came to power, the obsession with great power was further consolidated by appealing to feelings of pride. His affective regime has enthusiastically asserted the grand mission to deliver historical justice for China. It has made a concerted effort to restore national pride by deploying a more direct, positive, assertive mode of emotional expression. The production of the hope and optimism of the Chinese Dream is built on the strong sense of global competition, arduous pursuit of technological progress and 'Belt and Road' projects; it also inevitably relies on the political technology of emotion to cultivate super national identity and loyalty to the party, on the other. . . . The project of great rejuvenation of the country requires an active penetration and embodiment of individual nationalistic sentiments as a collective endeavour. (Pun and Qiu 2020: 624)

Creating an economy of excitement for the national ideal is central to Xi's redistribution of emotions. The six-episode TV documentary *Amazing China* (*Lihai le wode guo* 厉害了我的国, 2018) offers a utopian promise by glorifying what the Xi administration has achieved and demonstrating that the country is moving towards autonomy, modernity and prosperity against the restructuring of global power. The enthusiastic sentiment is generated by the imaginarised transformation of a humiliated and oppressed past into a great mission of national rejuvenation and world leadership. At work is a new dialectic of enjoyment, which imagines China as growing into its new role and the right place to redeem itself. Its positive energy articulates the deep-seated aspiration for a strong nation. In *Wolf Warrior II*, 'other government units also make courtesy appearances . . . police from the Public Security Bureau in the China-set scenes, regular PLA troops, the ambassador and his diplomatic staff, Chinese Embassy guards, doctors at a state-invested hospital – nearly all of whom are painted in a noble light' (Wu H. 2017). The film portrays the state as a defender of national pride and promotes identification with state interests. It is through such a glorification of the state that Xi's utopian vision is embodied.

TAKING REVENGE ON THE WEST THAT STEALS OUR ENJOYMENT

[N]ationalism can easily be transformed into enmity . . . nationalist hatred emerges when another nation is perceived as threatening our enjoyment . . . social groups deal with their lack of enjoyment by attributing it to the presence of an enemy which is 'stealing' it. (Mouffe 2005: 28)

The new geopolitical context opens up new possibilities for recovering lost dignity and enjoyment, and the image of the strong-nation subject in *Wolf Warrior II* manifests such utopian possibilities. At the heart of Xi's project lie complex renegotiations with previous affective articulations. At work is a double affective investment: the new fantasmatic subject inherits the anti-Western sentiment of the revolutionary period *and* rearticulates the desire for Western-style modernity and technological power in the reform era. First, the tension between China and the West, primarily expressed in the embodied antagonism between Leng Feng and Big Daddy, resonates with the political films produced during the Mao era. In the Mao era, imperialism – one of the three mountains – was seen as a threat to 'our' enjoyment. The revolutionary-nationalist discourse was sustained by the double projection of imaginary internal and external enemies. This logic of representation underpinned the war films that focused on anti-imperialism during that time. In the face of the constant threat of foreign invasion, the movies during that period, such as a series of films on the Korean War (e.g. *Shang gan ling* [上甘岭, 1956], *Surprise Attack* [*Qi xi bai hu tuan* 奇袭白虎团, 1957] and *Heroes and Children* [*Ying xiong er nv* 英雄儿女, 1964]), showed that the once-humiliated national subject displayed strong will and determination against US imperialists, who were characterised as 'paper tigers' that were defeated by the Chinese and North Korean armies. The US was characterised as using its power to prevent China from realising its potential and getting back its lost enjoyment.

In the recent transformation of national identifications, Xi's affective regime has also associated the US with injury and 'us' with victimhood, defining the former as the source of jeopardising the Chinese ideal. In *Wolf Warrior II*, there is a similar distribution of emotions at work. The film features three racial groups: the capable Chinese (e.g. Leng Feng), the arrogant and evil Westerners (e.g. Big Daddy) and the helpless Africans. Among them, Big Daddy represents the source of wounds and pain, constituting the object of Chinese resentment and revenge. In this film, Chinese anxieties about the West are projected onto this imaginarised enemy who is fantasised as a mean-spirited figure blocking the dream of regaining China's status. If Big Daddy represents the enemy responsible for the loss of Chinese enjoyment, Leng is portrayed as a utopian promise invested with the enormous capacity to deliver justice for the motherland wronged in modern history.

For Leng, the historical emotions of resentment and revenge, which are transformed into hate, are so deep that they drive him to resort to physical violence. A critical logic underlying the film is the masculinisation and militarisation of the self to deal with historical hate. Emotions such as hate, according to Ahmed (2009: 251), 'work to secure collectives' and 'align some subject with some others and against other others'. His love for the nation motivates hatred. Through its portrayal of the emergence of a vengeful pride, the film depicts an eruption of embodied nationalist hatred, which unfolds through Leng's physical act in the name of love. Emotions 'work to shape the "surface" of individual and collective bodies', through which individuals and collectives are brought into being by making a distinction between 'us' and 'them' (Ahmed 2004: 1). The story depicts the Sino-Western encounter as a violent contest, where Leng represents the affective becoming of the new national body, which is imaginatively brought into being through the competition.

At the beginning of the film, when Big Daddy says 'Your nationals are timid and weak, and you should be oppressed for the rest of your life,' Leng does not respond immediately but avenges himself later through violence. The violent scenes of physical fighting reveal that 'China is anxious to flex its muscles in front of domestic and international audiences after hundreds of years of shame. Driven by the slogan of "anyone who offends China will be destroyed no matter where it is", the film appeals to the most simplified and rough national imagination' (Liu 2017: 258). The manifestations of violence and vengeance become metaphors for realising the Chinese Dream. By featuring Leng's military capability and physical strength, the film *naturalises* violence and privileges it as the *only* way to recover national dignity. This militarism is also manifested in other films of the same period, such as *Sky Hunter* (*Kong tian lie* 空天猎, 2017) and *Operation Red Sea* (*Hong hai xing dong* 红海行动, 2018). In these films, military strength and great power are celebrated. The fantasy of a strong nation finds its true expression in expansive bodily performance.

The film features several scenes calculated to induce indignation and resentment among the Chinese. Differing from past formulations, the subject of the Chinese Dream not only defends the nation but also aspires to take the place of the West. The Maoist 'surpass' trope is played out throughout this film and resonates with the notions of restoring 'China's rightful place on the world stage' celebrated by official discourse. The film marks the desire to overtake the West as a great power and stand on an equal footing with the West, which reveals a great deal about Xi's ambition and the nostalgia rooted in the historical memory of China's imperial past (Chen 2010: 208).

When Big Daddy is defeated, China's shameful history is redeemed and the utopian subject is elevated:

> After Leng Feng struck a counter-attack and hit Big Daddy, he said, '[T]hat was in the past!' This conversation at the time made me shocked. It took me quite some time to remember what Big Daddy said when he took the upper hand, like 'Chinese people are sick and useless' . . . Leng Feng finally defeats Big Daddy after desperate wrestling and he speaks out proudly, which almost releases the repression of the Chinese people in the past hundred years. (Chen 2017)

In this triumphalist depiction, reminiscent of Maoist emotional dynamics, the subordinate position is imaginatively reversed. China humiliates the West and gets its revenge as promised. The West is no longer superior to 'us', nor is it a model to be emulated. Instead, the West represents a declining influence whose narcissism can no longer cause 'our' injury. The fantasy subverts the metaphor of the previous teacher–student relationship by taking the superior position. Underlying the moment of affective encounter and status reversal is a profound desire to reimagine past humiliation as a form of recovering national fullness:

> [H]umiliation is not just about passive 'victimization'. National humiliation discourse involves a very active notion of history and recovery. (Callahan 2004: 203)

Leng's victory represents the recovery of 'our' collective self-esteem and face. Saving face is central to Chinese nationalism, which symbolises China's aspiration for great power status (Gries 2004: 24). Intense feelings of national enjoyment associated with regaining face ('it's our turn, finally') are generated by the emotional transformation from shame to victory and the fantasmatic ending of Western dominance. Through such an inscription, the ecstasy of national rejuvenation temporarily suspends the jealousies and victimisation complex as bodily histories. The production of fantasy, however, runs the risk of reproducing the imperial desire 'locked in the binary opposition of China versus the West' (Chen 2010: 41).

AFFECTIVE ENCOUNTER WITH AFRICA

The enjoyment of what feels national also encompasses the projection of China's strength and desire for Africa, which is characterised as weak and chaotic. Historically, Africa has been proof of China's global influence and solidarity with the Third World. When the split between China and the Soviet Union occurred during the Cold War, China started aligning with countries in Asia, Africa and Latin America and supporting their anticolonial struggles. During the postwar period of decolonisation, China assumed leadership across these countries.

Such a historical tie and sense of solidarity have been reimagined in *Wolf Warrior II* through the utopian construction of China's self-image as a global soft power. The film offers an expression of Sino-African solidarity (Harper 2017). Africa has been a key partner of Xi's Belt and Road project. In the film, feelings of aspiration stick to the bodies representing Africa, whose enjoyment is also stolen by the West. Leng Feng is positively portrayed as an assertive and fearless protector of vulnerable African people. He is depicted as offering promises to people in Africa (e.g. his care for his adopted son Tundu, his rescue of Tundu's mother and African citizens trapped in territories controlled by the rebels). There is a scene where he protects African captives and Big Daddy threatens him, saying, 'You will die for them.' Leng Feng responds, 'I was born for them.' Here, the fantasy of saving African people, which implies a shared historical experience associated with Western aggression and the possibility of recovering fullness, is reminiscent of Mao's ambition to liberate the Third World in the 1960s.

The film also reveals the reaffirmation of previous forms of identification. The renewed Maoist heroism is articulated with metaphors of modernisation and development, such as the construction of factories and infrastructures in Africa, which resonates with Xi's Belt and Road initiative. Through relaying the narrative of 'saving the Third World', the current sense of pride is no longer driven by the actions of workers and peasants who used to be the 'master' of the nation, but by China's new global engagement. Compared to the historical image of the West as causing only destruction and war, the film features China's global influence by demonstrating that China brings modern construction and technologies to Africa. Furthermore, by constructing the ideal of saving innocent African civilians, Leng Feng represents China's growing assertiveness as a rising superpower and its promise of fulfilling its global destiny. This ideological affinity is the main reason that the Chinese state supported the film, including by supplying human resources and military equipment by the Nanjing

Military Region. Since its release, various official cultural agencies, film-related associations and research institutions have hosted events to discuss the film to evoke feelings of pride (Zhang 2017).

The film's dramatisation of Africa also reveals the emotional effects of racial othering. As Chen (2010: 83) observes, 'third-world nationalism inevitably reproduced racial and ethnic discrimination'. Throughout the film, Africans are portrayed as unable to govern and protect themselves, and lacking the ability and autonomy to speak for themselves. As the adoptive father of Tundu, Leng Feng represents a father–son relationship with Africa, which is nothing more than a *voiceless, deficient and incomplete object* onto which the desire for great power status is projected. This racial representation is nothing more than a copy of Western colonial prejudice and 'a weird exercise in what might be called a "yellow savior" mentality – a slant on Hollywood's problematic "white savior" complex' (Hsu 2017). Under the gaze of the Chinese father, the Africans are depicted as premodern tribes who can only ignite bonfires, bang tambourines and pray when they are in danger. Through the film's articulation of this father–son metaphor, 'a feminine, childish, and racially inferior African image is shaped' (Liu 2017: 259). As a result of such emotional operation, pride gets stimulated into sentiments of triumphalism and superiority. The racial organisation of enjoyment is only part of China's broader affective investment concerning the African Other. A similar portrayal of African people, emphasising the benefits they have derived from Chinese investment and their gratitude to China, was shown in the Spring Festival Gala produced by China Central Television in 2018, which triggered widespread criticism of state-approved racial stereotypes. Underlying this formation is the desire for a superior national-racial ideal.

CONCLUSION

This chapter has attempted to illustrate how the affective space of Chinese nationalism has transformed under the Chinese Dream. The enquiry into nationalist affects is an intervention in the political discourse of our time. By situating the cultural representation of nationalist affects in *Wolf Warrior II* in the broader geopolitical context of the emotional production of national fantasies and ideals, we analyse the complex historical process and mediation of this affective space. The film offers a powerful tool for constructing political subjectivity.

The analysis here sheds light on how certain affective bonds, mechanisms and trajectories are historically formed and operate as sites of political investment. It focuses on the cinematic articulation of emotional economies of national feeling, which offers utopian promises and the excitement of rejuvenation. This chapter traces new ways of distributing emotions, particularly why and how some emotions become sticky and fixed. By historicising the traumatic sentiments of national weakness and humiliation, our analysis examines the shifting emotional operations of utopian possibilities in political films and conceptualises their manifestations in terms of the theft of enjoyment. It delineates the changing ways in which films have dealt with the historical lack of national enjoyment. It also demonstrates the complex ways in which such enjoyment is deployed by fantasmatic narratives of loss and recovery, and how they contribute to the ideal of the Chinese Dream that projects the nation as an emerging global superpower. A central issue is how affective sovereignty addresses its shifting identity and reconnects it with the ideological agenda. The utopian subject formation that underpins Xi's affective regime combines and reinvents previous political dynamics to produce new passions. Centring our analysis on the imaginarised promises the film provides and the broader regime, we suggest that the film is more than just propaganda and the extraction of affective energy. Instead, it brings to light the nation's affective residues, as well as the political possibilities and contradictions of the affective geography created by the Chinese Dream. It illuminates the contradictory politics of nationalism.

The analysis presented in this chapter illustrates how the film mediates the affective space of nationalism. Yet it has avoided the question of the wider emotional impact of Chinese nationalism. More specifically, what has not been explored so far is the emotional response to the Chinese Dream. We will consider this issue by shifting our analytical focus to the affective dynamics in Hong Kong. What are the emotional experiences of Hong Kong people under Xi's affective regime? What kinds of emotional subjectivity and politics are constructed against 'China' as an emotional other? How do specific emotions intervene in the local process of political formation, hold the social body together and fuel popular discontent? What local strategies are deployed to organise enjoyment, and how do they produce fantasies of loss and fullness? These questions constitute the primary interest of the next chapter, which focuses on the highly controversial political film *Ten Years*.

CHAPTER THREE

The future as an injury

Fear projects us from the present into a future. But the feeling of fear presses us into that future as an intense bodily experience in the present ... one's whole body becomes a space of unpleasant intensity. ... So the object that we fear is not simply before us, or in front of us, but impresses upon us in the present, as an anticipated pain in the future.

Ahmed 2004: 65

China's 71st National Day in 2020, which coincided with the Mid-Autumn Festival, was supposed to offer a much-needed day of relaxation during the coronavirus pandemic. However, Hong Kong's prevailing atmosphere was tense and depressing, mixed with conflicting emotions. Unlike the usual festive scenes of mainland shoppers filling the streets on previous national days, there was no joy of celebration but heightened security concerns in a city that has just experienced waves of anti-government protests against an extradition bill. Some empty streets were decorated with national flags, with scores of redshirt citizens waving more flags and chanting patriotic slogans. Ironically, the official flag-raising ceremony, viewed by Chief Executive Carrie Lam and hundreds of participants at the Golden Bauhinia Square, was met with roadblocks, heavy security and dozens of arrests in the business zone, including two protesters allegedly throwing petrol bombs. Against this backdrop of ritualistic mobilisation of national identity, pride and love for the nation, hundreds of protesting bodies were trying to make their emotions felt. In contrast to the patriotic event staged by the government, the protesters – who had been educated to love China since the intensification of anti-China sentiment in the enclave – defied the social distancing measures and the ban on public gatherings, expressing feelings of discontent, agony and anger by illegally gathering across

98

the district of Causeway Bay and chanting the slogan '*Liberate Hong Kong. Revolution of our times*'. Some sought to incite hatred by cursing the police. The political divide, deepened by a Beijing-drafted national security law enacted in the wake of recent social unrest, was condensed into a purple flag raised by riot police as a warning against acts that might violate the law, which had generated an emotional impact of fear on the territory.

If National Day constitutes a brief emotional moment for constructing the nation as a love object, where is the national enjoyment among Hong Kong people? Why are so many Hong Kong youth, who are learning to belong to the nation (Mathews et al. 2008), turning against China, and why are negative emotions such as anger, hate and fear so pervasive and intense? The consideration of Hong Kong's 'postcolonial awareness' (ibid. 66) should be situated in what Chen (2010) refers to as the emotional structure of sentiment that has become the material basis of the ensuing conflicts. As far as the psychic dimension of the conflict is concerned, Hong Kong's identification is bound to produce its Other. In light of Hong Kong's postcolonial trajectory, the current dilemma is locked in a hyper-essentialised 'us vs them' emotional structure that has been reproduced as the foundation of antagonism whereby the subject often sees the Other in strongly negative ways. In this binary structure of feeling, each side is charged with profoundly negative emotions and treats the Other as immoral, deceitful and threatening (Hong Kong's fear of losing freedom and autonomy versus the mainland's outrage over unpatriotic 'troublemakers'). Each side constructs its version of emotional imaginaries and narratives depicting the Other as a primary source of hurt. Therefore, the ongoing blame game over national love can be understood as a product of the conflictive emotional structure *and* the affective investment of friend/enemy distinction, which must be maintained in order for political conflicts to be waged (Ost 2004: 240). The tensions in Hong Kong offer an example of how political struggles are saturated with emotions and how emotions mediate power relations and produce boundaries. If the current predicament in Hong Kong is largely caused by parallel, contradictory and unreconciled logics of organising enjoyment, the emotional subjectivities shaped by these investments are constitutive of broader political formations that shape people's social psyche through the work of emotions.

The emotional conflicts exhibited in Hong Kong, a symbol of China's past weakness and an inalienable part of the nation for many

Chinese, provide an opportunity for rethinking the manifestation of affective space in the region. Our reflections propel our thinking about the Hong Kong question on the role of identification and emotional memories in sustaining the hostilities between mainland China and its margins (Shi 2007; Liu 2005, 2008, 2018). Since the 1997 handover, tensions between Hong Kong and mainland China have been rising despite the changes in political intensity. The strained relationship is driven not only by the deep-seated contradictions embedded in the 'One Country, Two Systems' arrangement but also by a historical accumulation of emotionally charged experiences and imaginaries. Widespread feelings such as anxiety, uneasiness, powerlessness, frustration, indignation and fear have become the most prominent components of the crisis, evoking a range of political practices and effects on Hong Kong's postcolonial landscape. Although multiple factors drive the conflicts, emotions have been a component of shaping Hong Kong's self-image.

TEN YEARS AS A SITE OF AFFECTIVE ANTAGONISM

Compared to mainland China, Hong Kong has a radically different economy of desire and subjectivity derived from the colonial era. The fundamental problem of Hong Kong over the past few decades has been one of how to deal with the increasingly assertive country. This chapter explores the emotional disposition of the politically controversial film *Ten Years*, through which a set of local feelings and historical antagonism are captured and materialised. This cinematic text, which is explicitly critical of Chinese dominance, offers a snapshot of Hong Kong's loss of enjoyment after the handover, especially under Xi Jinping's Chinese Dream. The Xi regime's growing assertiveness and desire to restore national pride have created an enormous emotional effect on the enclave. The fantasy offered by the film, which works through narratives of loss, 'explains' how Hong Kong's enjoyment is threatened and stolen by 'China', which is depicted as destroying Hong Kong's way of life with its excessive enjoyment. Under this logic, China is imagined as preventing the territory from delivering the fullness of its fantasmatic promises of freedom, autonomy and prosperity. By offering an outlet for popular discontent, the affective investment of the film has created tremendous emotional effects and offered a fantasmatic site of political intervention. In terms of the style of Hong Kong films in recent years, *Ten Years* is seen as the 'most eye-catching Hong Kong film since the handover' (Zou 2016). Produced on a modest budget of HKD 500,000, this independent film was a surprise hit after it was released in Hong Kong at the end of 2015, recording a full house on each showing and setting a record by grossing HKD 6 million for a low-budget film (the best in the past twenty years). After being taken down from cinemas, it continued to be shown in colleges, streets and neighbourhoods. It was awarded Best Film at the 35th Hong Kong Film Awards in 2016, attracting contrasting film reviews.

The film comprises five short stories that show the viewer what Hong Kong might look like in 2025 (hence, ten years from 2015). The dystopian film recounts the theft of enjoyment as a consequence of the imaginarised 'Chinese invasion'. In *Extras*, the central government officials conduct a false flag 'terrorist attack' to assassinate local politicians during an official event in 2020 to promulgate the National Security Law in Hong Kong. Two gunmen, a South Asian man and an unemployed immigrant from the mainland, are killed when the national security law can be passed. The second episode, *Season of the End*, depicts a young couple who wish to preserve rapidly destroyed objects in Hong Kong to keep memories of the past alive. The story narrates that as the city develops too fast, the speed of destruction is getting more astonishing. In frustration, the hopeless actor attempts to create his own body as a specimen to overcome the feeling of weakness. The third story, *Dialect*, reflects the marginalisation of the Cantonese dialect: a Hong Kong taxi driver suffers employment discrimination because he cannot speak Putonghua (Mandarin Chinese). As the territory becomes further integrated with the Chinese mainland, he is required to speak Putonghua with his son, who is ready to start secondary school. In the form of a mockumentary, the fourth episode, *Self-Immolator*, tells of a young activist who is jailed because he violates national security law. Following his death during a hunger strike in prison, a fierce conflict occurs between students and riot police. Protesting against police brutality, an old woman commits self-immolation outside the British Consulate-General to express her anger with the government. The last story, *Local Egg*, focuses on shopkeeper Sam, who sells local eggs to make a living. Under political pressure, however, all the local grocery stores in Hong Kong are forcibly closed down. Sam's son is mobilised to join the 'Youth Guards' to conduct routine inspections on local businesses. The portrait of these affective activities can be seen as a renewed political manifestation that responds to Xi's hegemonic norms that dictate what people ought to feel. The film has sought to redistribute emotions by creating an economy of fear. Fear in *Ten Years* is constructed by the representation of hardships or difficulties that Hong Kong people may experience in the future. All the characters representing Hong Kong are fearful about the negative situations threatening their existence. Underlying these stories is the profound desire to recover Hong Kong's lost enjoyment and reconstruct its lost ideal of self-determination.

Ten Years stirs up emotions that have been pervasive since the late colonial era. The film's emotional intensity has also motivated public contestations that generate political valence. Interestingly, neither positive nor critical commentaries of *Ten Years* focus on the film's artistic value but instead on its political stance and psychic effects. Supporters of the film have acknowledged that there are some flaws in its plot settings, narrative structure, shooting techniques and use of film language. However, considering the extensive political impact it has made, 'it makes no sense to just focus on the astringent skills' while missing the point that 'the most valuable component of art is creativity, which comes from the author's independent spirit' (Zhang 2016). Critical reviews then hold that 'it is politics that kidnaps professionalism and politicizes the film award' (Lin 2016). Nevertheless, what allows for the persistence of politics and how the film sustains its energy remains to be understood.

The film depicts the lack of total enjoyment by prioritising some negative emotions associated with 'China', a structural fixture in Hong Kong's cultural imaginary. It calls into question the treatment of Hong Kong people under the disposition of 'One Country, Two Systems'. It provides an affective surface through which deepening emotional contradictions are inscribed. Although *Ten Years* points to the imaginarised 'future' of the city, its roots are deeply embedded in the present political crisis and a fantasmatic past. Because of its explicitly antagonistic expression, which strongly echoes the popular sentiments after the Umbrella Movement, some see *Ten Years* as a 'prophecy of Hong Kong society' (Liao 2016).[1] As one jury member of the 35th Hong Kong Film Awards commented, 'The film speaks for the era, and you will understand why the film was awarded the Best Film in 2016 when looking back in the future because it is very representative of the year' (Chen 2016). Similarly, the introduction to the Best Film also pointed out that it:

reflects the current anxiety and fear in Hong Kong, regardless of politics, language, or people's livelihood, as the local living space is being eroded. After the Occupy Central campaign, Hong Kong people have no outlet to release their depression but to take this film for catharsis and healing. (Li 2016)

These remarks imply that the fear conveyed by *Ten Years* resonates with the broader structure of feeling in Hong Kong. Some critics suggest that the film provides an interpretive narrative to articulate and reproduce popular sentiment about the uncertainty of Hong Kong's future (Zhang 2016; Chen and Tu 2016). As a result, the Chinese media outlet *Global Times* strongly criticised *Ten Years* and called it 'a reflection of the deep anxiety of some Hong Kong people . . . Hong Kong's extreme thought has deeply influenced Hong Kong people and made them lack confidence or even have fear about the future' (Wang 2016). Fear, as an unpleasant form of intensity (Ahmed 2004: 65; Evrigenis 2008: 20) that anticipates an undesirable outcome, is often coupled with a paralysing sense of hopelessness and constitutes an emotional foundation for politics. Fear is a primary political emotion (Barbalet and Demertzis 2013) that can produce chain reactions and cultural imaginaries about selves and others. It reveals a collective experience and creates uncertainty, tension and struggles. If fear is crucial to the formation of collectives (Ahmed 2004: 71), it creates emotional fixity and coherence in a local community in response to uncertainty.

Economy of fear

In retrospect, *Ten Years* has evoked widespread repercussions. For example, although the film was popular, no cinemas were willing to continue screening it (Zou 2016; Li 2016). As one commentator observes, 'what the five stories in *Ten Years* express is fear, and the fate of *Ten Years* also reflects fear' (Zhang 2016). Not one celebrity was willing to present the award at the Hong Kong Film Awards. Finally the chair of the awards, Derek Yee, presented the award in person, quoting the former US President Franklin Roosevelt in his speech: 'The only thing we have to fear is fear itself' – thus revealing unexpected vectors of fear that the film has induced. Mediating a negative apprehension of the future (Demertzis 2013), fear establishes a ground of moral and political judgement and evokes a sense of righteousness. This chapter attempts to understand how fear, as the anticipation of a future injury or hurt (Ahmed 2004: 65), is represented in the film, specifically focusing on how the climate of fear intervenes in the territory's affective space. Although most commentaries have acknowledged the profound emotional impact created by this film, there has been insufficient scholarly analysis of how fear as affective energy works (Lyon 1998; Ahmed 2004; Reed 2005; Hoggett 2009) to intensify psychic insecurities and depression in the territory. If Hong Kong's postcolonial subjectivity is constructed 'in the very process of negotiating the mutations and permutations of colonialism, nationalism, and capitalism' (Abbas 1997: 11), it remains unclear how post-handover feelings tighten the territory's boundaries. When scholars talk about a 'more politically conscious Hong Kong' (Lo and Pang 2007: 351) and its 'postcolonial self' (ibid. 354), it is unclear how such notions of consciousness and selfhood can help us to understand the emotionally charged political landscape.

Fear is relational and turns against others. It presupposes the prospect of undesirable events and always seeks an investment object (Barbalet and Demertzis 2013: 184). Our analysis conceptualises fear not as a subjective property of the person or some feeling rules entirely constructed by society (Clarke et al. 2006b), but rather as an intensity that flows and circulates between individuals and societies, inscribing them into a relational power network. Hong Kong's fear is driven by specific events and conflicts associated with government acts. Here, fear is a site for constructing political subjectivities and motivating political actions (Grossberg 1988; Ahmed 2004; Harding and Pribram 2004). It is in 'its capacity to circulate meanings, to transmit social relations and to constitute subjectivity' (Harding and Pribram 2009: 18) that fear creates political effects. This chapter explores how the politics of fear shapes Hong Kong's response to Xi Jinping's promotion of national pride, which has paradoxically raised fear among many Hong Kong citizens. Given that *Ten Years* is widely regarded as a 'Hong Kong Manifesto' (Lv 2016) against the Chinese regime, we are interested in how fear is represented in the film and how it reveals Hong Kong people's emotional experiences. As a product of the broader affective dynamics driven by decolonisation, the film produces fantasies of loss and theft vis-à-vis the Chinese Other. It also offers an example of how Hong Kong's enjoyment, as the ambivalent foundation of solidarity (Stavrakakis 2007: 201), is reorganised in the broader historical context. We will explore how fear intervenes in the local political process and reinforces the emotional organisation of nativist enjoyment, which is affiliated with a way of life and a set of values. If the rendering of China as a negative object of disidentification relies on the ability of nativist discourse to offer a convincing explanation for the theft of enjoyment, how does the film, as a means of rechannelling affective flow towards the figure of China, create imaginaries of loss and threat? How does it shed light on the shifting projection of nativist fantasies when China has increasingly grown into a great power on the world stage? How does the film represent a multiplicity of emotions associated with mainland–Hong Kong tensions – including love and hate, optimism and disappointment, depression and fear (Huang 2020: 7)? How does it inspire different forms of imaginary and reflect the affective material basis of ongoing conflicts? What are the sources of fear, and how does fear work in Hong Kong? How does the politicisation of fear articulate a sense of unbelonging and turn isolated individuals into unified people? The enquiry into Hong Kong's state of fear should address the complex dynamics of emotional (dis)identification and historical experiences through which the dialectics of enjoyment is played out. A central issue is how the film captures a set of emotional experiences of Hong Kong's social subjects and reconnects it with nativist politics.

THE CHINA SYNDROME

In Hong Kong's emotional structure of feeling, China is a ghostlike figure, an intimate enemy. The 'othering' of China as a cultural-political logic, as a means of inscribing the lack, can be seen in contemporary Hong Kong cinemas, where it is often through fantasising about China as Other that Hong Kong subjectivity is constituted. However, such a fantasmatic process is always inconsistent and contradictory. As Lo observes, 'Hong Kong's Chineseness is a site of performative contradictions. It is a crack in the edifice of Chineseness. Its existence is simply a living and contingent contradiction, in the sense that the city's culture both exaggerates and negates Chineseness in the vicissitudes of its sociopolitical milieu' (Lo 2005: 4). In other words, Hong Kong's subjectivity cannot be understood without considering its negativity towards China.

Historically, Hong Kong has wanted to keep its distance from China. Its collective sense of uncertainty, insecurity, anxiety, depression and fear about the future – which are frequently mixed with distrust, sadness and anger – can be traced back to the signing of the Sino-British Joint Declaration in 1984, which determined the fate of Hong Kong after 1997.[2] Fear needs and sticks to an object (Ahmed 2004: 64). Change itself, especially the social agent's perception of a loss of power and the possibility of social dislocations of various kinds, is a primary source of fear (Barbalet and Demertzis 2013). This is because change may cause 'the possibility of deteriorating prospects for subjects whose power is insufficient to provide compensating or mollifying adjustments' (ibid. 169). Hong Kong's fear results from possible actions by the two countries that make it vulnerable to deprivation. It also stems from frustration in recuperating enjoyment caused by political changes that stimulated a sense of anxiety and fear about the future. These emotions are responses to destabilisation, which has also prompted Hong Kong's citizens to reflect on their identity and culture. Hong Kong people became more sensitive about their identity status during the 1980s than at any other time (Chow 1995a; Teo 1997; Abbas 1997; Kar 2001; Cheuk 2003). During this period, the enclave gradually developed a distinct sense of local self and sentiment, including feelings of superiority in relation to the economically disadvantaged mainland (Law 2009). During the late colonial era, a discourse emphasising the uniqueness and autonomy of Hong Kong's culture was entangled with the binary political imagination formulated during the Cold War, which was increasingly framed as the dichotomy of 'totalitarian China versus democratic Hong Kong'.

At the time of the Sino-British negotiation, Hong Kong's emotions towards mainland China were ambivalent and complicated. They were stimulated by the double experience of dealing with colonial and national powers. Multiple historical factors produced Hong Kong's emotional experiences. During the colonial period, Hong Kong's local sentiment was not mutually exclusive with the Chinese ethnic and cultural identity. Meanwhile, the experiences of British colonial rule and Cold War antagonism cultivated a sense of nativism (Law 2007). After Britain and China reached a consensus in 1984, China as an intimate yet ambivalent Other began to take shape in popular culture. Experiences of transition, which generated the possibility of social displacement, stimulated the struggle for alternative distributions of emotions. Academics and artists began exploring Hong Kong's cultural and historical roots, emphasising the uniqueness of the city's lifestyle and cultural milieu as well as the complex nature of the historical colonial experience (Abbas 1997; Law 2009; see also Chun 2017). The deep sense of intimacy and unease implicated in the ambivalent relationship between Hong Kong and China can be understood as 'China syndrome', which has profoundly influenced Hong Kong cinema since the mid-1980s. Local filmmakers 'asserted their identity in terms of its difference from what they presented as China's but they at the same time attempted to come to terms with China' (Teo 1997: 224). In her reading of Johnny Mak's *Long Arm of the Law* and Yim Ho's *Homecoming*, Yau highlights the importance of border crossing in understanding the complexity of Hong Kong's popular perception of China, 'an internal experience found inside a mythic "China" that encompasses obviously racial and political differences and transcends arbitrary boundaries' (Yau 1994: 194). In the late 1980s and early 1990s, China as an intimate Other became even more intense in such nostalgic films as Stanley Kwan's *Rouge* (1988) and *Center Stage* (1991). The strategic play between the present and the fantasmatic past intervenes in the linearity and continuity of history, thus dissolving the taken-for-granted historical imaginary. As Chan observes, those nostalgic films signify the 'introspection of the past, the anxiety of the present, and the uncertainty of the future of the city', providing an alternative means of emotional expression and '[giving] a "voice" to the suppressed subjectivity of the historical writing of Hong Kong' (Chan 2000: 268–9). They provide fantasies to recover fullness. As an intimate yet alienated Other, the anxiety and worry brought by China at this stage was more of an anticipation of the uncertain future.

During the transition period, the cultural imaginary of China shifted dramatically. Fragmented, inconsistent, contradictory imaginaries about China continued to unfold in the late colonial transition period. The figure of China tended to be represented as old-fashioned, traditional and incompatible with modern society. In contrast, Hong Kong was often figured as modern, Westernised, educated, open-minded and desiring individual freedom; the most famous example of such a portrayal is *Her Fatal Ways*, a 'Chinese cousin' serial of the early 1990s (Shih 1999). The shifting of Hong Kong's cultural imaginaries of China shows that the affective space is a dynamic entity, transforming as events unfold. Hong Kong's uneasiness, vulnerability and insufficiency of power were featured in cultural narratives. Some scholars described Hong Kong as struggling to survive between its two colonisers (Chow 1995a: 94); 'nativism' was regarded as a rebellion against colonial rule. As Hong Kong's return was not a voluntary choice, and particularly because of the shock of the crackdown on the Tiananmen protest in 1989, the fear of an unambiguously repressive, despotic, tyrannical China triggered feelings of depression, frustration and desperation. The previous intimate, nostalgic feeling had been dissolved by the sense of alienation, hopelessness and despair – this was especially evident in Fruit Chan's '1997 Trilogy': *Made in Hong Kong* (1997), *The Longest Summer* (1998) and *Hollywood Hong Kong* (2001). These films share a depressing sense of powerlessness in that the protagonists cannot freely decide their own ways of life or futures. The othering of China was at this point no longer limited to the projection of fear; instead, China was imagined as being insidious, malicious and unscrupulous towards Hong Kong, as prominently featured in *Hollywood Hong Kong*. Alienation, frustration and loss are common and recurring emotional tones in these films, mixed with an uncooperative and resisting sentiment towards the destiny set by China (Lang 2003; Shi 2008). The fear of losing identity and freedom has never faded but has become the driving force of the territory's subsequent political activism.

Since the transition period, nativism has constituted one of the main emotional forces for creating Hong Kong's affective space. The transition has driven a series of identification acts to recover fullness in the territory. Throughout the 1990s, local resistance to 're-nationalization' (Erni 2001) and the popular movement against the Chinese state have combined to reinforce a sense of nostalgia for the colonial period and an obsession with the uniqueness of the local culture. Some scholars have noted the risk of Hongkongers becoming fixated on nativism (Lo and Pang 2007), the 'Great Hong Kong Chauvinism' and the essentialised 'us vs them' structure (Hung 1997; Ip 1997). As a result, the colonial mindset that sees China as underdeveloped, barbaric and backward is well preserved. As Chow (2015: 103) observes:

> The thought of 'Great Hong Kong' has been deep-rooted into the minds of the Hong Kong people, who believe that everything about Hong Kong is superior to mainland China, so they look down on mainland Chinese, and disdain their own Chinese identity.

This sense of superiority is why cultural critic Chan Koon-Chung (2012) urges the need to reflect on the essentialising tendency of

Hong Kong nativism. After the handover, cultural superiority was combined with a growing sense of victimhood, as presented in Fruit Chan's 1997 Trilogy, where the victimised subject is no longer the well-off urban middle class but disenfranchised youth, ex-soldiers, and a butcher of inferior social status. With the increasing regional integration of the enclave into the Guangdong–Hong Kong–Macau Greater Bay Area, the former British colony no longer enjoys a unique status. Meanwhile, mainland China is no longer lagging behind Hong Kong in terms of modernisation and economic power.

In the face of new affective sovereignty, there has been a growing tendency to search for a more definite identity and to highlight a sense of powerlessness and anger in the nativist discourse. Underlying these efforts is a growing fear of the annihilation of 'the local' in the renationalisation process (Erni 2001: 409). Despite the affective investment in Hong Kong's youth to 'keep national humiliation in mind, [and] develop China vigorously (*wuwang guochi, zhenxing zhonghua*)' (Ren 2010: 1), the Chinese identity remains unpopular and unfashionable among local youths. In response, efforts have been made to reconstruct purified local identities around which anti-Chinese political forces are organised. Much energy is directed towards legitimising local identity, which entails aggression and hatred. The inability to satisfy the desire thoroughly fuels nativist politics marked by the rejection of any activity that seems to threaten 'our' enjoyment, through which China is seen as blocking the economy in the city's ideal. Nativism allows for the persistence of local attachments and offers the social agent a form of enjoyment. The years after 2008 saw a phenomenal rise in nativism and 'strands of pro-independence and self-determination thinking' (Ma 2018: 46–7). This new nativism, invested with a renewed desire to preserve the cultural heritage of the colonial period, enjoys emotional legitimacy among youths and legitimises adverse affects that reject the post-handover status quo. To find mass support, it has desperately sought new objects representing China, such as mainland immigrants, students and tourists. Since then, the idealised local image has increasingly been reasserted as a mark of autonomy and pushed the rising tide of fear politics.

INTENSIFICATION OF FEAR

Such sentiments accumulate over time as emotional value saturated with moral sensibilities. Obsession with the local as an object of identification relies on the ability of nativist discourse to offer a convincing narrative for the loss of enjoyment. The perception that people in Hong Kong cannot freely decide their own future and way of life culminated in 2015 with the release of *Ten Years*. Released in the wake of the Umbrella Movement and against Xi's call for national rejuvenation, the film is a turning point in the intensification of Hong Kong's politics of fear. Compared with earlier fantasies of loss, the fear in *Ten Years* has become much more intense, embodied and pervasive, where the logic of othering turns China into absolute hostility. If the fear and insecurity in earlier Hong Kong films were more vaguely and allegorically expressed, then they have found their full expression in *Ten Years*. In this film, 'China' is no longer the ambivalent object of nostalgia and discrimination but is fantasised as being unscrupulous, malicious and evil towards Hong Kong. China has now turned into an oppressor against a vulnerable Hong Kong. Under this fantasmatic construction, Chinese factors are depicted as not only dominating Hong Kong's politics (*Extras*) but also attempting to erase its local cultures, traditions and lifestyles such as Cantonese (*Dialect*), local products (*Local Egg*) and Hong Kong's autonomy (*Self-Immolator*). The destiny of Hong Kong's people is depicted as tragic and miserable, ending up in self-immolation (*Self-Immolator*), suicide (*Season of the End*) or the deprivation of dignity (*Dialect* and *Local Egg*). Invested with 'us vs them' antagonism, the film articulates a range of emotions including frustration, insecurity, distrust, indignation, hostility and even hatred. It changes the political metaphor often used in the past, and 'employs a candid way to express the fear of people' (Zou 2016).

Fear is the product of specific social relations embedded in historical contexts. It is deeply embedded in concrete social interactions and is thus closely associated with power hierarchy and conflict. The fear in *Ten Years* is activated by the representation of the loss of enjoyment or ideal that Hong Kong people would experience in the future, such as the gunmen who lose their lives (*Extras*), the taxi driver who is not allowed to use his native language (*Dialect*), the grocery shop owner who is not allowed to sell local eggs (*Local Egg*) and the desperate antiquarian, students and citizens (*Season of the*

End and *Self-Immolator*). All the protagonists are faced with different threats from China. They cannot maintain their way of life or their dignity, and ultimately cannot control their destiny, due to the rapid disappearance of local history and culture.

The film reveals the complex emotional experiences of Hong Kong's economic integration with China. Despite the opportunities and accompanying feeling of optimism afforded by integration, the rise of China as a geopolitical power and its pro-development agenda have further intensified the sense of insecurity, worry, aversion and fear among the majority (Huang 2020: 10). Chow (2015: 126) describes the collective feelings of the Hong Kong people in the following terms:

> After its return to China, Hong Kong people feel fearful of their home country, as they are afraid that the Chinese government will impose the governance approach for the mainland Chinese on them. Moreover, due to the different systems, things that happened in mainland China might appear ridiculous and unacceptable to Hong Kong people.

As mainland scholar Qiang Shigong (2008: 90) observes, when faced with Western notions of human rights, the rule of law, democracy and universal suffrage, China is 'in a state of aphasia' and unable to offer competing discourses. The failure has made it immensely difficult to win the hearts and minds of Hong Kong's people. The governance issue coincides with growing cultural tensions intensified by the cumulative effects of mutual contact. A series of social and political events led to the radicalisation of nativism. Mainland immigrants, parallel traders and students are targeted as evidence of Chinese encroachment into the territory. Psychoanalytically, they embody an excess of Chinese enjoyment. The influx of mainland tourists is seen as intrusive, destroying Hong Kong's way of life:

> [I]t drove up rents in malls and tourist districts, which in turn made it difficult for ordinary retailers to survive. It also inflated consumer prices, hurting local consumers. Small shops were soon replaced by chain stores, with their goods mostly catering to Mainland visitors and not local needs. (Ma 2018: 41)

This quote provides the context in which post-2008 anti-Chinese sentiments are nurtured. Public grievances over the stress being placed on the territory's public resources are transfixed by discontent and fear that 'our' living space is being taken over by newcomers.

In *Ten Years*, predatory China is pervasive and penetrates the private sphere of ordinary people's everyday life. The enactment of the national security law, as predicted in *Extras*, is represented by the false flag political murder plotted by the central government. The story reveals the distrust in the central government and anticipates the fate of self-destruction caused by any form of cooperation with Beijing. In *Self-Immolator*, the bloody conflict between police and protesters and the suppression of student protest can be seen as refreshing the 'June 4th' memory of Hong Kong people and the unhealed anxiety for the political tension at that time. The mainland tourists in *Dialect* and the disappearance of local values in *Season of the End* all predict that Hong Kong's culture will be destroyed and go extinct at an astonishing speed. In *Local Egg*, the younger generation is brainwashed and acts the same way as the Red Guards during the Cultural Revolution. Such a fearsome image contrasts with the Chinese Dream's underlying triumphalism.

Existing studies focus on how the state evokes fear as a means of social control (Robin 2004; Barbalet and Demertzis 2013; Shalhoub-Kevorkian 2015). They depict how authorities construct threatening Others who need to be either excluded or controlled, thus legitimising the violence imposed upon them (Ahmed 2004; Robin 2004; Kinnvall 2013; Shalhoub-Kevorkian 2015). In the case of *Ten Years*, the flow of fear is two-way. Fear is productive in circulating imaginaries and formulating or destroying social solidarity. Meanwhile, fear can bind the social body together and identify a visible target as the enemy (Clarke et al. 2006b; Ahmed 2004; Harding and Pribram 2004, 2009). The film represents fear by highlighting the threat, danger and destructiveness of an omnipresent, powerful and violent China whose narcissism causes 'our' injury. This Other is fantasised as making the lives of Hong Kong people difficult and miserable, through which China is imagined as the source of Hong Kong's loss of enjoyment. That is to say, the film is not just a representation of the social atmosphere but draws emotional boundaries between 'us' and 'them'.

As such, Hong Kong is represented as a trapped, victimised and 'injured subject' (Smaill 2010) whose enjoyment is stolen. In this film, the injured subject is characterised by a set of lower-middle-class protagonists such as a taxi driver and a local shop owner, whose sense of frustration, depression and fear arises out of their social marginalisation and the increasing loss of autonomy. The pessimistic mood depicted in *Ten Years* reflects the directors' sensitivity to the emotional trauma that Hong Kong people experienced during the political conflict in 2014. This traumatic experience was collective and widely felt across the political spectrum. As the producer of *Ten Years* Andrew Choi said: 'Hong Kong people cannot imagine some of the things that happened during the Umbrella Revolution, so I want the whole tone and atmosphere of the film to be more pessimistic' (Qian 2016).

EMOTIONAL TRANSFORMATION

Fear and insecurity can motivate political action: 'Fear of harm, the emotion that triggers our concern with our preservation and security, becomes the enemy, the rallying point for political awareness, vigilance, and meaningful collective action' (Evrigenis 2008: xviii). The affective dynamics unleashed by *Ten Years* constitutes a distinct political manifesto for change. Unlike the characters who choose the means of self-paralysis to avoid confrontation with threatening China in Fruit Chan's 1997 Trilogy, *Ten Years* addresses fear by featuring radical action. The injured subject in the film is characterised as uncompromising and rebellious; the characters attempt to change their fates in more direct and confrontational ways. For example, the male character in *Season of the End* hopes to turn himself into a specimen to rebel against the irresistible force. Other characters sacrifice themselves to awaken the public (*Self-Immolator*) or suspend China's infiltration in their everyday lives (*Local Egg*). They are more self-determining and capable than helpless victims, showing a strong desire to choose their destiny. As a hunger striker in *Self-Immolator* says, 'It's not hatred that keeps me going. But hope.' This statement also indicates how the injured subject becomes more hopeful of regaining lost enjoyment and insistent on struggling with China. The narrative of loss has gotten rid of the implicit, indirect and ambiguous strategy and invested more with subaltern groups, victims of political oppression and rebels.

Such an emotional transformation reflects the political ambition of the film's directors, who are aware of their connection to the Umbrella Movement and conceive of their work as constitutive of broader political activism against China. The film offers the myth of local destiny and stimulates their desire for change. As a planner of the film recalled, the initial inspiration for *Ten Years* started from the bewilderment of Hong Kong's destiny:

> It is not a resolution that we just let the pessimism prevail in Hong Kong
> ... we need to imagine the future of Hong Kong. Even though it may
> not be a good result, the imagination is powerful and can lead us to get
> rid of the scary reality. (Liao 2016)

The intense mood of uncertainty and insecurity, which constitutes a collective response to the perceived threat to Hong Kong, prompts the filmmakers to incorporate emotions into their work. The film aims to stimulate political motivation and intervention. The story creates a fantasy that 'we' must take action towards the fearful Other. In this sense, the film opens up an affective space for gathering resistance. As the director of *Self-Immolator* commented,

> The film hopes to surprise the audience to take concrete action to change
> their situation. . . . We need freedom of thinking, and I think we should
> fight for such freedom. Many people have asked us whether we are
> scared. We have to fight, and how we conduct ourselves in a frightening
> atmosphere requires fearlessness. (Liao 2016)

In the same vein, the director of *Local Egg* said, 'if Hong Kong people don't want to see the situation in *Ten Years*, they should do something now, and they should control their destiny'. This reflection explains why some hailed the film as the 'Umbrella Movement in the Hong Kong film industry' (RTHK31 2016).

Ten Years illustrates how fear motivates a politics of resentment and hatred expressed in the form of nativism. It visualises Hong Kong's affective struggle over identity and the future. Two fantasies are offered by the film to recover nativist fullness. The first is taking up a resisting and uncooperative attitude in the practice of everyday life. The grocery shop owner in *Local Egg*, the collector of cultural relics in *Season of the End* and the taxi driver in *Dialect* display their refusal. As the man in *Season of the End* says, 'I don't want to give up the principle until this moment.' The second fantasy mobilises vengeful and heroic passion by featuring the sacrificing and dead body, as illustrated in *Self-Immolator*. Acts of self-immolation create traumatic effects by generating 'a heightened sense of anxiety and a dread of the unknown' (Kinnvall 2013: 150). Representations of traumatic events produce powerful emotional meanings that enable witnesses to share in the sense of injury and loss (Hutchinson 2016). The film's affective investment focuses on the trauma of self-immolation for shock, sorrow and anger to emerge. Through the work of investment, the vulnerable and dying body becomes the imaginarised body of the native, a shared object of nativist love. The director admitted that 'self-immolation is a very radical means, which will make people think, and this is my original intention' (Ho 2016). The death protest is invested with the meaning of martyrdom. Shock and sadness can bind the social body together. As the character in the film says, 'the reason that Hong Kong people failed to fight for democracy is that no one is dead'. The episode implies that sacrifice is inevitable if Hong Kong wants to overcome its loss of enjoyment.

Despite their contextual differences, in many ways the film's fantasies of loss resemble the Chinese political films made during the Cultural Revolution. The most typical films of this kind – namely the 'revolutionary model operas' –served to cultivate revolutionary passion. The subjects in these films are fantasised as the oppressed and victimised class. Fear nurtures the imaginaries of the enemy. These films were about how the masses struggled with their enemies and finally obtained freedom under the leadership of the Communist Party. In these narratives, the people can only live happily by eliminating the enemy. In Mao's period, emotional mobilisation was crucial (Perry 2002). As Mao once pointed out, 'there is absolutely no such thing in the world as love or hate without cause or reason' (Mao 1991: 871). The opposing emotions – love and hate – were evoked to draw political boundaries between friends and enemies. Hateful passion has been central to the revolutionary drive: 'No "enemies", no indignation, and no indignation, no fuel for revolution. Paranoia was no longer considered revolutionary "excess"' (Liu 2010: 342). *Ten Years* reproduces a similar logic of the 'us vs them' confrontation in moral terms (good vs evil). In such emotional narratives, all the emotional relations presented in the film – including romance, family affection and friendship – are invested with fear and hatred of the enemy.

AFFECTIVE DISJUNCTURE

This chapter has thus far contextualised the emotional forces that have gathered to formulate Hong Kong's affective space. It also addresses the importance of enjoyment in structuring local identification. One has to understand the role of enjoyment in the formulation of anti-Chinese sentiment in order to make sense of nativism. The contextualisation of the dialectics of enjoyment helps explain what sustains the tension between Hong Kong and mainland China. Both parties have their own affective lives, subjectivities and dynamics embedded in different historical experiences, memories and trajectories. Both are seen as sources of disturbance preventing 'us' from living up to 'our' ideal and from satisfying our desire fully. Both recapture the particular enjoyment by bolstering identification with the self and disidentification with the Other, eliciting divergent economies of desire, distributions of emotions and attachments.

Due to the different historical and psychological forces at work, each entity has developed different emotionally charged imaginaries. On the part of mainland China, Hong Kong has been a historical object of sovereign desire. The Hong Kong question permeates the entire historical experience of modern China (Ren 2010: 28). The territory has never been a purely foreign Other in the Chinese perception. Rather, it has long been seen as a compatriot once ruled by the West – a victim of colonial humiliation and a loss of sovereignty. Its existence is evidence of the arrogance and greed of colonialism. Its colonial past is why the nationalist narrative frames the 1997 handover in terms of recovering the Chinese people's common ancestry and history of suffering. Likewise, in the binary relationship between Hong Kong and mainland China, British colonial modernity is always an 'absent presence' in Hong Kong's fantasies. This internalised Other is invested with various cultural imaginaries, such as modernity and civilisation, that cultivate a sense of superiority. In this sense, Hong Kong's anti-China and pro-West sentiments are inseparable. They are marked by the relegation of China into signs of disgrace, pain and fear that fail Hong Kong's ideals. Its cumulative emotional energy is exemplified in a series of nativist actions.

The emotional conflicts exhibited in *Ten Years* provide an opportunity for rethinking how the two entities are interlocked with their otherness. Both entities follow very different paths. Both deal with their lack of enjoyment by attributing it to one another, entailing two opposing emotional structures that have become the material basis of ongoing conflicts. When both shift the object of identification towards the self and become utterly self-centric, the political possibilities are foreclosed. The affective disjuncture also provides an opportunity to understand the emotional impact of the rise of China. Underlying Xi's affective sovereignty, which promotes the triumphalist sentiments of pride and hope, is the perception that Hong Kong's nativist politics disrupts the ideal image of the nation. The regime's extraction of affective energy ignores and erases Hong

Kong's complex emotional experiences and appeals. Recent changes in geopolitical status between the two have further solidified the disjuncture. Fear represents Hong Kong's uneasiness and anxiety about these changes, while pride signifies China's emotional transformation from a weak to a powerful position. Although their paths are historically connected and overlapping, they have run parallel to each other and never intersected. Each entity sees the Other as a symbol of loss and pain. Each side is limited by its narcissistic logic and privileges its own experience to ignore that of the Other – an approach that has made mutual understanding and reconciliation more difficult. There is a deep, shared refusal to acknowledge the Other's anxiety, hope and frustration. With both parties imagining the Other as antagonists, only resentment, hostility and hatred are cultivated. We suggest that juxtaposing these two axes of feeling helps to identify the internal psychological mechanisms of the present political predicament.

The affective dichotomy can be seen as a consequence of different aspirations for and pursuits of modernity. We agree with Baik Youngseo's (2016) claim that the key to reconciliation is the subjects' ability to 'share each other's agony and sufferings' and to feel for and understand one another. The critical question is: what dialogic space could be opened with this emotional divergence? How can the emotions of each side be mutually recognised? How can both sides avoid the dangers of parochial identity politics and narcissistic self-centredness? These questions demand a new mode of enquiry and intellectual practice to overcome the platitudes of the political domain. The ongoing tensions may offer a starting point for attending to the emotional dimensions central to China's future.

CONCLUSION

Hong Kong's affective space is a product of shifts in geopolitical emotions and nativist passions under the gaze of Chinese nationalism. This chapter explores how the film *Ten Years* expresses mainland–Hong Kong tensions and highlights some salient emotional contradictions in Hong Kong society. By contextualising the film-produced fantasies through which Hong Kong's loss of enjoyment is imagined and organised, we investigate how a range of emotional dispositions constitute affective tendencies and antagonism leading to political conflicts. Embedded in the broader historical traces of Hong Kong's traumatic encounter with China, these film-mediated emotional intensities resonate with off-screen development. *Ten Years* provides a fantasy through which the current contradictions are registered. Our analysis considers fear's configuration of popular imaginaries and how it plays out in the emotional split with mainland China. It reinvents Hong Kong's emotional subjectivity and contributes to the ongoing confrontation. The film also illustrates the impact of geopolitics on the distribution of emotion in Hong Kong. The fear channelled by the film signals a refusal to perform the positive emotions demanded by the regime.

The analysis presented in this chapter illuminates Hong Kong's landscape of fear and its underlying structure. It offers an assessment of the ways intensities of fear open up an affective space for political intervention. Our analysis has focused on the cumulative effect of emotional attachments on a historical relation, treating fear as a representation of geopolitics. What is lacking is a more specific description of the experience of fear as a bodily symptom. If fear conveys discontent, how is it manifested in concrete political practices in ordinary people's everyday life? How does fear capture political subjectivity by circulating across bodies? How does fear intervene in the micro-process of struggle? What remains unaddressed is the question of the body. More specifically, Chapter 4 will explore the embodied aspect of fear by shifting our attention to the transmission of bodily feelings.

NOTES

1. The Umbrella Movement was a sequence of street protests that unfolded in Hong Kong between 26 September and 15 December, 2014. The protests were triggered by Beijing authorities' decision concerning Hong Kong's electoral framework, introducing a candidate pre-screening procedure for the Chief Executive of Hong Kong. The movement derived its name from the protestors' subversive use of umbrellas to shield themselves from the police's pepper spray, resulting in a widely covered global media event.
2. The agreement declared that the Chinese government would reclaim the governance of Hong Kong from 1 July 1997. The declaration promised to keep Hong Kong's social and economic system unchanged for fifty years to ensure Hong Kong's prosperity and stability. It also pledged to give Hong Kong a high degree of political autonomy by establishing it as a Special Administrative Region (SAR) under the authority of the Chinese central government.

PART II

Body, Social Media,
Affective Struggle

CHAPTER FOUR

The body in fear

'HOW CAN I LIVE ON IN THE FUTURE?'

During the summer of 2015, we carried out a series of field observations and interviews at a clothing factory in Shenzhen. Our research was motivated by the actions of a group of female workers who publicised their non-violent protests on social media. Between 2014 and 2015, conflict associated with social insurance contributions became a component of an ensuing social crisis. Many protest events were triggered by widespread outrage at the violation of workers' legal rights to social insurance and other forms of welfare security. This chapter continues the interest in the politics of fear by shifting the analytical focus to the body as a site of affective investment. It attempts to demonstrate the centrality of fear to China's sociopolitical order and how this influences the expression of discontent. We seek to understand the role of fear in the embodied protest by exploring the emotional dynamics of the protesters' struggle and the political possibilities created by emotional forces. Our analysis investigates the complex ways these workers experienced and articulated the distinctive passionate politics that binds peasant workers with the state. In doing so, it captures the ways in which fear serves to maintain power while opening up a space for struggle.

'How can I live on in the future?' This problem has particularly worried Zhongfen, a female worker whom we interviewed. Zhongfen, over fifty years old, started working in Shenzhen after moving from Yulin, Guangxi Province, in 1984 and began her job in the factory of the subcontractor Artigas in 1994. As of July 2015, although she had worked for the company for nearly twenty years, Artigas had only paid her pension insurance for less than two years.

She would not be entitled to social security on her retirement at the age of sixty, because the years paid into it would be less than the fifteen-year minimum stipulated by the state. Zhongfen keenly hoped that the factory would pay back the pension insurance from the year of her recruitment, but such hope was rapidly fading as she attempted to negotiate with the employer. Since there was no guarantee that she would have the means for basic survival after retirement, Zhongfen felt uncertain about the future that market forces would determine. She was overwhelmed by an intuitive fear of losing her job and social security, which is a future-oriented experience and anticipates adverse outcomes.

Fear is a negative and unpleasant emotion that involves intense bodily experiences. It mainly works by anticipating a lack of predictability and security or an injury, pain and suffering imminent in the present (Ahmed 2004). The Artigas workers deeply felt fear as emotional anticipation of the gloomy prospect of a threatening and injurious future (Barbalet and Demertzis 2013: 170). It was a component of their collective experience of protracted struggle. Another female worker, Meizi, was also fearful of being exposed to the uncertainties of life. She had worked twelve hours almost every day for more than twenty years and, worse yet, her overtime pay was often deducted by her employer. In 2010, the company began to pay her social security funds but was unwilling to make up the previously unpaid fund. Therefore, if she wanted to receive a pension after retirement, Meizi, who was fifty years old, would have to continue working for eleven more years. These experiences had made her feel like she was just a disposable object:

> We started to work in Shenzhen in the early 1990s when there was no pension insurance system, but after the pension insurance had been rolled out, the factory did not want to make up for the unpaid pension insurance. How many eighteen years can I have in my life, and my best eighteen years were spent in the factory. Back then, we were young, but now when we grow old, the factory just sweeps us away like garbage. (Interview, 21 July 2015)

Restless anxiety, insecurity and fear made Zhongfen and Meizi unwilling to resign themselves to fate. In December 2014 and June 2015, they took part in a series of strikes requesting that their employer make up for the pension insurance. Many of the protesting workers – primarily women who had been eager to leave their villages and sell their labour in the city when they were young – had worked at Artigas for more than a decade.

This research focuses on the affective struggle of this group of female workers at a UNIQLO supplier in Shenzhen, exploring how their fears for the future played out and how their emotional feelings of insecurity motivated collective action and configured their emotional subjectivity in the face of extreme risk. As a subsidiary of Hong Kong-owned Lever Style, Artigas was founded in 1992, serving as a subcontractor for UNIQLO and G2000. Its workforce was mainly made up of women from rural areas. Although Artigas is a well-known enterprise in the Pearl River Delta region, its treatment of workers has been notoriously fraught with problems such as long working hours, low wages, poor working conditions and harsh punishments.

In response to global economic downturn, an increase in China's labour costs and the Chinese government's control over the renminbi, the firm eventually started to cut production scale in China. From 2011 onwards, the number of its employees in China dropped by one-third and the firm transferred its main production base to Vietnam, whose worker salaries were only half of those in Shenzhen in 2013. When, in late 2014, Artigas announced it had merged with other Lever Style factories and planned to shut down, many of the Shenzhen workers became anxious about their future. At this point they learned that the company had not legally paid social security in full since their recruitment – and not only that, but it had even transferred their deducted social security funds to those of some management staff. This situation rendered the workers intensely indignant, requesting that management make up the pension payments as soon as possible. However, instead of meeting their demands, the company continued to shirk its responsibilities and persuaded workers who had just turned fifty to resign. The angry workers united, staged strikes and fought for their future by seizing the factory and appealing to the government. This chapter draws upon these events to explore the affective dynamics of fear in economic restructuring.

Similar evasion or non-payment of workers' social security funds has been a pervasive problem in China and emerged as a legal rights issue in the Pearl River Delta region,[1] triggering waves of labour struggle on a national scale (Gao 2015; Su 2017). The enmity, anger and fear expressed during these protests are emotional reactions to a perceived threat to the protesters' status as workers. According to official statistics, the number of peasant workers in China totalled 273 million in 2014, of whom those over 50 years old represented 17 per cent – that is, more than 46 million. If the age group of 41–50 years is included, then the proportion of those over 41 years old is 26 per cent, for nearly 120 million people. Since the existing social security system for peasant workers is poorly implemented at the local level, more than 100 million workers will live in fear without social protection in the next ten to twenty years (NBS 2015).

UNDERSTANDING WORKERS' EMOTIONS

The negative mood of uncertainty and insecurity – a collective response to destabilisation and perceived threats to workers' identity – prompts us to consider the role of emotion in the struggle. There is an extensive body of research on Chinese workers: many such studies have documented the situation of peasant workers (for example, Zhang 2012; Pun 2005; Yang 2013; Chang 2009; Pun et al. 2010; Li 2012; Goodman 2014). Although some have tried to incorporate culture into their analyses, how the production of emotion shapes workers' identity and politics remains largely unexplored. The field pays much attention to the living conditions and experiences of peasant workers from traditional sociological perspectives, including their vulnerable social positionality and unfair treatment (Zhang L. 2001; Chang 2009), their class attributes associated with specific political and economic structures of domination (Pun 2005; Yang 2013; Goodman 2014), and their contingent strategies of resistance (Lee 2007a). Emotions such as expectation, worry, joy and disappointment are present in every aspect of workers' daily lives, but politically excluded. Experiences of subordination or unfair treatment can stimulate the struggle for different distributions of emotions (Goodwin et al. 2001; Clarke et al. 2006b). Although Chinese workers are emotional subjects who actively produce different emotions in response to different situations, and their identity experiences are saturated with emotional conflict, the role of emotion in social and political processes has largely been overlooked by the existing research.[2] Since traditional scholarly approaches tend to see the political actor as motivated by the instrumental pursuit of interests (Mouffe 2013), much work remains to be done to examine politics and emotions (Berezin 2002).

124

This research attempts to fill the void by examining the embodied resistance of peasant workers under Xi Jinping's regime. Our analysis suggests that emotion is central to the formation of worker subjectivity because it is a resource to be mobilised (as presumed by rationalist thinking). It is also a form of cultural practice (Harding and Pribram 2009) that enables the emotional subject to become a collective force. We chose to investigate workers' emotions because it was evident that anxiety, insecurity, frustration and anger were present at every stage of this struggle: the workers' feelings motivated their actions, while their actions, in turn, affected their feelings. An observable emotional intensity drove their actions, and their emotional appeals generated tremendous energy for political intervention. Emotions enable workers to cultivate the capacity for collective action, through which 'the body and the mind are simultaneously engaged, and that similarly reason and passion, intelligence and feeling, are employed together' (Hardt 2007: x–xi). We are not only interested in how emotion triggers political action but also in the way a broader regime of political culture shapes its production of subjectivity. Emotional feelings and energies at the group level, which are produced and manifested in various activities of workers, play a crucial role in shaping their subjectivity. We see worker action as being driven by the emotions produced by adverse experiences of social dislocation and dispossession, rather than just the rationally motivated pursuit of benefits.

As a form of sociality, emotion's constitutive role in popular political activity has now been recognised: powerful emotions can take possession of people (Hoggett 2009), create political identities and open up potentially subversive moments (Mouffe 2013), and influence political organising (Hardt 2007).[3] Emotions prepare individuals for political action and constitute an 'important microfoundation upon which more complex political processes and outcomes depend' (Clarke et al. 2006b: 10). The collective emotion released in the protest movement can manifest itself through bodily sensations, conversation, gestures, voices, narratives, body language and other forms of expression (Buechler 2000; Goodwin et al. 2001; Ahmed 2004; Reed 2005).

Originated and embedded in concrete social interactions and relations, the production of emotional subjectivity – especially in the politicised emotions of subordinate groups – is closely associated with social hierarchy, inequality and conflict. The specific emotions

that subordinated people experience mainly 'arise out of the structure of the relations of power and status in which they are implicated'
(Barbalet 2002: 4). People sharing common structural circumstances
may experience common emotions. In the case of Artigas's workers,
their chaotic emotional experiences resulted from their loss of status
and the threat to their identity as workers. The emotions aroused
by their collective experience of frustration, outrage and fear about
negative situations constituted the motivating force of their militant
action. Informed by a relational understanding of emotions, this
research investigates the complex ways in which the proliferation of
fear, as a response to the anticipation of pain in the future, articulates
the process of subject-making in the face of increasing instability and
precarity.

Fear, as an expression and product of social inequality, is inherent in every form of domination, where the powerful can decide
the life chances of the powerless but are uncertain about the latter's
response. In 'repressive systems', writes Flam (2005: 23), 'the fear for
life chances is joined by the fear for one's physical freedom and life'.
This perspective is particularly pertinent to the emotional experience
of subaltern groups in China. In the contemporary political history
of China, fear has been a fluid, pervasive and widely felt emotion
that is deeply associated with and embedded in the state's political
institutions and practices (Barbalet 2002; Berezin 2002: 43; Clarke et
al. 2006b). Especially after 1949, the economy of fear was produced
and amplified by a series of state-led political campaigns and thus
intensely institutionalised and politicised. It involves the fear of both
the powerless and the powerful (Robin 2004: 20). Fear can promote
fear – it can become highly contagious when instigated by the state.
Powerful elites can use it to promote their agenda and make people
consent to their power. To prevent and deter any potential threats to
the status quo, the Chinese state took fearful actions and constructed
political fear as its instrument.

Instead of discussing emotion in general, we will focus mainly on
the unpleasant intensities of fear produced by a loss of power and
a threat to workers' identity formation – mainly how fear is constructed, performed and felt through a range of concrete emotional
practices and dispositions. The fear experienced by workers results
from negative situations that threaten their survival. It is worth
investigating how their fear articulates with other emotional expressions such as moral shock, insecurity and indignation by investing

in an object (Laclau 2005). In our analysis, fear is not something embedded in a preexisting subject or object as its property, but a kind of energy circulating across social bodies and relations. In other words, fear is produced in fluid, intersubjective processes and has no residence. Rather than asking what fear is, we investigate what fear *does*. In addition, we also consider how the workers' affective practices of solidarity, strategy and identity construction served to 'provide instant evaluation of circumstance . . . [and] influence the disposition of the person for a response to those circumstances' (Barbalet 2002: 3).

The empirical data of this study are mainly drawn from first-hand interviews with Artigas workers and NGO activists amid heightened surveillance by the local government. During the fieldwork, some workers tried hard to avoid us for fear of being punished. Even a motor tricycle driver, on learning that we were going to approach the workers, became suspicious of our identities, worrying that he might get into trouble for helping us. Under such circumstances and given the limited time available to us, we were only able to talk with a dozen workers who were still hoping to have their pension problems solved.[4] In considering these conversations, it is necessary to contextualise the politics of fear.

TOP-DOWN DISTRIBUTION OF FEAR

[T]he object of fear is conceptualized as the prospect of an undesirable event or outcome . . . the specific objects of fear will include the prospect of social dislocations of various sorts. (Barbalet and Demertzis 2013: 184)

Peasant workers' fear – a complex product of the one-party-dominated political culture, state attitudes, policies, market conditions and business decisions – is deeply embedded in a rapidly reconfiguring society since Deng Xiaoping's reform initiatives. Their fear has to be understood in the specific context of a complex, multifaceted process of dispossession of workers, where

the worn-out yet still-existing hukou system (the population registry system); the parochial nature of urban governments with expanding administrative power; the strict control of the population and economic development all dictate a specific process of proletarianization and struggle in contemporary China. (Pun 2005: 5)

Workers' experiences reveal the complex ways in which fear is 'stimulated by specific experiences of power and status' (Barbalet 2002: 3) and raise questions about how the state and capitalists mobilise it to perpetuate domination. The state's ideological politics, rural–urban disparity, and workplace control contribute to the production of fear that can hardly be reduced to a single factor. The varied experiences of peasant workers provide clues to understanding the making of their emotional subjectivity from above.

FEAR OF INSTITUTIONAL DISPOSSESSION

Peasants, the largest population group who formed the base of the communist revolution, were often the target of political mobilisation to confront perceived enemies. The CPC, which took power by successfully mobilising the peasants, is undoubtedly aware of the peasants' subversive power and potential threat to regime stability, so containing and controlling them and keeping them in a subordinate position has always been central to its rule. Although the regime claims to represent the interests of the working class, it has ironically relied on peasants to build up legitimacy. The 'notion of class was no doubt alien to the Chinese peasantry' (Pun 2005: 11). This ambivalent attitude towards peasants is manifested by separating them from class enemies while endorsing them with an empty sense of moral superiority. During Mao's era, rural areas were endowed with higher moral-political status, and youth from urban areas were sent to the countryside to receive 'reeducation' from peasants. Despite their strong support of the communist revolution, Chinese peasants were not allowed to enjoy the same status as urban residents.

The urban–rural separation policy of the *hukou* (户口, household registration) system was first implemented in 1958. It 'proved to be one of the most effective mechanisms for population control and distribution during the process of constructing the socialist state' (Pun 2005: 179). The system determined not simply where a person could reside but also their social rank, food rations, entitlements and other life chances (Cheng and Selden 1994; Fan 2002). Mao's industrialisation prioritised the city and was based on the extraction of rural resources; urban development was prioritised at the expense of rural interests (Yang 2005; Pai 2012). Since then, a vast social chasm of inequality between the urban and the rural has been created. The urban population enjoyed the benefit of social status, employment, wages, food supply and housing. By contrast, the rural population could not enjoy such benefits, and their social status and living standards were significantly inferior to those of the urban population (Liu 2007). The state has legalised this deep-rooted divide and inequality (Solinger 1995; Lee 2007b). Inferiority, insecurity and fear for their own survival have become familiar emotional experiences for many Chinese peasants.

This tremendous social divide has also nurtured a collective desire to migrate to the city. Deng Xiaoping's reform policies depended on the mobilisation of cheap rural labour, creating new opportunities for peasants while exacerbating the unequal development between rural and urban areas. The state's loosening of control on population mobility, which aimed to meet the urgent need for economic growth, set peasants on the move – a vast number of peasants from across the country were driven off their lands with great hopes and desires for a better life chance in coastal cities. The *mingong* (民工, peasant workers) tides signify 'the fusing and struggling of individual and collective desires to fill the social chasm as the only hope of escape' (Pun 2005: 73). However, their migration experience is replete with a mixed sense of frustration and injustice. Rural bodies are often labelled as 'floating population' or more discriminatory terms such as *mangliu* (盲流, blind flows). Regardless of how long they live in the city, they are seen as outsiders (Zhang L. 2001). Thus, the construction of peasants as inferior Other is closely associated with the legitimisation of social space that allows those urban bodies to claim their existence while excluding those rural bodies.

Hierarchies of power and status can 'generate certain kinds of emotions depending on where one is in these hierarchies and to whom one is reacting' (Goodwin et al. 2001: 10). Peasant workers' fear is a crucial element in forming their emotional subjectivities, which are caught between 'the master of the nation' on the one hand, and the inferior position in the city on the other. The term 'peasant workers' blurs the lines of identity between peasants and workers: when they are no longer needed as workers, their identity as peasants becomes an excuse for the state to expel them from the city. As Li (2012) observes, the exploitation encountered by peasant workers is a kind of 'multi-level deprivation' whereby members of this group are subject to many forms of dispossession successively during their lifetimes. At the local level, although state laws claim to protect the interests of peasants and migrant workers, most local governments fail to provide adequate protection and often formulate policies that are not entirely consistent with the laws or even against them.

In the case of Artigas's workers, their rights should have been protected by the Labour Law, under which both employers and workers have to pay pension insurance for fifteen years in order to obtain access to pension funds after retirement. If employers fail to do so, then they shall be obligated to make it up and pay an additional fine. However, these legal regulations have been poorly implemented in Shenzhen and many other cities. To protect the interests of employers, the Shenzhen government makes a special provision that employers only need to set up a pension for two years at most if they have failed to pay in the past. Such a policy provides justification for employers to reject workers' demands for compensation, as Liu (2007: 475–6) observes:

> [T]he monopoly of local governments in policy implementation has created barriers that keep rural migrant workers in particular out of social protection. The introduction of market principles, whereby entitlement to social welfare depends, both qualitatively and quantitatively, on the payment of social insurance premiums by individuals and employers, discriminates against low income earners, rural migrant workers and those who are not in formal employment.

MICROPHYSICS OF WORKPLACE FEAR

Chinese workers' fear, expressed mainly through a 'paralysing sense of hopelessness' (Gould 2016: 3498), arises from different forms of politico-economic and cultural hierarchies. Business power immediately affects their job security and thus often becomes the main target of labour conflicts. As in many factories in China, in the case of Artigas workers were vulnerable to exploitation, deprivation and punishment by management, which sought to maximise working time and the extraction of labour power. The workers' fear was embedded in productive relations and linked to their subordinate position in the workplace. Their fears included the fear of punishment and losing their job, losing life chances and being denied access to social security and a liveable future. A kind of 'workplace authoritarianism' was visible in Artigas's management style that is familiar to China's production regime, especially in special economic zones:

The minimal state intervention in management-labor relations in most of the developing zones, along with the lack of independent labor forces, means that practices of excessive control, long hours, low wages, and poor living environments are often the rule in contemporary China. (Pun 2005: 108)

Structural changes in labour conditions, usually manifested as merging, restructuring, streamlining and layoffs, often result in a decrease in workers' bargaining power and thus produce negative emotions such as anxiety, insecurity, and fear:

[C]hange itself is a potential source of fear [. . .] . Not all changes lead to fear, of course, but under conditions of the social actor's perceptions of insufficient power, the experience of changes is likely to lead to fear. This notion matches the intuitive supposition that change is to be feared which raises the possibility of deteriorating prospects for subjects whose power is insufficient to provide compensating or mollifying adjustments. (Barbalet and Demertzis 2013: 169)

As a negative emotional aspect of the experience of unemployment (Barbalet 2002), fear can prevent the unionisation of workers (Barbalet and Demertzis 2013: 175) and increase monitoring and punishment in the workplace: 'Wielding threats of firing, demotion, harassment, and other sanctions,' writes Robin (2004: 21), 'employers and managers attempt to stifle speech and action, to ensure that workers don't talk back or act up.' Many Artigas workers shared with us their fear of being punished and losing their jobs. Workplace fear had become part of their subjective experience of migration and dislocation. Meanwhile, unfavourable business practices and government attitudes, which workers perceived as a threat to their survival, constituted the primary sources of their actions, reinforcing other negative emotions such as frustration and anger.

PROTEST ACTION AS A MANIFESTATION OF WORKER EMOTIONS

The subjectivity of peasant workers is embodied in productive relations and their resistance to conditions of insecurity. In China, negative emotion often manifests itself in protest action. In the Artigas factory, the workers were desperate to find ways to channel their anger and fear and express them in the form of defiance and refusal. Embodied feelings such as fear and frustration can paralyse people and motivate them to act up (Goodwin et al. 2001; Harding and

Pribram 2009; Jasper 2014). There is, as some scholars indicate, an inherent connection between emotion and protest action:

> [P]rotest emerged when a structural strain – for example, an economic depression – disrupted the normative order and provoked feelings like alienation and anxiety, leading individuals to turn toward rash, frenzied, disruptive group behavior. (Gould 2016: 3466–7)

In a regime where political opportunities for struggle are severely limited, emotions such as fear, desperation and indignation often combine to stimulate action in the face of extreme risk and uncertainty (Gould 2016). In the case of Artigas, the workers' anger was sparked by a business decision on factory closure. When the decision was disclosed, the workers' intuitive fears were further intensified and transformed into anticipation of 'hurt' caused by the deprivation of a liveable future. All these experiences gave rise to a process of emotional accumulation that provided the grounds for collective action and sustained their struggle.

Fear is not necessarily disadvantageous to popular protest but 'leads to an actor's realization of where his interests lie, and points in the direction of what might be done to achieve them' (Barbalet 1998: 149). From a strategic perspective, workers can deploy fear as a resource for mobilisation (Goodwin et al. 2001). Fear transformed the Artigas workers into transgressive subjects of resistance. If their restless insecurity and fear were driven by their negative experiences of discrimination and dispossession, their sense of anxiety and uncertainty about the future – which is central to the making of their subjectivity – also provided a source of political vitality and tactical resistance. The fear of worse consequences enabled them to develop an affective capacity for disruptive action. In the past decade, Chinese workers have staged mass sit-ins or traffic blockages, organised petitions and strikes, and in some circumstances occupied workshops as part of their attempts to increase their bargaining power. Emotional feelings are present in every aspect of their protests, where workers often threaten with sheer numbers that constitute a coercive power (Jasper 2014).

EMOTIONALLY CHARGED RESISTANCE AND SOLIDARITY

The Artigas workers' emotions affected the embodied activities through which they lived out their body politics in confronting the factory's disciplinary power. The disposition of workers' bodies is situated in a disciplinary production regime that monitors and restricts the movement of the labouring body to specific spaces (Ahmed 2004; Shalhoub-Kevorkian 2015). Despite the regime's efforts to normalise and individualise heterogeneous rural bodies as a unified, obedient, submissive and productive workforce, workers could still find chances to seize some moments, turn their bodies into agents of resistance and hold 'interstitial power' (Pun 2005) in negotiating with disciplinary forces. The body, through which multiple emotions are circulated and a relational field of practices is formulated, is central to workers' resistance. The assembly of working bodies around a factory area, for instance, is a show of threat and constitutes an ad hoc site for the investment of fear. The defiant body amasses, speaks and acts in concert so that the workers' voices cannot be silenced.

Here the body is understood in embodied relationality in a specific situation (Prokhovnik 2014). The two strikes at Artigas demonstrated how the workers' bodies created a site for claim-making within the disciplinary space and had the potential of redeploying that space for their ends. In addition to sit-ins and strikes, the workers also sought to subvert disciplinary power by blocking the gate. At the peak of the protest, they seized the factory as a way of claiming the properties. The symbolic meaning of seizing the factory is that it belongs to the workers and that they possess the right to keep it. These embodied practices of disruption paralysed and frightened the employer and, more crucially, turned the factory into a temporary 'political theatre' that allowed workers' grievances to be seen and heard: 'We guard all workshops day and night just to get back our hard-earned money!' This slogan, which was displayed during the strike on a banner made by the workers, conveyed the message that their fight for survival and dignity was finding its expression in their physical control of the workshop. It aimed at preventing the employer from taking machines out of the factory. The seizure was a way of gaining a political platform and securing the material conditions for resistance. The workers' disruptive actions created a situation, transformed the workshop's hegemonic meaning and function, and opened up an ad hoc space for struggle. Facing the risk of

133

police evictions, they took turns to keep an eye on the equipment for more than forty days during the summer of 2015. They slept in the workshop and took care of each other to counter the individualisation of their bodies. Through these embodied practices, the workers waged their struggle for survival and exerted some control over the workplace, albeit short-lived.

The workers' embodied actions were motivated by multiple fears about their situation. Fear is an intersubjective experience (Demertzis 2013: 13) that can produce a series of unpredictable responses and chain reactions to state and business elites. Fear bound these workers together and turned them into a united group. As the struggle unfolded, their embodied practices formed an emotional bond that produced a feeling of solidarity, including mutual trust and concern for the collective, embodying the spirit of 'we are all here together, we must share something' (Berezin 2002: 44). This affective investment in the group was based on preexisting kin and ethnic networks of *tongxiang* (同乡, native–place relationship) familiar to the majority of Chinese peasant workers in the city (Pun 2005). Fluid affective networks of relationality offered the most intimate support to the workers, most of whom came from rural areas of Guangxi province.

DISILLUSIONMENT

Fear as a bodily symptom has an object (Ahmed 2004), and during this struggle, the object of fear had shifted and reconfigured the workers' sites of embodied resistance. There were different points of resistance created by the workers: the embodied actions driven by their fears targeted the employer and the government at different levels. They made their demands visible by gathering around government buildings, deploying symbolic resources in an attempt to make the factory management concede and gain leverage with the authorities. Since appealing to the government is a familiar tactic for Chinese workers seeking recognition from the state, such processes usually involve affective encounters between workers and local authorities.

During the first strike, Artigas workers who had lost their guaranteed pensions hoped to win the support of official trade unions, and thus submitted petitions to the Guangdong Province Federation of Trade Unions. During the second strike, the workers took their appeal to local district offices, the municipal petition office in Shenzhen, and the provincial petition office in Guangzhou respectively, making the provincial leadership aware of their plight. In the beginning, the workers carefully demonstrated obedience to the state and voiced their discontent with the employer. They created a scene of disorder near the boundary of official channels and blamed the employer for the problem. However, the response from these authorities was largely disappointing, leading to the proliferation of negative emotions of frustration and anger among the workers. As Duan told us:

> In the beginning, we believed that we should turn to trade unions, labor authorities, and appropriate national authorities once we encountered any problems. That is why we approached these units first. Their responses, however, were always disappointing. We also went to the Guangdong Federation of Trade Unions to complain about this problem last year. However, the Federation did not do anything from January to June, and we were disappointed . . . that is why we could not help feeling depressed when this was not possible . . . (Interview, 23 July 2015)

As in many other labour protests in China, the Artigas workers sought their rights through expressive actions of defiance such as staging sit-ins, strikes, rallying outside government offices and paralysing traffic – actions that were illegal but helped to widen public visibility. These protests are risky in a country where workers have been deprived of the right to strike, a right removed from the Chinese Constitution in 1982 for fear of regime-threatening labour unrest. Often, demands are framed in moral claims to subsistence and government responsibility. Although the workers' dramatic actions were somewhat successful in attracting official attention to their cause, a profound moral feeling of betrayal by the government was fomented during their interactions with local officials:

> They [governments] never stand by us. They asserted that they would uphold justice for us. But they didn't. . . . A staff of the labour inspection department told the workers that 'the factory will be closed down if you keep making trouble!' They always stand by the factory [owner]. I worked for the factory for more than eighteen years. How many eighteen years can I spend my life, and my best eighteen years were spent in Shenzhen. I will indeed spend the rest of my life here. (Interview with Duan, 23 July 2015)

A new worker-subject struggled to emerge amid growing suspicion of the government's attitude. As the tension increased, the workers invoked the notion of 'people' to exert moral-political pressure on the government. During the previous socialist period, the 'people', which nominally encompassed the majority of peasants and workers, were branded as 'masters of the nation' in official discourse, and the idea of 'serving the people' was the moral source of regime legitimacy. Satisfying people's needs, helping them to solve their problems, and working for their benefit were considered the primary responsibilities of the benevolent state. However, local governments' indifference and bureaucratic manner were seen as violating this moral commitment. These perceived breaches of humane governance gave rise to negative emotions such as anger, frustration and indignation. In petitioning the government, the negative feeling of disillusionment prevailed, contributing to growing distrust. The moral emotion (Jasper 2014) invested in the idea of the people was mobilised as a political resource. Another worker, Ou, then said:

> I have no faith in the words 'Serve the People'. I am incredibly disappointed in the government. How could Shenzhen become prosperous without our peasant workers? Now the city has become rich and we are old, the government does not need us anymore, they want to kick us out of the city. (Interview, 22 July 2015)

For the workers, the protest was about having their demands for respect and dignity recognised:

> If authorities demand respect, ordinary people earn their respect not by obeying the authorities, but by challenging them. [. . .] whereas the 'feeling rules' for authorities are to expect respect and compliance. When these two sets of feeling rules are confronted with each other, the result is likely to be conflict and the intensification of emotions on each side. (Yang 2005: 85)

Dong, who was beaten by the police during the strike, recalled:

> We complained about our problems to the government, only to be told that we should obey the boss's arrangement since we are working for him, and wherever the boss needs us, we should go there [. . .] . This is something that we might not forget forever. I told people that bodily injuries could recover quickly, but the wound in my heart . . . might be kept for a lifetime. This is the sadness of being a peasant worker [. . .] . We are not fighting only for the money, at least not entirely for money, but our dignity as peasant workers. (Interview, 22 July 2015)

When the workers discovered that the experience of 'people' was contradictory to what the state proclaimed, their sense of disappointment would prompt a repoliticisation of their subjectivity. The gap between official narratives and realities created an affective space where fear, frustration and anger were inscribed. In reshaping their political subjectivity, the workers' actions were intensely invested with the desire to 'be their own master'. Meanwhile, the CPC's enlargement of the terrain of social rights, as driven by its fear of social instability, provided a strategic space for the defence of collective persistence.

ACTING OUT IN THE NAME OF THE CITIZEN

With the expansion of social rights, Chinese workers have tended to employ hegemonic discourse to protect themselves (Pun 2005: 78) and garner moral support. Since Hu Jintao came to power in 2002, there has been a visibly greater emphasis on the institutionalisation of citizenship and the protection of ordinary people's legal rights, especially those left behind (*ruoshi qunti* 弱势群体) (Froissart 2009: 156). Since then, the state has enacted laws to ameliorate social tensions. Although these new labour laws did not overcome the problem of non-compliance among employers and local governments (Jacka et al. 2013: 77), they did provide the language of rights to be strategically exploited by the workers. The enumeration of legal rights has stimulated higher social expectations about rights protection and produced a rights consciousness. Labour protests have also been increasingly framed in legal terms, with protesters becoming emboldened to employ state laws to justify their actions in defence of 'citizens' legitimate rights' (*gongmin de hefa quanyi* 公民的合法权益) against abusive employers and officials (Goldman 2005; Pei 2010). As Lee (2010: 55) observes:

> Economic and legal reforms entail not just the transformation of institutions but also shifts in cognitive categories and moral subjectivity. The promulgation of laws, and the associated discourse of citizenship and legal rights, for instance, allow workers to view the self as public and to recognize the discrepancies between legal prescriptions and experiences of the absence of legal rights.

The widespread abuse of labour rights has led to strikes across the country (Perry and Selden 2010: 25–6; Ren 2013: 137). Compared to the socialist moralism espoused by workers of state-owned enterprises, peasant workers have resorted to the law as a basis for their actions. The Artigas workers deployed official discourses and acted in the name of state laws and citizens' rights to gain legitimacy. They defended the social rights to which they were entitled, namely *weiquan* (维权), through which they constituted themselves as active rights-bearing citizens. Being citizens means that they are entitled to legal protection and the benefits and rights guaranteed by state laws. In many such embodied protests, workers demand that local governments comply with state rules. When the struggle unfolded, it became apparent that the workers began identifying themselves as rightful citizens, entitled to negotiate with the employer and the government.

According to the provisions, employers should negotiate with employees' representatives when they decide on significant issues concerning the employees' interests. With the assistance of a local NGO, the workers developed a rights consciousness and framed their demands in legal terms. They selected their representatives and entrusted a law firm as their consultant to defend their rights. These efforts made possible the transformation of the abstract 'people' into concrete political subjects. With minimal resources at the workers' disposal, the legal rights of citizenship became a legitimate means of countering local governments. As a worker put it: 'They said they acted by the law? Did they do like that? We must ask them!' In the workers' online posts, there was an allocation of blame onto local governments for not addressing the wrongs. They constructed themselves as victims of local abuse of power and sought to arouse public compassion for their cause. A post under the title of 'Artigas Workers' Safeguarding Rights' circulated during the first strike in December 2014:

> The workers' hope is constantly crushed [by the government]. What does the government do? Does it stand by the factory? Can we expect the government to do something for us? We need to fight for our rights to the end all by ourselves! This is not only for us but also for peasant workers' fundamental interests.

FEAR AS A CHAIN REACTION

Widespread labour unrest has increasingly raised worry and fear for the state. Since 2003, *weiwen* (维稳, the maintenance of stability) has been prioritised as a way to contain the impact of social upheaval. The workers' disruptive actions necessarily generated caution and fear. The state's fear of labour protest has been translated into preventive action amid the drastic increase in public spending on stability preservation. This fear reaction is more likely when power elites feel threatened by the powerless: 'given the great disparity in power, for one with greater power a strong fight response is usually available at relatively low cost' (Kemper 2002: 61). With this mentality, the 'insecure state' (Berezin 2002) has made concerted efforts to discipline and punish the unruly body. Protesting workers are often conflated with troublemakers or criminals by local governments, whose fear works by characterising the workers as dangerous and threatening to stability. The language of fear, writes Ahmed (2004: 72), 'involves the intensification of "threats" which works to create a distinction between those who are "under threat" and those who threaten'. As a result, groups that are considered a threat to authorities are usually harshly suppressed through quotidian surveillance, harassment, arrests, detention, imprisonment and bodily injury. Police surveillance, intimidation and physical violence were all part of the Artigas workers' bodily experiences of fear:

> We just defended our rights and interests without offence. Why did the police arrest us?

The above quote was a question many workers felt confused about during the strikes. During the first strike, the employer agreed to negotiate with the workers under the coordination of lawyers. However, on the morning of the agreed-upon negotiation, police and security guards were called in to force the workers to resume work with threats of arrest. During the second strike, about one hundred workers who had petitioned the Shenzhen municipal government were repatriated to the factory by police. After the workers staged sit-ins with the authorities in Guangzhou for more than a week, no high-level officials were willing to meet them, but the police escorted them back to the factory. Before they were set free, the police forced each worker to sign a confession. Even after the strikes, the factory and the residential building were still filled with plainclothes police.

Because fear always moves and slides between bodies, it can produce emotional chain reactions: the repressive actions of the powerful can easily arouse fear in the powerless (Robin 2004: 29). After the local government intervened, surveillance became more intrusive and thus terrorised the Artigas workers, whose bodies were placed under constant surveillance and control. As a worker said:

> It was exceedingly terrible then. Large numbers of monitors were installed everywhere, on the streets, outside the factory and in every corner of the workshop. . . . I saw some people who passed by the factory taking photos. Then, the police searched their bags and took them to the local police station. The police asked them the purpose of taking pictures and then confiscated their mobile phones. It was exceedingly terrible! [. . .] Plainclothes officers were everywhere and remained around our residence. The employer knew our address and gave it to the police, so some workers were arrested based on inspection. Everyone felt highly terrified. (Interview with Lin, 23 July 2015)

Another worker, who was seized by the police during the strike, described the frightening experience of her days of imprisonment:

> I was seized because I was accused of 'disrupting the work order of the factory', and I had to accept this accusation; otherwise, I would continue to be detained . . . I don't want to be detained again. I could only have a steamed bun for one meal, and there was no bed. I could only sit, stand or lay on the cement floor. (Interview with Wen, 21 July 2015)

Fear and trauma did inhibit the workers' risky actions and create a heightened sense of insecurity. Nevertheless, despite the risk of bodily harm and their anxiety over the unknown, the impact of police repression on the workers' emotional state yielded mixed results: the 'presence of a large and impressive police contingent could intimidate the protesters or, on the contrary, stir anger on the side of the protesters' (Rucht 2016: 770). We observed that rough police treatment evoked broad emotional resonance among the workers and reinforced their distrust and moral indignation. There was a strong sense that the government should be held accountable:

> They [the government] always claim that China has already been a society ruled by law. Shouldn't the government practice what it propagandises? Honestly, what aspects could the government be said to be ruling according to the law? With police officers arresting people arbitrarily, government authorities keeping information to themselves and

doing everything they like, how can our action be successful? They treat us like three-year-old kids. (Interview with Xia, 23 July 2015)

The police action also triggered a battle over blame, with moral emotions playing a crucial role in arousing public concern and sympathy. As the struggle unfolded, workers used the emotional force of their moral argument to mobilise public support. They used social media to raise doubts about the opponent's morality:

> Does [the boss] take us 1,000 workers as fools? Who will believe that the problems can be resolved after we resume work? The factory has agreed to negotiate with the lawyers to defend workers' rights. How can it go back on its word and suppress the workers with the police? Does this solve the problems?

The workers' stories and images of action, suffering and solidarity became an indispensable resource to stimulate a heightened sense of moral anxiety, sympathy and urgency that was part of the chain reaction of fear.

CONCLUSION

This chapter investigates bottom-up emotional struggles by focusing on the political subject formation of a group of peasant workers who protested against the infringement of their rights to social insurance. It incorporates emotions into research on Chinese labour protest and argues that specific feelings, which link the individual to the broader social terrain, matter to labour politics. It investigates the emotional processes, dispositions, practices, reactions and conflicts involved in the shifting contours of worker struggle shaped by a broader affective regime. Power differentials result in different ways of distributing fear. Fear stems from negative experiences of subordination and power hierarchy. It arises in social interaction with others, such as rural bodies. Moreover, fear can generate caution and be incorporated into state governance. To understand the complex mechanisms of fear production and their intensity, we identify different causes and manifestations of workers' fear and consider its political impact.

However, fear is not simply an instrument of power. A perceived threat to status, security or identity will lead to a climate of fear that galvanises political intervention. Fear was the predominant emotion in the Artigas workers' struggle and articulated with other negative emotions such as anxiety, insecurity and anger. This chapter analyses how fear, a form of energy and a driving force for political action, circulates among social bodies, creates political possibilities and sustains political processes. We also identify the emotional sites and strategies that have become a motivating force of workers' rights struggles. The fear of the uncertain and the unpredictable is not confined to the powerless. The politics of fear functions as a two-way, mutually constitutive sequence of interaction and negotiation. It enables workers to reconfigure their subjective experiences of subalternity with broader sociopolitical processes. 'Top-down' fear, for example, constructs rural bodies as inferior and is bound up with the securing of hierarchy. Nevertheless, it can also produce emotional spillover effects and chain reactions on bodily feelings and provoked forms of disruptive action. Through the articulation of multiple fears, political boundaries are drawn. In describing workers' lived experiences of fear and how they communicate embodied feelings in the emotional dramas they create, this chapter illustrates the ways the economy of fear, which springs from pervasive social inequities, produces widespread repercussions. The politics of fear performs through the control and resistance of the body. Although the workers' fear links to their subaltern experience, it has the potential to politicise the body. We hope that the analysis presented in this chapter can open up new ways of thinking about political subjectivity.

Our analysis finds that social media, like the body, offers a crucial space for mediating workers' political expression and forging bonds of affective solidarity. It enables the social body to expand its physical, bottom-up emotional struggles by enlarging the terrain for fluid intersubjective communication. It allows workers to engage with others beyond their physical locale and to transmit affects. It is a place where political intensity spreads across borders and affective encounters occur. How do emotional subjects communicate and interact on social media? Does the Habermasian ideal of a public sphere apply to their online engagement? How do their interactive dynamics create an affective space of cybercommunication? These questions constitute the next chapter's analytical focus.

NOTES

1. Becker (2014: 28) categorises migrant worker disputes into four types: unpaid wages, labour injuries, illegal dismissal and unsafe working con-

ditions. He observes that protests over a lack of social benefits, including pension insurance, are growing. In 2014, the failure of China's largest footwear manufacturer, Taiwan-owned Yue Yuen, to properly handle workers' benefits and insurance by-laws caused over 30,000 workers to participate in a major strike that lasted for twelve days. This event caught the attention of other workers in the Pearl River Delta region regarding pension insurance and benefits. Finally, the employer promised to pay back the social security funds and grant increased subsistence allowances. Still it did not respond to the workers' demands, including pay raises, the reorganisation of trade unions and the execution of collective contracts. Intervention by the police eventually ended the strike.

2. Pun Ngai's research is an exception which is attentive to the emotional feelings of female peasant workers in China, particularly how they defeat boredom and fear through gossip, rumour, jokes and laughter. 'During joking and laughing,' writes Pun (2005: 157), 'women were more capable of articulating their feelings and emotions, albeit conflicting and ambivalent, such as love and hatred, desire and fear.' However, Pun's analysis does not account for the emotions associated with rights protest.

3. In social movement studies, 'most discussions portray collective identity as the drawing of a cognitive boundary rather than as affection for group members and, frequently, antipathy toward non-members' (Goodwin et al. 2001: 8–9).

4. With the help of NGOs, the protesting workers set up Weibo and WeChat accounts to publicise their struggles. To protect the privacy of interviewees, we use pseudonyms for all of them in this chapter. Our empirical sources include media coverage, workers' social media accounts and a very limited range of news reports. Although the government frequently blocked these channels, some valuable resources were left for our analysis.

CHAPTER FIVE

Affective publics' encounter

Political events, especially if they involve ideological rivals, can often elicit instantaneous and contrastive emotional responses. The United States politician Nancy Pelosi's high-profile visit to Taiwan on 2 August 2022 is a case in point. The CPC has long claimed ownership over Taiwan, and tensions have intensified under Chinese President Xi Jinping. Before Pelosi's plane landed, the Chinese government had frequently sent warplanes into Taiwan's air defence zone. Pelosi's trip, regarded by mainlanders as a political provocation to upgrade America's official interaction with Taiwan and encourage Taiwanese independence, prompted China to conduct military drills in retaliation. In contrast to the mainland's widespread upset and outrage at the visit, supporters held welcome banners out of Pelosi's hotel. The Chinese military operations, which took place in the waters and skies near the island, were driven by nationalist sentiment and intended to cause feelings of insecurity and fear among the Taiwanese. Some missiles even landed in Japanese-claimed zones. This expression of Chinese military threat showed not simply force and strength but deep frustration, irritation and resentment at an imagined loss of national dignity. Pelosi's visit damaged cross-Strait relations, tipping the region into a geopolitical crisis.

Contradictory emotions about national sovereignty and identity were dispersed virally across the Taiwan Strait. They permitted ordinary people of different political persuasions to feel their way into regional geopolitics, usually dominated by the state. The anger and fury felt by the Chinese revealed a hyper-essentialised 'us vs them' structure of feeling, which had intensified since the 1990s. On the night Pelosi's plane landed, emotional posts flooded Chinese cyberspace, calling out enemies who invade 'our territory' and traitors who cause 'our pain'. Patriotic claims that 'Taiwan is an inalienable part of China' and calls for 'unification with the motherland' mediated feelings of connectedness and served as a source of emotional solidarity among mainlanders. Taiwan's Internet was imbued with distrust, worry, uncertainty, anxiety, defiance and hatred towards mainland China, especially its regime. Both sides felt a sense of threat caused by each other's actions. Each side produced an emotional narrative portraying the other as a source of hurt. No matter their passionate positions, hostilities permeated across the Taiwan Strait, accompanied by a subtle exclusion of other emotions that prompted each subject to see the other in a negative way. Emotions overwhelmingly characterised their political expressions. They are political statements in themselves.

In this incident, emotions operated like libidinal energy, driving both sides to connect with the broader public and express their views. Mainstream discussion mainly focused on the military and security aspects of the crisis, ignoring the affective intensity of the political subjects involved. The passion unleashed by the event invited people to feel their place in developing news stories. This affective process, however, was far from rational and consensual but unfolded within a broader, deep-seated historical magnitude of geopolitical emotions that articulate binary oppositions of memories about the US and Japan. The escalation of emotional conflict caused by the Pelosi incident offers a lens to understand how the affective space transfixed by divergent structures of feeling operates through the psychic terrains across the Taiwan Strait. What causes and sustains the ongoing emotional contradiction remains unclear in the current discussion. What affective flows shape contradictory structures of feeling 'beneath the surface of explicit life' that are collective and saturated with implicit knowledge and memories (Berlant 2015: 194)? In the current standoff, there is no dialogue between the two sides. Their emotional trajectories are parallel, unreconciled, and never intersect. Given the profound ideological ramifications, is a dialogue between opponents still possible? If so, where could it take place and in what form, especially in historical moments?

This chapter addresses these questions by exploring how the extensive public outpouring of emotion across the Taiwan Strait brings into existence a porous, liminal affective space for intersubjective engagement. We seek to go beyond the conventional political rhetoric of democracy versus autocracy, to identify sites where non-official, people-oriented exchange and communication are made possible and political boundaries are negotiated. Our purpose is to examine the emotional dynamics of cross-Strait tensions and the (im)possibility of mutual understanding through popular affective investment.

CRITIQUE OF THE RATIONALIST APPROACH TO CYBERCOMMUNICATIONS

In the emotional reverberation triggered by Pelosi, as in many other political events, the Internet plays a central role in mediating and displaying everyday casual affective expressions (Bensky and Fisher 2014). Social media in cyberspace constitute a rich repertoire of popular emotions binding and dividing individuals (Garde-Hansen and Gorton 2013). They facilitate emotional disclosure, activate feelings of engagement and make people feel reenergised about politics (Papacharissi 2015). Because of the Internet's immediate, anonymous and spontaneous nature, much online communication is emotional (Knudsen and Stage 2015; Tang 2009). Its ubiquity and mobility provide an accessible and fluid communicative space for evoking the emotional states and reactions of others, giving rise to various forms of emotional exchange. It also serves as a 'storytelling infrastructure', inviting ordinary people to tune into current events and formulate issue-based, ad hoc and transient affective publics across geographic boundaries (Papacharissi 2015: 3). Affective publics are connected and disconnected through emotional interactions (ibid. 125). They are formulated by structures of feeling, which support meaning-making and disrupt the state's distribution of emotion by presenting underrepresented viewpoints or reinterpreting dominant narratives (ibid. 24–5; 130). In China, social media functions as a safe space for disclosing and circulating emotionally charged micronarratives (Gan et al. 2017; Tang 2009). This process creates a public of intimate strangers bound together by emotions. Their engagement facilitates the political formation of affective publics and provides a means to formulate the affective space.

Theoretically, the present political standoff is also a test of the Habermasian conception of a rational public sphere. The public displays of antagonistic sentiments open up questions about what types of popular expression are dominant and how people belonging to different political regimes communicate with each other in a fraught relationship. The rationalist approach, emphasising reason and the will to consensus, fails to explain political processes driven by emotions (Karatzogianni and Kuntsman 2012). It marginalises emotion as a critical factor in political participation. This chapter addresses the omission of affect from much of the theoretical discourse on the political public sphere. Many Internet studies have employed the Habermasian conception of a public sphere to explore the democratic potential of social media as a space of public deliberation for facilitating rational-critical debate and fostering democratic culture. At the core of the model of deliberative democracy is an assumption that political antagonism and conflict, which are charged with passion and desire, can be eliminated through deliberative procedures to create a universal and impartial consensus that meets everybody's interests equally (Dahlberg 2001; Tanner 2001; Janssen and Kies 2005). Rationality is construed as an essential element of a healthy public sphere. Advocates assume that all participants, free from the structural effects of power relations, are able to leave behind their feelings; driven by aspirations of rationality, they can critically examine their values and show sincere respect towards others. However, political talk is about more than just information sharing and rational exchange. This chapter suggests that the deliberative model loses sight of the potential of affect in mobilising popular political participation. Consequently, the absence of a proper analysis of sentiment-driven publics in situated antagonism has led to our growing inability to grasp the region's challenges.

This chapter considers the emotional dynamics and reverberations of online chats to consider how historically shaped affective stickiness formulates the Internet-mediated affective space. Online emotions are contagious and can grow exponentially in emergency situations (Zhou et al. 2019). They have the potential to constitute the sociopolitical. Their affective flow nurtures togetherness, solidarity and hostility. In the case of Pelosi's visit, online political participation was energised by emotion. Political solidarity on both sides was shaped around the public online display of emotions, which served as a snapshot of historical structures of feeling. The affective process leads to an important question: If the 'connective affordances of social media help activate the in-between bond of publics' (Papacharissi 2015: 9), what does the mediated feeling of connectedness afforded by social media do for cross-Strait reconciliation? We are interested in the ambient, atmospheric and dispersive effects produced by such sequences. By examining a range of emotional exchanges observed in

Internet forums and chat rooms, we argue that although the rationalist perspective is a valid approach to thinking about what democracy ought to be like, it cannot adequately account for the political energy of online discussions that do not fit the normative criteria set for an idealised public sphere. Such conversations result in affective connections that attach participants to specific exchanges, groups and threads (Paasonen et al. 2015). This chapter attempts to fill that gap by examining the emotionally charged conversations and interactions in online chat rooms concerning cross-Strait relations. It contends that emotions are not unmediated, unintelligent affective impulses, but embodied thoughts and value judgements that involve a complicated cognitive process and the use of reason to determine what is good and what is wrong (Hall 2002; Nussbaum 2001). Emotions are essential to ethical reasoning and a vibrant public sphere.

This study also benefits from the critique of liberal thought contending that the negation of affect eventually leads to political impotence, especially when confronted by antagonism. Political theorist Iris Marion Young, for example, mounts a forceful critique of the rationalist approach on the grounds that the ideal of impartial reason is predicated on a strict, hierarchical and mutually exclusive division of reason and affectivity that reduces plurality to unity and identifies the former with universality and the latter with particularity. 'Impartiality', writes Young (1990: 100), 'seeks to master or eliminate heterogeneity in the form of feeling. Only by expelling desire or affectivity from reason can impartiality achieve its unity.' For critics, the normative ideal of an impartial consensus that stands above all particular desires and identities will eventually exclude those subjects who do not fit the model of rational citizen from the public (Fraser 1997; Nicholson 1999). The ideal of impartiality 'expresses in fact an impossibility, a fiction. No one can adopt a point of view that is completely impersonal and dispassionate, completely separated from any particular context and commitments' (Young 1990: 103). Mouffe (2002: 16) argues that democratic politics 'needs to have a real purchase on people's desires and fantasies'. She points out that the deliberative model seeks to eradicate the antagonistic aspects of politics, which makes us 'incapable of thinking politically, of asking political questions, and of offering political answers' (ibid. 3). Further insights can be gained from the work of Carl Schmitt, who insists that politics is impossible without a political frontier being created and a political moment of discrimination being defined. Rather than being partisan-free and non-adversarial, democratic politics always consists in the identity formation of an 'us' counterposed to a 'them', and the phenomenon of the political 'can be understood only in the context of the ever-present possibility of the friend-and-enemy grouping' (Schmitt 1996: 35).[1] In a similar vein, Dahlgren (2006: 277) maintains that the restrictive and formalistic version promoted by Habermas and other proponents 'delimits the kinds of cultural practices that should characterize civic agency in the public sphere, pushing to the margins certain kinds of communicative competencies and practices that are important for robust democracy'. It not only suppresses the heterogeneity of lived forms of popular cultural expressions that may not be qualified as formal speech by strict deliberative terms, but loses sight of the potential of affect that brings the needs and desires of subjects into the political agenda. The analysis in this chapter illustrates how the format of the online discussion thread invites emotional contestation and leads to divisions among the chatroom users.

In what follows, we extend this line of argument to the virtual settings of Chinese cyberspace and investigate a range of emotional statements and struggles mediated by online forums. These statements and struggles mix facts and political viewpoints with emotion in a manner that stimulates heated conversation. We compare the various emotional states – such as anger, hatred and indignation – through which popular subjectivities and identities are reproduced in terms of 'us' and 'them'. This study is framed at the particular moment of the sixtieth anniversary of the victory of the War of Resistance against Japanese Aggression (15 August). Taiwan's Retrocession Day (25 October) in 2005 – during which time online interactions were driven by the unsettling forces of nationalist sentiment, and the us–them relationship quickly became the locus of a friend–enemy struggle. The two dates constituted a brief emotional moment for cross-Strait interactions, during which emotions were formed in a group setting. There was a growing nationalism during that time (Lam 2006: 212). Compared to Jiang Zemin, then-President Hu Jintao was more enthusiastic about the 'great revival of the Chinese nation' (*zhonghua minzu weida fuxing* 中华民族伟大复兴). Anti-Japanese and anti-Western protests were tolerated during his term. China's growing wealth and strength had given rise to a new structure of feeling highlighting national pride on the mainland.

We focus on several cross-Strait-related Internet forums hosted by two mainland-based commercial portal websites, NetEase (www.163 .com) and Yahoo! China (cn.yahoo.com), where people across the Strait actively participate in reproducing the friend/enemy relationship.[2] There are plural voices and rich stories in these forums, which offer a site for divergent structures of feeling to intersect. The forums constitute a shared space of emotional memories and experiences. Their participatory settings invite always-on feeds and improvised contributions to unfolding events. They also serve as a medium for storytelling and co-creation that sustains emotional engagement and belonging. The digitally enabled cross-Strait interaction facilitates a new political space that allows antagonists without decision-making power to negotiate existing political boundaries and share emotional feelings. The affective zone created by online emotional clashes constitutes what we visualise as the affective space of a terrain of contestation. In this space, the unrestrained outpourings of contradictory and hostile sentiments, which often take intense and extreme forms, carry more weight than high-minded arguments in articulating the antagonistic cross-Strait relationship. Instead of envisaging the affective space as a neutral domain, we propose to rethink the tension in terms of 'undomesticated hostilities', which acknowledge the ineradicable nature of antagonism and the impossibility of a fully actualised unity of 'the people'. The idea of undomesticated hostilities and affective space can help us recover the political potential of emotion that has too long been dismissed as prerational, irrational or inappropriate and excluded by the liberal perspective. It permits us to grasp the deep-seated emotions inherent in cross-Strait relations in a more productive way. Specifically, we describe how participants use the politically infused forums as a 'site of memory' (Nora 1989) to articulate and contest divergent affective memories that are intricately entangled with traumatic pasts.[3] In this chapter we will attend to the unfolding web of emotional energies, the spectacular encounters of emotional subjectivities and the negotiation of power relations in these chat rooms.

THE CREATION OF A DIALOGIC SPACE

This analysis examines the texture of the storytelling that fills online forums, which bring together individuals connected by different feelings. Since the early 2000s, various online forums have been created by portal sites to discuss cross-Strait relations and Taiwan issues. Because these forums filter out physical and non-verbal traits in an anonymous setting, they tend to encourage emotional disclosure. Compared with the mainstream public space dominated by the voice of the government and elites, this online space, as articulated with conflictual forms of national/ethnic identity politics, accommodates a wide array of unorganised, unbridled conversations over cross-Strait relations. It links strangers by enabling co-creation and inviting affective investment into historical conflicts. Participants share their emotional fantasies in the form of textual narratives. Group formation is based on different senses of shared emotional memories and experiences. In this political space, antagonism is intense and pervasive, and the political frontiers between 'us' and 'them' are constantly being created in moral terms.

What is happening in this virtual setting is very different from what theorists of deliberative democracy would have expected in their hope of objective consensus. In this unofficial space, spectacular outbursts of popular emotion dominate conversations about cross-Strait relations. Plain and sometimes vulgar emotional expressions carry more weight than critical-rational debate in these conversations. Practices of flaming evoke emotional reactions among chatroom users and produce antagonistic intensity. No common interest or general will is being recognised by the different groups, and it seems illusory to believe that such emotional clashes, which are not simply battles of unthinking forces but involve forms of value judgement and ethical reasoning, can be eradicated or neutralised. In online forums, issues about Japan – particularly the complex historical relationship between China, Taiwan and Japan – have always been the most emotionally charged topics, where different experiences and memories are entangled and contested. Much discussion deals with controversial topics about Japan and its colonial past. The intense emotional energy invested in such forum themes as the two Sino-Japanese wars, the Nanjing Massacre, Japan's wartime responsibilities, and Japanese prime minister Koizumi Junichiro's controversial visits to the Yasukuni Shrine shows the participants' strong desire to reckon with war memories.

Online forums help to extend popular participation in debating highly contentious historical issues and expose users to opposing sentiments (Morris-Suzuki and Rimmer 2002). They are alternative sites of emotional antagonism between Taiwanese and mainland

Chinese participants based on their radically different attitudes towards Japan. Opponents define one another in moral terms as an 'absolute' enemy against the virtuous and innocent 'us', and both sides collide with and reject the emotional memory of their rival groups. The mainland chatroom users are most concerned with the hundred-year suffering of the Chinese people and their bitter history of humiliation under colonialism and imperialism. For this group, modern Chinese history since the mid-nineteenth century is a history of foreign aggression and Chinese resistance. The War of Resistance against Japanese Aggression, among other conflicts, has been a recurring theme eulogised by mainland users. Their nationalist sentiment of victimhood is predicated on a relatively fixed, oversimplified image of Japan reinforced by Chinese mainstream media. The sense of rage, hatred and indignation runs deep when they speak of the history associated with Japanese aggression. The defeat of the Qing Empire in the first Sino-Japanese War and the subsequent separation of Taiwan from the mainland are seen by many as evidence of China's weakness and national humiliation (*minzu chiru* 民族耻辱). The sentiment towards Taiwan, therefore, is deeply implicated in the collective psyche of national weakness and humiliation. Reclaiming Taiwan, as articulated in narratives of unification, is thus imperative to realising the dream of becoming a 'strong and wealthy nation'. As long as Taiwan is separated from the mainland, as one scholar puts it, 'the Chinese humiliation would not be washed away' (Zheng 2001: 35). When the issue of Taiwan's sovereignty is raised, the affective investment becomes much more intense. The forums are flooded with the rhetoric of blame and the sentiment of national suffering. There are, however, always dissonant voices in the chat rooms. Emotional disclosure often solicits further emotional support, which gives group members a sense of solidarity and encourages more disclosure. The forums' anonymity and openness support the expression of marginal and ideologically disparate viewpoints, engendering multiple meanings and constant emotional tensions. Ideologically divergent publics are convened around similarities and differences in historical emotion. Various taboo topics in mainstream media – particularly those concerning Taiwan's sovereignty and independence – are brought under the public spotlight and trigger contestation. The unrestricted expression of Taiwanese identity – based on the affirmation of an irreducible difference from 'China' – is unambiguously perceived by mainland groups as fragmenting and threatening their identity and existence. The two groups split according to their remarkably opposing national identifications and sentiments. Some Taiwanese participants, who represent the marginal minority group in the forums, form affective alliances and raise challenging questions regarding Taiwan's national identity and independence. Although the system administrators of the forums have the power to delete messages, it does not seem to be the case that the forums can effectively crack down on or take complete control of the circulation of politically sensitive content. The threads often amplify sentiments denied by mainland authorities. In a Yahoo post titled 'A Question for the Chinese', for example, the author puts forward a query about why the Chinese have taken different attitudes towards the history of the cession of Taiwan and that of other ex-Chinese territories: 'Why don't Chinese people reclaim the estimated 1.5 million square kilometers' land ceded to Russia, but only stick to Taiwan that is only about thirty thousand square kilometers? Haishenwai [Chinese appellation for Vladivostok] was a Chinese city. Why don't the Chinese ask the Russians to return it to China?' Taiwanese solidarity is shaped around the public display of 'deviant' emotions.

This 'deviant' post, which can be seen as a characteristic attempt to cope with the stigmatised status of Taiwan and to undermine the 'authority' of Chinese nationalist discourse in the forums, immediately provoked intense emotional responses taking offence at the Taiwanese participant. The tension leads to the cultivation of particular emotions. The following two posts, which register the territorial division of China as a token of national shame, represent the most typical emotional reaction of mainland participants:

> Are you a *Yanhuang zisun* [descendant of Yandi and the Yellow Emperor]? Should a person who refuses to recognize his *minzu xuetong* [national descent] still be considered human?

> We grieve for all the lost lands. Though the Qing Dynasty was incompetent [and should be responsible for the lost territories], Taiwan remains the primary issue [for China]. The Taiwan issue really makes the Chinese heartbreaking.

These two posts reveal the affective stickiness of historical memories, which carry more weight than a reasoned argument. They also illustrate how the issue of Taiwan's sovereignty is articulated with the members' sense of national humiliation and their desire to return to a primordial Han Chinese essence. Showing their emotional attachment to the motherland, these participants seem indifferent to and ignorant of the historical resentment felt by their Taiwanese counterparts, whose predecessors are claimed to have experienced the formal dispossession of Taiwan by the motherland and the brutality of the authoritarian rule of the Kuomintang (KMT) regime. It is also clear that, apart from the excessive rhetoric of blame against the 'disloyal' and 'untrue' Taiwanese, a majority of the mainland participants feel disparagement and disdain towards those Taiwanese who oppose the narrative of national loyalty and anti-Japanese discourse. Their interaction with the Taiwanese unfolds beyond the deliberative pattern of a traditional public sphere. When negotiating with the Taiwanese in the forums, the memory of foreign aggression continues to shape the subjectivities and identities of mainland participants. Their emotive articulation shows that the memory of humiliation has remained a trauma in China's national psyche.[4] This, however, does not seem to be respected or understood by Taiwanese members of the forums. They seem to have forgotten Japan's brutal militaristic past and the Taiwanese anticolonial resistance movement. Instead, it is a sense of the perceived 'backwardness' of China and a 'savage' and 'uncivilised' image of the Chinese that dominates the emotional discourse of Taiwanese participants.[5]

The Taiwanese groups' identity politics is deeply implicated in a historically inscribed triangular relationship with mainland China and colonial Japan. Unlike the mainland participants, these groups use the chat rooms to articulate their particularistic identity and their desire and struggle for recognition of their cultural-political difference. Since the colonial period, the triangulation has, as Ching (2003: 8) has noted, 'formed the terrain where contradictory, conflicting, and complicitous desires and identities were projected, negotiated, and vanquished'. The half-century-long colonisation of the Taiwanese population (1895 – 1945) has made Japan an indelible point of reference in the construction of Taiwanese identity and subjectivity and thus differentiated the notion of 'Taiwaneseness' from the 'spectre' of China. Despite recognising that most Taiwanese share similar languages, dialects and customs with mainland Chinese, the majority of Taiwanese participants think their identity cannot be reduced and sublated to the homogeneous and essentialised conception of Chineseness. Their storytelling practices facilitate engagement and produce the potential for disruption. As one post puts it:

> I am a Taiwanese brother. My ancestors came to Taiwan from the mainland's Quanzhou 300 years ago! Our ancestors [had the experience of becoming] Dutch, Ming-Dynasty [subjects], Qing-Dynasty [subjects], Japanese, Taiwanese, and Chinese. . . . In our generation, actually most people don't know which nation we belong to. Sometimes we want to become Chinese immediately . . . sometimes we want to become truly Taiwanese.

In this narrative, the participant tactically invokes various subject positions (i.e., 'Dutch', subjects of Ming and Qing dynasties, 'Japanese') to justify a Taiwanese identity that is not unitary and undifferentiated. In doing so, they argue that such a hybridised identity cannot be encompassed by the homogeneous category of Han ethnicity or by the long organic relationship with China, as espoused by mainland Chinese members. An ambivalent sense of belonging and not-belonging characterises this sort of identity narrative demanding acknowledgement of its unique status.[6] Taiwanese members complain that the Taiwanese people's yearning for the 'motherland' has been distorted and exaggerated and that the mainlanders, obsessed with racial identity and cultural heritage, are incapable of adequately understanding Taiwan's peculiar historical relationship with Japan. The attempt to negotiate or reject a homogeneous ethnonational Chinese identity has frequently led to strong moral condemnation from mainland chatroom users who vent their anger against what they call *hanjian* (汉奸, traitors) and *minzu bailei* (民族败类, scum of the nation) for the latter's explicit or implicit pro-Japan attitude. There is no universal will or consensus that can accommodate different subjective expressions. Instead, the mainland groups tend to see the presence of different voices as a damaging intrusion by the wrong people, so they often ask Taiwanese members to keep out of 'their' space.[7] The public display of emotion becomes a political statement. It seems to be the case that the forums constitute a site of emotional division and struggle rather than one for achieving consensus, reconciliation and understanding.

The affirmation of difference and a 'them' are the preconditions for reassuring a coherent Taiwanese self-identity. The sense of not belonging to China, and the associated desire for obtaining an independent national status and standing on an equal footing with China (and with Japan in a much less autonomous sense), can be better apprehended and analysed concerning the deep-rooted *guer xinli* (孤儿心理, orphan mentality). This term refers to a sentiment of

155

homelessness and parentlessness constitutive of the Taiwanese (especially *bensheng ren*'s)[8] identity ever since Taiwan was ceded to Japan in 1895 after the first Sino-Japanese War. The image of the orphan, drawn from Wu Zhuoliu's novel *The Orphan of Asia*, conveys a deep sense of historical pain and resentment at being abandoned by and dispossessed from the mainland (the 'motherland'). The following two posts are self-explanatory and require only minimal framing:

> The poor Taiwanese were abandoned by their mother and became Japan's *huang min* [皇民, imperial subjects] for half a century. During this period, tens of thousands of anti-Japanese martyrs were killed, since they were reluctant to accept the culture and education alien to their ancestry. When Taiwan was returned to China, [the Taiwanese people] found that they had to face a familiar and yet totally blurry culture.

> I hope that my mainland compatriots could sometimes change your standpoint and think over again. . . . Nowadays Taiwanese can be divided into three kinds. The first kind are native Taiwanese. The second kind are those mainlanders who migrated to Taiwan with Zheng Chenggong [also known as Koxinga] during the late Ming and early Qing [usually known as *bensheng ren*]. The third kind is the mainlanders who retreated to Taiwan with Chiang Kai-shek after the Civil War between the Kuomintang and the Chinese Communist Party [usually known as *waisheng ren*]. Except for the Taiwanese of the third kind who have never been betrayed by their motherland, the others were abandoned to Japan. Today, the people who grow up in Taiwan have never lived under the communist system. To be honest, if you were Taiwanese, would you identify yourself as a citizen of the PRC?

These threads are not entirely devoid of reason, but they convey a deep ambivalence and reluctance towards China. For mainland chatroom users, the trauma of foreign invasion and the consequence of *ge rang* (割让) – the ceding of Taiwan and its surrounding islands to Japan under the Treaty of Shimonoseki – is unforgettable. For their Taiwanese counterparts, as the two posts above show, the historical perception and feelings about *ge rang* imply more than a sense of loss and disgrace. Instead, it is a mixture of sentiments of abandonment and betrayal, of solitude and despair, that shapes the psychic structure of the Taiwanese people. It is this conflicted sense of lament and anger, as Ching (2003: 179–80) cogently argues, that 'constitutes Taiwan's collective psychic formation and enables the Taiwanese to eulogize their "national" history as one of betrayal and abandonment'. Such division should be understood by referring to what

Chen (2010) conceptualises as the 'emotional structure of sentiment' that constitutes the material basis of cross-Strait conflicts. The historical sentiments of the Taiwanese and mainland chatroom users are disarticulated from and run parallel to each other on the affective terrain. Although both are the product of conflictive emotional structures, the affective investment of the friend/enemy distinction afforded by the forums furthers the difference. The strong sentiments of humiliation and indignation felt by the mainlanders do not occupy a central place in the collective identity of the Taiwanese, just as the feeling of abandonment and betrayal is almost completely effaced in the emotional structure of the mainlanders. Each group uses its own emotions to refuse the possibility of acknowledging the other's sentiments. Negative emotions such as resentment and hostility are intense. It is unlikely that the two groups can transcend their sentimental positions and reach an 'objective' consensus in this space.

In cyberspace, according to Mitra (2001: 31), the marginal group 'can call out to the dominant and put the dominant in the difficult position of either having to acknowledge the marginalised, or further distance the dispossessed by ignoring the call'. In the forums observed here, the interactions between the dominant group formed by the mainland participants and the marginal alliances formed by the Taiwanese appear more intricate and do not seem to conform to Mitra's argument. The presence of pro-Japan sentiment among the Taiwanese frequently provokes intense emotional conflicts with mainland participants. The emotional discourse may sometimes cause a collective fear of losing control of the public space, although it does not appear that it could result in a complete reversal of the dominant status of Chinese nationalists and give effective validation to the minority group. Generally speaking, the dominant group is attentive and responsive to the call of the marginal group and does not appear to be passively pushed into the 'difficult position' described by Mitra. Moreover, the affective public formulated in this forum is not always virtuous, egalitarian or inclusive when it comes to contesting rival discourses that bind subjects to opposing identities. Both groups often shade into a parochial and exclusivist nativism or nationalism that cancels out the historical emotion of the other. The blame game over national identity is not a simple dichotomy of domination and resistance, but is best understood as a set of complex social practices permeated by historical imaginaries and sentiments. The emotional constitution of both the dominant and the marginal, no longer confined in a closed national space, has gone through an irreducible process of disfiguration, displacement and dispersion that reveals the contingent status of all affective subjectivities. The spectacularly emotional encounter in the Chinese forums, in the words of Sun (2002: 6), 'compels us to leave the integral entity of "selfhood" which gives people a sense of safety, and to rethink the fluid and self-sufficient notion of subjectivity in a network of relationships'. The highly permeable and contestatory zone created by online encounters constitutes an ad hoc affective space in which the flow of historical emotions, rather than the abstract notion of communicative reason, plays a more prominent role in articulating alternative cross-Strait interactions.

HISTORICAL MAGNETIC FIELD

> Emotions tell us a lot about time; emotions are the very 'flesh' of time. . . . Through emotions, the past persists on the surface of bodies. Emotions show us how histories stay alive, even when they are not consciously remembered. . . . The time of emotion is not always about the past, and how it sticks. (Ahmed 2004: 202)

History retains a trace in popular memory and manifests itself through the texture of online threads. The emotionally charged memories and counter-memories scattered across the forums operate as a means of us–them distinction and the constituent of affective communities. Multiple emotions infiltrate the texture of memory narratives, prompting the mainlander and Taiwanese chatroom users to turn against each other. The historically constituted emotions not only constrain but also enable the possibilities of the struggle for recognition; they are both limiting and productive to these sorts of struggles in the circuit of emotions (Grossberg 1997b: 242–4). The affective space as a contested terrain is animated by uninterrupted flows of people coming to negotiate their collective memory of a national past and engage in sharing, debating, protesting and struggling over historical meanings and interpretations. Memory does not have an intrinsic property to be retrieved but, as Kim (2000: 462) has noted, 'selects from the flux of images of the past those that best fit its present needs'. It is a site of struggle articulated to different ideological fantasies. Collective memories of Japanese colonialism are deeply split between opposing modes of remembering that are bound up with the political divisions across the Taiwan Strait.[9] Online chat rooms provide an indispensable outlet for different imaginations and desires about the past; the discussion threads provide momentary feelings of such imaginations. As traversed by the distinct form of us–them imagination, tactical performances of memory become the key locus of online cross-Strait antagonism. Although the speech acts that originate from the outpouring of historical memory do not seem to facilitate the formation of coherent public opinions, they shed light on how affective memories emerge as the dominant expression prevailing over the rational in the chat rooms. We propose that collective engagement in the politics of remembering and forgetting – as shaped by the structures of power and desire that 'variously sustain, erase, and transform memories of past events' (Fujitani et al. 2001: 2) – creates a unique political horizon that allows a tactical mobilisation of collective memories and theatrical performance of emotions.

The political energy associated with cross-Strait relations is manifested in the conflict over historical memories. In the chat rooms, each grouping wishes its own interpretation of historical truth to become hegemonic, yet they are often, as Olick (2003: 7) has noted, 'caught in webs of meaning they themselves participate in creating, though not in ways they necessarily could have predicted'. The mainland participants' perception of Japanese colonial rule in Taiwan is fuelled by strong nationalist sentiment condemning the Japanese authorities' oppressive rule and inhumane treatment of the Taiwanese. For the mainlanders, Taiwan's territorial sovereignty evokes painful memories of Western and Japanese imperialism. Taiwan symbolises national shame and disgrace and the loss of dignity. As such, they eulogise the great spirit of liberation struggle and resistance of the Taiwanese against the Japanese colonisers. Historical accounts and images of major events, such as the defeat and surrender of the Japanese empire and the retrocession of Taiwan, as well as biographical profiles of famous Taiwanese anti-Japanese heroes such as Luo Fuxing, Yu Qingfang, Mona Rudao, and Jiang Weishui, are widely circulated and commented on by interested Chinese members in the forums. Some zealous forum participants present historical texts narrated through the simple imperialism/resistance dichotomy to contend that Chinese compatriots on the mainland did try to support Taiwan's anti-Japanese uprisings in various ways. Contrary to this liberation trope, the Taiwanese groups maintain a more ambivalent sense of intimacy and attachment to Japan, in which Japanese colonialism assumes a relatively positive image associated with civilisation, progress and modernity. They rarely join the discussion of anti-Japanese movements and the Chinese experience of suffering or demand an apology from Japan. They have come to view Japanese colonial legacies with fairly positive emotions and nostalgia, characterising Japanese colonial rule as munificent and beneficial to the Taiwanese. In the postcolonial era, the Taiwanese tend to speak of colonial Japan's modernisation and development projects rather than its exploitation and oppression of Taiwan. 'Japan' has been internalised as an object of desire in the Taiwanese ideological fantasy.[10]

The mode of remembrance of the Taiwanese groups has, with very few exceptions, reproduced the pervasively fond memories of Taiwan's ex-coloniser, Japan. Affection for Japan runs deep in the articulation of Taiwanese identity and the 'forgetting' of Japan's colonial oppression is at the heart of Taiwanese 'national' self-understanding. Many Taiwanese members believe Japan did a good thing for Taiwan during its occupation. The arrival of the Japanese in 1895 is seen as having provided salvation from backwardness, scarcity and chaos. Some emphasise the extent to which the colonial administration helped transform Taiwan from a feudal society into a modern society, and the significant improvement of the infrastructure and health standards of the island during the period of occupation. The Japanese colonial administration is perceived as a benevolent occupying power that provided the Taiwanese with better living conditions and raised them to a higher cultural level. Traumatic issues such as the 'comfort women', among others, are almost entirely out of sight of the Taiwanese chatroom users. Moreover, they tend to emphasise the cultural/racial superiority of Japan and the Japanese in contrast to the inferiority of China and the Chinese. Many Taiwanese members contend that a 'higher culture' (of Japan and Taiwan) must not be ruled by a 'lower culture' (of China). As a NetEase post puts it: 'The Japanese are genuine "descendants of Dragon". Our mainland friends might be upset when hearing this. But in fact, Japan is the leader of Asian cultures. If [we] compare Taiwan's cultural essence with that of Japan, the Taiwanese would feel ashamed.' This post exhibits the wishful sentiment of an ex-colonial subject who embraces an uncritical identification with the superior status and flawless image of the ex-colonial master, accompanied by disdain for the tradition and culture of the motherland. This dislike and negation of everything related to China, as Chen Yingzhen (1998) observes, is a clear manifestation of the profound psychological effect of Japanese colonialism on the subjectivity of the Taiwanese. The superiority-vs-inferiority worldview, a hierarchical way of thinking about race and culture, has left the Taiwanese with profound spiritual trauma, the effect of which has reinforced the dependency complex and the feeling of self-negation.[11] However, within the affective space of online chat rooms, we should recognise participants' active and creative use of memory and other symbolic resources for emotional struggle. Acts of collective remembering and forgetting played out in antagonistic online interactions may well be tactical manipulations that enable the participants to pursue identity politics and define their relations with the other. What needs to be problematised for intersubjective understanding is not simply memory itself but also the formation of *lishi cichang* (历史磁场, historical magnetic field) where the reproduction of memory and identity takes place (Mizoguchi 2001). As this research demonstrates, online forums provide a unique symbolic space for engaging in collective acts of remembering that negotiate the existing power relations emanating from the historical magnetic field.

In the present mode of interaction, memories of modernisation frequently collide with memories of liberation and resistance among the two major groupings, thus tightening political boundaries. Much of the conversation is marked by parochial self-centredness. The mainland chatroom users usually become furious over news stories about some high-profile Taiwanese celebrities or politicians expressing fondness for Japan. A Yahoo post, 'Do the Taiwanese people really appreciate Japanese colonial rule?' generated a highly emotional conversation. This and the follow-up posts illustrate how the tactical deployment of memory provokes discussions of political relevance. The first post states: 'You should hear the story of Yoichi Hatta, and then you will realise [why the Taiwanese people appreciate the Japanese]'. Many older generation Taiwanese will know that Yoichi Hatta was the Japanese chief engineer behind the construction of the Chia-Nan Irrigation Waterworks during the colonial era and has been acclaimed by local Taiwanese residents as the 'Father of the Chia-Nan Irrigation River'. He represents the prominent contribution of the Japanese colonial administration to Taiwan's modernisation. The post is a one-sided exaltation of Japanese colonialism as benevolent and beneficial, downplaying the fact that Japan's modernisation project in Taiwan was carried out primarily to exploit the island's natural resources and indigenous economy more efficiently (Chen 2005). This post reveals how the tactical use of memory works to harden the China–Taiwan boundary. As the following post demonstrates, the use of memories of colonial Taiwan emphasises the negative image of the 'corrupt' and 'backward' Chinese regime in the wake of the defeat of colonial Japan. The tactical forgetting of colonial repression and remembering of postcolonial state violence – as marked by the February 28 Incident (hereafter '228 Incident') in 1947 – aims to construct a discursive equivalence between two opponents of Taiwanese nationalism: the KMT and the CPC. The 228 Incident was a brutal military crackdown on Taiwanese civilians who rose up against the corrupt KMT administration less than a year and a half after the end of Japanese colonial rule. Contrary to the mainland participants' strategic emphasis on the KMT regime's effort to resist the Japanese invasion, the Taiwanese members often describe how badly the regime treated the people of Taiwan after it reverted to Chinese rule in 1945. Events associated with the KMT regime are often presented as the worst kind of tragedy and destruction. In such a selective, one-sided mode of remembering, the Taiwanese insist that although the Japanese colonial administration was at times oppressive and discriminatory against the Taiwanese, it brought tremendous progress to Taiwan. Under colonial rule, they claim, the Taiwanese enjoyed more political freedom, greater law and order, and higher living standards than in the precolonial and postcolonial eras. In contrast, the liberation from Japanese rule simply brought with it familiar experiences of subordination and oppression.

> During the Japanese occupation, many councillors in Taiwan could participate in the congress. As you mainland fellows may have known, the Taiwanese people do not care so much about which regime governs them; but we care about suffrage and political influence . . .
>
> In terms of hardware construction:
>
> Railway construction: the Japanese continued to use the railway constructed by the Manchu regime and expanded it into an island-wide railway network that linked up the north and south . . .
>
> During that time, for the Taiwanese, there was no distinction between the Taiwanese and the Japanese because they were all Japanese. There was no such thing as colonialism because Taiwan was part of *Riben guo* [日本国, Japanese nation]. The sense of righteousness, preciseness and

162

honor, as well as the spirit of Bushido of the Japanese police and civil servants, were highly admired by the older generation of the Taiwanese!! According to the older generation, Japanese civil servants did not take any red envelopes [*hongbao* 红包, a common form of bribery]. For them, corruption was disgraceful and humiliating. Moreover, from the perspective of a Taiwanese, Japan already had aircraft carriers, while the Chinese government was still corrupt and the Chinese were still fighting against each other [*ziji ren da ziji ren* 自己人打自己人]. They are as far apart as heaven and earth if you compare the two.

Such storytelling practice appeals to both emotion and reason to reinforce affective identification with the ex-coloniser. In this narrative, 'Japan' is a positive emotional symbol for constructing an alternative Taiwanese identity. In addition to the affective investment in these stories, evidence and rational logic legitimise the emotional position. In April 2005, the chair of the pro-independence and pro-Japanese political party Taiwan Solidarity Union, Su Chin-Chiang, paid a controversial visit to the Yasukuni Shrine, where the spirits of approximately 28,000 Taiwanese and indigenous people who died serving in the imperial army were enshrined. The forums were immediately mobbed with raging mainland participants protesting Su's visit and condemning the act as a sign of a 'slave mentality'.

The tactical act of memory sparked considerable outrage and insult from Chinese members, who called for 'the weeding out of traitors and pro-Japanese elements' from the forums.

The following two posts insist that it is unfair and unacceptable to equate the KMT regime with the CPC and to ascribe all of the former's wrongdoings and failures to Chinese mainlanders:

> Why should the mainlanders be blamed for the bloody 228 Incident caused by the reactionary faction of the KMT? It was because of its disregard for the appeal for stability and its suppression of the people that the KMT regime on the mainland was overthrown.

> The Communist Party will never repeat the same mistakes made by the KMT. Many Taiwanese people fear that the People's Liberation Army will launch a new 228 Incident after it disembarks on the island. There is no cause for such worry. The PLA is different from the KMT troops; it has strict military discipline.

These examples suggest that real-life identities are not entirely decentred or dismantled in cyberspace, as claimed by some Internet enthusiasts. They also exemplify the persistence of unreconciled memories in producing emotional subjectivities. Our observation supports that online talks in the postcolonial world tend to be framed by real-life configurations of power, such as colonialism and racism (Ignacio 2000). The act of remembering encourages popular participation in various contentious historical issues and invites a multitude of competing desires and imaginations central to political subject formation. Chatroom users' manipulation of state-sponsored memories is crucial in articulating the antagonistic us–them relationship online. The undomesticated hostility in the chat rooms challenges Habermas's idealistic conception of rational consensus grounded in communicative reason. It shows how immanent division and conflict open up a political space for different hegemonic subjects to struggle for emotional power.

ENTERING THE MESSY TERRAIN

This chapter explores how the historical trajectories of geopolitics leave affective traces in cybercommunication. Theoretically, the emerging affective space of Internet chat rooms is incompatible with the normative image of a consensual public sphere. First, online talk is permeated by upheavals of passion rather than purely rational forces. The emotional interactions rarely meet the normative conditions for an ideal speech situation. Most conversations do not facilitate rational-critical debate but rather create a terrain of contestation where politicised identities, desires and memories, inextricably entangled with the contradictory forces of colonialism, nationalism and racism, perform and compete with each other. The militant us–them distinction of cyberpolitics is unlikely to be tamed or defused. Moreover, although affective communication is hardly thoughtful or reasoned for consensus-making or immediate action, it nevertheless creates a dialogic space in which opponents can speak in their own voices and reckon with different memories. Second, the affective space, lacking a genuinely unified political will and coherent objective, is not created to mediate between civil society and the state or to formulate public opinion furthering political action. Instead, it serves as an alternative communicative space that broadens the political horizon of imagined communities across established boundaries. It is a rare communicative space for the subjects to 'feel' each other's sentiments and negotiate their relationships with their contradictory affective energies. Cyber-interactions have brought a confusing array of new possibilities for the clash of ideologically bounded affective energy, which makes the subjects realise that there always exists an incommensurable 'outside', an irreducible dissonance and heterogeneity, to what has been taken for granted in their everyday political lives. Although their conversations are often unfriendly and intolerant, as the space continues to give public visibility to different subjects and voices, it helps facilitate people-to-people interaction, exchange and dialogue that can democratise access to matters of cross-Strait relations.

Our analysis has also contributed to the discussion of what counts as politics. Through an analysis of the circulation of affective energy online, this chapter contends that democratic politics needs to touch people's desires and fantasies and recognise affect not as a dangerously undermining force but as a critical starting point for rethinking contemporary discourses of democracy and identity politics. Cross-Strait reconciliation should not be understood simply in political and economic terms but involves a psychic terrain suffused with the imbrication of geopolitics, history and affect. Given that the divergent sentiments explored in this chapter hardly intersect and continue to create geopolitical tensions, the idea of affective space and affective public offers an analytical lens to capture the emotional subjects and intensity that the regimes across the Taiwan Strait fail to absorb fully. It acknowledges the aggressive instincts of nationalist sentiments rather than seeking to eliminate them for the sake of moderation. In the context of cross-Strait opposition, the us–them relation is understood as undomesticated hostility derived from the unparallel collective identifications. A democratic project for transforming the antagonism, in the words of Mouffe (2002: 9), 'requires that the others be seen not as enemies to be destroyed but as adversaries whose ideas should be fought, even fiercely, but whose right to defend those ideas will never be questioned'. Instead of trying to rule out the enmity inherent in political processes, a more productive strategy should seek to distinguish potentially just and beneficial forms of desire from unjust and oppressive ones and disarm the destructive potential of the latter. The main challenge is not how to eliminate emotions to achieve unity but how to mobilise them towards democratic projects. We can only begin to identify the sites and strategies of alternative political intervention by entering the messy, contradictory terrain of affective struggles.

This chapter demonstrates social media's political potential in facilitating feelings of engagement. Social media creates a fluid, temporary affective zone of political encounters and contestation. The public display of networked sentiments stimulates political interest and unites individuals despite emotional differences. Emotional stories connect social subjects and invite collective improvisation by participants. The dynamic practice afforded by social media facilitates the emergence of affective publics, whose emotional outpouring is not necessarily in line with state-orchestrated narratives. Social media's connective affordances help activate the in-between bond of affective publics (Papacharissi 2015: 8–9). Casting a sharp contrast to state-dominated modes of communication, the affective public contests the state's distribution of emotions. Affective publics are united and divided by feelings. Social media's storytelling infrastructure invites spatially dispersed individuals to feel their way into an unfolding event and create a shared space for emotional disclosure and spontaneous commemoration. Its modes of public reverberation sustain affective feedback loops and formulate alternative archives of feelings.

Chapter 5 mainly focuses on how social media liberates collective imaginations associated with historical stickiness and national identification. Social media's affective flow raises further questions about the blurring of public and private boundaries in formulating affective publics. How do users' digital connectivity and networked engagement create a safe space for authentic expression and turn everyday sentiments into an ambivalent and implicit political act? How do individuals contribute to ongoing emotional events by adding their personal stories and translating them into moments of dissent? How does daily life offer a source for the constitution of storytelling publics and attain political relevance? Chapter 6 will examine the transformation of a personal blog into a site of alternative meaning-making through the narration of personal experiences. It will consider how personal tragedy holds the social body together and the ambivalent political formation the emotional texture supports.

NOTES

1. Mouffe (2000) contends that the political unity of 'us', which requires a moment of closure and homogeneity, should be conceived more as a contingent and temporary hegemonic articulation of 'the people' and remains contestable.

2. In mainland China, major Taiwanese websites are, by and large, blocked. Only mainland-based forums are accessible to both sides. All posts presented in this chapter are drawn from the forums of NetEase and Yahoo! China between June 2005 and May 2006. All translations are our own.

3. The concept of affective memory refers broadly to the emotional trauma, feeling, subjectivity and mode of identification shaped by the historical effects of colonialism in East Asia. In this geopolitical region, intellectual enquiry into this concept is mainly concerned with questions of transcultural dialogue, intersubjective understanding, and reconciliation among conflictual national/ethnic groupings. The conceptualisation of affective memory in this essay is inspired by the following works: Sun (2002); Mizoguchi (2003); Chen (2001).

4. The notion of being 'carved up' (*guafen* 瓜分) by foreign powers is salient in the collective psyche of mainland China. See Wang X. (2003), chapter 11.

5. The sense of superiority is frequently mixed with the sentiment of resistance to China's 'big-nation' (*da guo*) consciousness and Sino-centrism.

6. The Taiwanese forum participants prefer to call themselves *huaren* (people of Chinese descent), rather than the China-centred appellation *zhongguo ren* (people of China).

7. Conversational impoliteness should be strictly distinguished from uncivility. Impoliteness, Papacharissi (2004) asserts, is often a 'sincere and spontaneous reflection of emotions'. Internet forums may foster heated exchanges that are at times rude and unruly but cannot be dismissed simply because of their explicit impoliteness. Yet apparently polite, cool-headed discourse that adheres to the norms of reasoning may be 'uncivil' for its chauvinistic and racist assumptions about the other.

8. *Bensheng ren* (本省人) is a local term used in Taiwan. It generally refers to those who immigrated to Taiwan before the years between 1945 and 1949. Those who came after 1945 are called *waisheng ren* (外省人). The largest group of *bensheng ren* speaks the Southern Fujian dialect and makes up about 73 per cent of the population of Taiwan as of 2008. For more information see 'Taiwan's Ethnic Distribution', www .hakka.gov.tw/public/Attachment/512722155971.pdf.

9. On the politics of remembering, see Anderson (1991).

10. In Taiwan, pro-Japan sentiment has surfaced dramatically with the

decline of KMT authoritarian rule in the late 1980s. Identification with the 'modern' image of Japan has been a powerful emotional base for pro-independence political parties to provoke anti-China and anti-KMT sentiments in major election campaigns.

11. Mizoguchi (2003) observes that the anti-China sentiment of the Japanese is mixed with the ideology of anti-communism and a sense of superiority derived from Japan's economic achievements. I have found similar sentiments in posts by Taiwanese users.

CHAPTER SIX

The wailing wall

On 2 February 2020, Li Wenliang, known for raising awareness of early Covid-19 infections in Wuhan, died after contracting the virus. His death sparked national mourning. Li was one of the few doctors who had warned about the coronavirus outbreak. Police investigated them for allegedly spreading rumours. Li's Weibo page was soon turned into a 'wailing wall' (*ku qiang* 哭墙) where netizens came to pour out their emotions. The circulation of negative sentiments towards authorities engendered a moment of dissent. In China, emotional expressions that are not in line with official stances are often regarded as potential threats to the regime (Yang 2018). This chapter takes the narratives posted on Li's last entry as the focus of analysis. It investigates how the emotionally charged narratives – which encompass many lived experiences – have resulted in a distinct structure of feeling and formulated an affective public. These affective traces are closely related to the nature of the unexpected event. Our analytical focus is on how ordinary people utilise social media to cope with pandemic situations and challenge official interpretations of the outbreak. Through analysis of the public reverberations, this chapter examines how online commemoration opens up a space of personal storytelling and subtly renders the personal political. Our analysis will provide insights into how social media and emotions intersect and what happens to people's emotional expression in an increasingly emotionally policed society.

'Here I am, Dr Li': How grief impels people to speak up

Finally, I got my nucleic acid test result today, and it's positive.

Starting from 10.41 a.m. on 1 February 2020, when this post was released, almost every day, every hour and even every minute, someone has left a comment.[1]

Hello, Dr Li. I forgot to say good morning to you this morning. Hey, good afternoon ~ It's raining heavily again. I don't like it.

It rained for a day, much cooler. I have to go on a business trip in the following days. Dragon Boat Festival is coming soon. I finally can meet the people I want to see. Good night.

My flower has blossomed. Hope you have a good day!

Dr Li: Get up and exercise! You can enjoy the morning breeze and hear the birds singing!

Dr Li, we can buy one chicken leg and get one free in Dicos tomorrow.

Recently, I rushed into the stock market. I am poor and too eager to make money. I hope to earn back the money that I lost over the years. Then, I can feel more confident to pursue a better self.

When I was in school, I felt still young. After graduation, I thought I was no longer a child. I need to face it, choose it and bear the consequences of my choice.

I am looking forward to payday every day, but I am still unhappy after getting the salary. Where is happiness?

Today, the temperature has dropped. The coldest time this year. There are still 15 days left in 2020. The year goes by so quickly!

These Weibo posts are driven by affection for Li and various personal experiences. They are usually presented in the form of short textual narratives. They talk about the pain of being crossed in love, pressure at work and tense family relationships; some complain about why their messages have been deleted again; some share a place for delicious cherries and fried chicken, and some say hello to Li casually. They reveal an intimate connection with Li. These people know that the blogger is no longer alive, and they still express their feelings on his blog. Geographically dispersed strangers participate in a virtual community of feelings formulated based on a sense of shared emotions. Their outpouring of personal sentiments also facilitates emotional connection. Although their affective encounters arouse contradictory emotions that resist state co-optation, there is no intense political passion for organising collective action. Since Li's death, many have used his blog to tell their life stories, entailing complex emotional attachments and dynamics. This phenomenon has been described as a 'miracle' on Chinese social media (True Exploration of Jellyfish 2020).

If Covid-19 had not occurred in Wuhan in early 2020, Li would have been just an ordinary ophthalmologist in the Central Hospital of Wuhan. On 30 December 2019, he sent out a short message in a WeChat group to caution against the reemergence of SARS. He was considered one of the whistleblowers who sounded an early alarm to society; however, the government regarded his behaviour as rumour-mongering and asked him to write a reprimand. Although the government continued to deny human-to-human transmission, Wuhan's urgent lockdown confirmed the warning of Li and several other medical staff. On 31 January 2020, Li himself was diagnosed with Covid-19, which he caught through contact with patients, and his condition deteriorated until his death in the early morning of 7 February. Unfair treatment can stimulate the struggle for different distributions of emotions and challenge the state (Goodwin et al. 2001; Clarke et al. 2006b). Li's tragic fate came as a moral shock, as many saw themselves in him:

> [A]t the time of Dr Li's death the pandemic situation looked grave, the tolls were high, and the prospects of containing the spread were gloomy. Life had never seemed so fragile. An acute sense of helplessness and pain hung in the air. . . . This sense of a common fate was heightened as netizens talked about how Dr Li was just like them – an ordinary person with the same human desires and weaknesses, likes and dislikes. (Yang 2022: 3602–15)

On the night of his death, social media platforms, including Li's Weibo account, were flooded with messages, poems, articles, pictures and music imbued with an intense sense of disbelief and anger. These emotional feeds co-produced by netizens turned the blog into a virtual monument. This monument's spectacular display of sentiment constituted China's most explosive emotional event in 2020 (Liang 2020; Zheng 2020; Yong et al. 2020).

The post featured at the beginning of this chapter was the last one that Li left on Weibo before his death, which invited massive participation, triggered a moment of dissent and formulated affective solidarity among strangers. His image as an ordinary, kind and humorous guy had touched many. The compassion towards him was contagious: millions of netizens persistently left messages under this post, making grief a pervasive emotion in early 2020 (Meerjump 2020). Grief reacts to the loss of life, causing moral shocks and moving individuals (Gharmaz and Milligan 2006). Grief is also an expression of love (Ahmed 2004: 130). From February to May 2020, there were typically more than 5,000 comments each day. Around Tomb-Sweeping Day, the average exceeded 10,000, with the highest peak reaching 100,000 a day. In China, 'only famous actors and pop stars may see such a large number of replies to their posts' (Yuan 2020). Because these posts often express disapproval of the state, the blog serves as an outlet for cultivating political agency. Nevertheless, Weibo is a highly monitored public space. Starting from June 2020, Weibo began to censor the messages on his blog and deleted many comments, especially those considered critical of the state. Some were worried about how long these memorial messages could be kept (Sanjiaojun 2020). Thus, it is difficult to estimate the actual number of messages. The exact number is likely to be in the millions or even more (Zhou and Zhong 2021).

Public displays of grief and sorrow are an old way of express-ing protest and dissent in China. Mourning enables a display of unapproved emotions. Not all lives are worth mourning; it depends crucially on the hegemonic norms regulating the scene of public rec-ognition (Butler 2005). If mourning can motivate political actions (Butler 2006), why do netizens spontaneously mourn Li and attach themselves to this site? How do they share intimate emotions with strangers, and how can we understand the political implications of their affective engagement? What kinds of political expression does it support? Our analysis selects posts from March to December 2020. It explores how they reflect ordinary people's everyday experiences and emotions and how they register their concerns online. Instead of seeing emotions as 'properties' owned by individuals, our anal-ysis conceptualises emotion as an embodiment of social practices informed by various social relations and encounters in everyday life (Williams 1975; Grossberg 1988; Ahmed 2004; Harding and Pribram 2009). In such practices, emotional expression is not just a psychic reaction of inner emotion itself but also constitutes a broader sociopolitical formation. The individualised, fragmented narratives on Weibo indirectly challenge state power and open up an affective space where a new feeling subject is brought into existence. In our view, grief is a rare emotional occupation and intense cultural practice worth exploring. We are interested in how an affective public and its underlying structure of feelings are brought into being via the unexpected outpouring of emotions. Our analysis will illustrate how online engagement with Li's Weibo temporarily blurs private–public distinctions and politicises grief and sorrow to formulate a personal politics of mourning.

CHANGING FORMS OF INDIVIDUAL EXPRESSIONS

Since 1949, individual expressions of personal emotions have been subject to state norms. Under Mao's affective regime, individualism was demonised as a symbol of a degenerate capitalist culture. Any spontaneous terms of individual emotions were considered bourgeois, selfish and harmful and thus were rejected entirely (Hansen and Svarverud 2010; Pang 2017). The conspicuous lack of reference to personal feelings began to change in the early 1980s. A massive body of personal memoirs, biographies and literary works, such as 'scar literature' (*shanghen wenxue* 伤痕文学), began to feature the unfortunate experiences of individuals during the Cultural Revolution. The Deng regime left more room for the personal expression of family affection, friendship and romance. However, such narratives, like the films of the Fifth Generation, were often deployed to construct a 'national allegory' symbolising the fate of the nation (Chow 1995b; Lu 1997; Dai 2000). Individuals were put under the nation's gaze and became absorbed into the social character.

By the 1990s, with the emergence of new realistic novels and the Sixth Generation films, personal emotions found their expression in ordinary ways of life. For example, the Sixth Generation films paid close attention to the daily struggle of urban youths, their sense of uncertainty and their defiance against mainstream values (Dai 2000; Zhang 2007; Shi 2008). In terms of visual style, these films were no longer obsessed with national allegory but documented the details of perceived reality (Cheng and Huang 2002). As director Jia Zhangke said, '"Crow Solves Crow's Problem, I Solve My Problem". No one has the right to represent the majority. You only have the right to express yourself. You can only represent yourself. This is the first step towards our liberation from cultural hegemony. Therefore, pain must be individual. Otherwise, one cannot understand the emotional world of young people' (Jia 2002: 367). The individual expressions presented in these films encompassed a wide range of unpredictable and ambivalent emotional states saturated with complex feelings of hesitation, uncertainty, contradiction, emptiness and displacement. Due to their incompatibility with mainstream ideology, most of these films were banned and labelled 'underground films' (Yin 1998; Lin 2002). Although these images and voices subverted the state's ideological uniformity, they were not expressed by ordinary people themselves. Due to the mediality of cinema, ordinary people cannot make themselves a part of the developing event.

The commercialisation of media sectors has provided new opportunities for expanding the sphere of individual expression. Some reality TV shows portray personal struggles (such as Zhejiang Satellite TV's *The Voice of China*), share emotional experiences (such as Shenzhen Satellite TV's *You Have a Letter*) or formulate criteria for spouse selection (such as Jiangsu Satellite TV's *If You Are the One*). These programmes enable individuals to express their sense of frustration and hope. Nevertheless, under growing commercial and political pressures:

> While these shows provide entertaining visual spectacles by dwelling on people's emotional turmoil and suffering, they seldom probe into the real origins of these conflicts or provide resources for resolving them. More often than not, the token psychological counselling offered on these shows was a superficial gimmick to give a sheen of professional value, and masking what was essentially media voyeurism: exploiting the audience's fascination for sensational stories and watching other people air their dirty laundry in public. (Kong 2014: 66)

In this operation, personal emotions are more like a selling point, making up for the lack of emotional resonance in such state-orchestrated narratives as 'harmonious society' and 'national rejuvenation'. The shows' production restricts individual repertoires of self-expression. Although these programmes often lead to heated debates over social values and personal choice (Ma 2014; Wang X. 2017), the agency of individual expression remains highly subject to commercial and political imperatives, making it difficult to express political dissent through such outlets.

Cyberspace invokes emotional states differently from traditional media. It has become a part of people's everyday emotional practices and liberated their imaginations. Social media anonymity

174

and connectivity invite people to feel their place in current events (Papacharissi 2015: 5). Its storytelling infrastructures encourage the proliferation of a plurality of personal narratives, configuring a new culture of disclosure. It enables individuals to constantly upload personal narratives and co-create critical interpretations of public events that challenge hegemonic discourses (Hansen and Svarverud 2010; Sun and Ma 2019).

AN ARCHIVE OF FEELINGS

Here is China's wailing wall.

Your microblog is like a wailing wall to everyone. I just want to tell you here that 2020 is ending. Because of you, many people can accompany their families at home, drink Coke and lead a simple and happy life. Thank you!

This has become a place where everyone can talk.

Dr Li's microblog has become a place where many people talk to him, making me full of tears every time I visit! At the moment, I thought of a text I learned in childhood (I can't remember the author's name): Some live when they are already dead; others have died but are still alive.

I came here to see what happened in the past six months. This has become everyone's wailing wall. I cried after reading a few posts. I don't know whether it was because of too much pressure or something. Sure enough, I still want to live well. I wish everyone all the best, and everything will be fine.

Weibo operates as a crucial terrain for the politically infused expression and circulation of emotions. It offers a storytelling infrastructure where online emotion is contagious and can grow exponentially with the development of forms of virtual memorialisation. The acts of remembering have created space for popular affective investment:

The social significance of people's expression of grief [is] perhaps that it articulate[s] a collective desire to speak out about the painful aspects of everyday life for many people – disappointments, losses, feeling let down – which are often born in silence. (Harding and Pribram 2002: 420)

Grief infiltrates the texture of Weibo posts. Mourning allows netizens to display various emotions that reflect their lifeworlds. Netizens have called Li's microblog a 'wailing wall'.[2] Driven initially by intense emotions of sadness and empathy, netizens resignify and reappropriate the virtual wall to pour out personal feelings, where everyone can talk and cry (Yuan 2020; Zhang et al. 2020; Chang 2020). Because of its immediate and spontaneous feature, much of the virtual wall's communication is emotional. It functions as an archive of feelings where netizens continually update emotional feeds and accumulate emotional values (Yang 2022). Weibo is more than a tool for social exchange but facilitates affective encounters. These encounters engender a highly fluid, permeable and contestatory zone of affective flows. While these individual experiences vary from person to person, they are primarily associated with daily joy, frustration and sorrow. Some messages are even one's most secret feelings that may not be shared with one's close friends or family:

> Dr Li, I have almost finished the final exam, and I am going back to my hometown to meet my parents and my good friends and teachers. I miss them so much. I hope you are happy. 😄

> An hour ago, my drunk husband asked for a divorce. The tone was as calm as what we should eat tomorrow morning. . . . I just couldn't sleep and wanted to talk to someone.

> I had an accident here. I hit an 86-year-old man. I dare not tell anyone. Luckily, the old man is okay. I accompanied him to the hospital for examination over the past two days. My butt is painful. Disaster cannot be avoided. People who want to die cannot die, such as me.

> Sometimes, I don't know which road I am taking. Life is really like a labyrinth.

> Today is the third day of my hard work. Sometimes, I think that I am too tired to live on. I have no more dreams and pursuits. However, I still need to live on for my parents. I hope time can cure me. I want to take a nap!

> Dr Li, why do people have to get married? I feel exhausted after only half a year of marriage. He's not good at talking. My mother does not like him and I have to mediate between them every time. He always says he's such a person and would not please his elders or say nice words. I am tired, regret it and don't know if I chose the right one.

> I went to the hospital today for a reexamination. All indices are normal and the sickness is gone! I am so happy!

> I'm gay.

The wailing wall facilitates the dispersion of personal emotions and blends public and private. It captures tiny feelings that are missing from official narratives. Those who posted messages here might be reluctant to share the same details with the people around them – that their marriage is unhappy; that they are gay; that they accidentally hit an old man – but they all choose to share their secrets here. The identities revealed by their narratives include college students, middle school students, businesspeople, public servants, workers, freelancers, etc.

> The high school entrance examination will be held the day after tomorrow. I am very nervous.

> My father is also a doctor. Why can't our voice be heard? I speak so loudly, but only I can hear it. Doctors are helpless. Why can't everyone sympathise?

> Today was my first night shift in the emergency department. One patient suffered from extensive burns, one suffered from a cerebral haemorrhage, one suffered from myocardial infarction and some suffered from heatstroke, headache and brain fever. I am too tired and weak.

> In the morning, the boss criticised me because of my work. What she said was harsh. My mother called, and I smiled and told her that everything was quite good.

From these posts' expressive themes and contents, we can easily detect that this form of social media participation is spontaneous, casual and random. Li's Weibo is regarded by many as a safe place to vent hidden sentiments. Some archive their private and probably unspeakable experiences in this anonymous space. The intensities unleashed from the archival practice help perpetuate social connectivity and sustain public memories framed in personalised narratives.

The wailing wall reveals the struggle over public–private divides central to the formulation of affective space. Private narratives often present as a record of personal emotions, such as diaries (Yang 2000). They offer 'the individual a way to narrate their own inner life (likes, dislikes, desires, and revulsions) to themselves and others' (Hemmings 2005: 552). In other words, an individual's self-expression is embedded in wider social contexts and relations, and the emotions conveyed through affective narratives often connect the individual with others. Through social media networking, this kind of personal emotional sharing makes the emergence of an affective public possible. Papacharissi (2015: 125) defines affective public as 'networked public formations that are mobilised and connected or disconnected through expressions of sentiment'. Alternative meaning construction is central to affective publics. Social media prompts people to venture into the situations triggered by public events and articulate their personal stories of moments of crisis. The wailing wall provides an affective space saturated with emotional feelings.

Although the netizens' affective engagement is scattered and fragmented, and their narratives are diverse, it constitutes a 'structure of feeling' reflecting the collective mood during the pandemic. Raymond Williams defines the structure of feeling as 'the felt sense of the quality of life at a particular place and time' (Williams 1975: 47), which is 'extremely difficult to recapture' (Harding and Pribram 2004: 867). It consists of emerging but ephemeral emotional experiences in ways that combine suppressed popular sentiments and unrealised potential. By contrast, 'social character' is the embodiment of the ideology of hegemonic groups (Williams 1975: 61), the official thought (Harding and Pribram 2004), or the idealised spirit (Williams 1979: 163) of an age. Compared with the social character, the structure of feeling encompasses and articulates the omitted or overlooked categories of existence (Harding and Pribram 2004: 868). The casual everyday expressions on the virtual wall can also transmit political affects. In response, the state has heightened Internet censorship (Yang 2009; Yang and Wu 2018; Peng 2021). Around mid-June 2020, censorship on the wailing wall began to intensify, and sometimes only the messages of the day or just a few hours can be seen. However, censorship has never successfully prevented new entries. Netizens keep the wailing wall alive by swarming and flooding it with posts.

Demobilising negative sentiments

The wailing wall has the potential to translate grief into more politicised emotions. Nevertheless, its political agency should be understood in the broader context of China's Covid war. Before the pandemic outbreak, Xi's regime had successfully established the positive image of a confident China. However, under his dispensation, media censorship has tightened. The state has sought to propagate positive emotions of hope and solidarity to reduce the sense of outrage aroused by lockdowns and grief. Since mid-January 2020, the state has managed to displace adverse emotions by framing the fight against the pandemic as 'everyone's war' (Shenzhen Media Group 2020). As a result, the outbreak has become a politically sensitive issue and nationalist celebratory narratives dominate the media. Personal diary-style records have mushroomed online when the regime starts orchestrating a uniform narrative about the pandemic war. The state ultimately co-opts these traces to its advantage. They are woven into narratives of national strength and solidarity. The official media reports and ceremonies feature individual contributions to the nation and their dedication and sacrifice 'for the people'. For example, 'The Sand Painting Diary of Doctors in Wuhan', a short video broadcast by CCTV and People's Net, inscribes the experiences of medical staff and volunteers with an ideological theme of sacrifice and unity (CCTV News 2020): healthcare personnel worked selflessly under high pressure, drivers picked up volunteers from work for free, police and soldiers provided timely help to those in need, and tens of thousands of construction workers built Huoshenshan Hospital, an emergency specialty field hospital, within ten days. These individual experiences are entirely absorbed into the triumphant, 'beating the virus' narrative that defines what an ideal person should be.

Some media portraits of individual experiences during the outbreak focused exclusively on the social role played by individuals and the actions they took to support compatriots. For example, the coverage highlighted how citizens across the country helped Wuhan residents during the lockdown (Sina.cn 2020). Although these stories portrayed individuals' daily encounters, they were ultimately inserted into the hegemonic narrative by 'integrating personal experiences, sentiments, and value judgments with the social context so that that individual experience could enter the "grand history" [*daxie de lishi*]' (Zhou 2020: 247).

In an attempt to turn popular emotions into a boost to nationalist sentiment, the propaganda machine formulated social characters by deploying the figures of father/son, mother/daughter and husband/wife to convey the sense of selflessness and sacrifice. It portrayed these characters by featuring their devotion to the nation at the expense of personal intimacy. In one piece of footage, a man wearing a mask kisses his doctor girlfriend in an isolation suit through the glass of a medical room – images like this function to turn individuals into an army of selfless, obedient citizens and brave soldiers united under the leadership of the CPC. Under this type of war narrative, individual needs and emotions give way to the national cause. Through such articulation, the individual is inscribed into the affective force of nationalism: 'Cheering for Wuhan is also to cheer for China; Wuhan wins then Hubei wins, Hubei wins then China wins' (*People's Daily* 2020). Winning the coronavirus war has also been constructed as a way to prove national strength and pride. Government officials promote gratitude as a positive emotion. As a result, the fear, worry, insecurity, grievance and indignation experienced by individuals are neutralised and depoliticised. Negative sentiments are redirected towards a common enemy. The 'Wuhan Diary' (Fang 2020), for example, has been fiercely attacked for its author's critical stance on state accountability (Xilisheng 2020). The publication of the English version of the diary was labelled as an 'act of treason'. Despite all these efforts, it is not easy to manage negative emotions towards the government's early missteps, especially when the moral principle is violated. The state's elimination of certain moral emotions makes the wailing wall a unique space for the exertion of political agency.

Silent protest

The wailing wall represents a bottom-up affective struggle over accountability, visibility and recognition. It creates a space for criticism and contestation that has the potential of inducing a trust crisis for the regime. In China, mourning offers an alternative avenue for expressing public outrage. The online mourning of Li is driven by the feeling that he was wronged (Yang 2022). Mourning enables emotional agency to take shape. Its storytelling facilitates feelings of political engagement and fosters empowerment. It also reveals how ordinary people use social media to make their feelings visible. Mourning questions who is worthy of grief and problematises the hegemonic distribution of emotion. Political possibilities are opened up when 'those who have been designated as ungrievable are grieved, and when their loss is not only felt as a loss, but becomes a symbol of the injustice of loss' (Ahmed 2004: 191–2). Although there is no explicit political statement, the space accommodates critical voices and adverse emotions towards the state.

> It's one year since you left the world. Just one year after you blew your whistle, 80 million people were infected and 1.77 million people died. . . . Today it snows in my city, and we will miss you forever!
>
> This place is afraid of something. Keep deleting posts. Poor editor, more pitiful than you.
>
> Fortunately, the wall has not fallen yet . . .

The more deleted posts, the stronger people's memories become.

This place cannot disappear.

I just came to this wall to write a note. Can you hear the voice of the people?!

Good morning! I thought the wailing wall was pushed down, so I came here to look. Fortunately, it's still there! Dr Li, will you tell me that the world will be better?

Because these voices convey a sense of resistance to censorship, they risk erasure and disappearance. They illustrate how social media participation opens up a 'space of appearance' (Arendt 1998; Butler 2013; Butler 2015), where people's feelings can be heard and seen. Their virtual appearance allows us to capture the affective intensity of ordinary people. This emotionally charged space does not produce passionate politics; it encompasses a multiplicity of heterogeneous experiences and imaginations not represented in official narratives. It is animated by popular sentiments and creates a domain for expressing dissent. These scattered and fragmented narratives cultivate affective intensity and political potential, which may not directly translate into political action, but constitute a force field that authorities cannot entirely ignore. Meanwhile, the wailing wall accommodates the plural emotions that the official social character cannot fully absorb. These fragments enable individuals to seek agency by connecting their sentiments with strangers in ways that are not in line with state-regulated sociality.

I haven't insisted on anything in my life, but if I don't insist on it, I may regret it when I get old. This is the best opportunity and the tale of youth. Dr Li, please bless me in the dark.

I feel that many classmates, colleagues and netizens are using the October 1 holiday to heal their wounds. Everyone chose to go home.

He does not appear in my dream anymore. Is he going to leave me soon? I have loved a boy for three years, more than three years. Why is his fate so unfair? I think I have no courage to live on.

I went to see the sea yesterday. I didn't expect that I could still see the scenic spots that made me feel good.

I have depression, but I wipe away my tears after visiting you every day and continue to live.

I have been down since yesterday's meeting. I hope we can all treat people gently and I have been thinking about whether I should change jobs at such an age, and whether I should study in a company that lays off employees every year. Should I move forward or quit as the boss doesn't like me or my performance? But now, I don't want to quit.

Today, I resigned because I suffered sexual harassment in the workplace yesterday. A disgusting man who is ten years older than me, and has two children, made obscene gestures and humiliated me at the dinner table after I rejected him. I could not get over this and resolutely chose to resign. I believe I must have a better future and work.

The wailing wall identifies who can be grieved and subverts the 'distinction between legitimate and illegitimate lives' (Ahmed 2004: 191). It also challenges standards regarding appropriate and acceptable emotions for public display. The growing dissatisfaction with the government's treatment of Li has pressured the state to acknowledge him as a 'national martyr' and turn him into a loyal citizen in line with state propaganda. By claiming Li as 'one of their own', the state attempted to co-opt the public memory to show that 'the party, too, was on the side of the people' (Yang 2022: 3824):

Dr Li is dead, yet the battle is not over! Li Wenliang's actions and wishes during his lifetime were to stop the pandemic and protect the health of his compatriots. We must continue to resolutely curb the spread of the pandemic and win this battle of prevention and control. . . . The Chinese nation has come through difficulties and hardships. . . . We will definitely win this smokeless battle. (China Media Group 2020)

Some netizens, however, do not appreciate the official gesture. Instead, they highlight his courage and honesty as a people's hero who dared to tell the truth.

I really miss you, hero.

Today is my first wedding anniversary and my lover and I admire you very much. I hope that the baby born in October will be a person with a sense of justice like you. We will tell him/her about your heroic deeds.

Salute my hero and we will not forget you.

If possible, I don't want you to become a hero. I just want you to be good, like an ordinary person, live happily with your wife and children, enjoy the dramas you like, travel and enjoy your life.

I hope you are not a hero, so that you can still accompany your wife, children and parents and there will not even be any celebration party.

You're memorable and trustworthy. I will remember you forever.

When President Xi Jinping recognised a select group of citizens for their contributions to the pandemic war, Li was missing from the list of 'national heroes', which prompted a moral outcry over standards regarding the official acknowledgement. Netizens contested the legitimate object of emotions. The following posts illustrate how personal emotions give rise to a temporary site of contestation:

> You are not at today's (official) ceremony, but you are in our hearts.

> There is no need for medals. We will not forget you. This is the highest honour I can give you, and the deadline may be until my death.

> You are in our hearts, and this is an invisible medal, more valuable than anything else.

> Your medal shames everyone. Thank you.

THE FRAGILITY OF THE VIRTUAL MONUMENT

The different interpretations of who deserves state acknowledgement are a matter of hegemonic struggle. They undermine the state's effort to secure popular approval. To many, Li is not a typical hero showing loyalty to the state, but like a neighbour or friend. They see themselves in his weakness, powerlessness and vulnerability as ordinary people facing the outbreak (Yang 2022: 3583). Such affective contrast signifies growing tensions with the uniformity of social characters and prompts the active pursuit of more autonomous and plural expressions. It brings dissents together. The demand for accountability mixes with a desire to contest censorship. The endurance of the wall becomes a focus of contention. In the absence of a unified political goal, these threads tend not to target the government explicitly but problematise the exclusion of negative feelings:

> I heard the comments were gone, so I came to see you.

> I want to tell the truth every day, but I can't tell the truth in this country.

> In addition to today's new comments, all the previous ones have been cleared. Over 1 million comments are all gone. Why not leave people a place to cry?

> It may not be possible to protect this microblog in the end, just like many things we cannot protect . . . there is no right to grieve.

> It was cleared, the wall was not torn down, but it was painted again, burying what they didn't want to see and what they didn't want others to see. Very clean, very bright.

I want to be positive, but unfortunately, this society is unfriendly to kind people. It's too painful.

We have opinions, but we cannot say them. We have words, but we cannot record them. We have 'negative energy', but it's not allowed. The so-called victory is not to control the pandemic but to control the people.

I saw the news yesterday that the Hero Medal was awarded. After the award, will those wicked people be blamed? When you told the truth, the police and reporters did not investigate but asked you to shut up and write a letter of reprimand. Even if they are not punished, God will punish them sooner or later. Today, we left you a message just to say a fair word for you, but these messages will be deleted someday, just like you were wronged initially. I cried when I saw that the comments were deleted.

What you see is what others want you to see, and what you can discuss is what others allow you to discuss. This society is too sensitive to hold any bad voices.

The wailing wall's semi-open structure channels flows of dissatisfaction with heightened censorship during the outbreak. When the moral act of telling the truth was punished, netizens responded angrily. The shared grief over Li reinforces the sense of anger over authorities, and disappointment with censorship further fuels the indignation. The growing discontent invites more participants to join. In their passionate participation, people contribute their emotional judgement to the current political environment.

This country is in a state of eternal stagnation. . . . The more carefully we look at this foolish country, the more disgusting it becomes. It has preserved the ugliest shape in the world for thousands of years. . . . Good medicine tastes bitter, and good advice is harsh to the ear.

The more good news I see in the morning, the sadder I feel, for myself and for others.

It's difficult to tell the truth and easy to tell lies. Our society is sick.

There is no standard for worldviews, value judgements and ideas about life. In the world of crows, swans are also a crime, but I'd instead choose swans.

No one can remove this wailing wall. Anyone who dares to delete it is against the people.

These narratives show that the wailing wall, underpinned by popular affective investments, symbolises the refusal to become a state-approved social character. They constitute an implicit form of antagonism that indirectly resists the state's attempt to totalise the social. Despite the state's policing of emotions, these sentiments refuse to disappear. They have struggled to display heterogeneous experiences that are not accounted for in the official narrative. They create an alternative scene that disturbs the unified image orchestrated by the state. Through the threads they post, netizens redistribute emotions that elicit many implicitly political meanings.

EMOTIONAL DEPENDENCE

Dr Li, we live for you.

I am not happy today, but life will continue. Hug you, I hope you can give me strength.

It's warm in Kunming today. It'd be great if you could have a look. Everything is slowly getting better. We can tell you.

It's drizzling today. It's not raining much! I feel a little relaxed, a little less sad at the moment!

How to become more brave and confident? I was pretty good when practising piano myself, but I couldn't overcome my nervousness in class.

It's December. Bad 2020 is almost over.

2020 has passed so fast. After this winter, I will be 20 years old. I will try my best to make my youth leave no regrets. I hope all the bad memories will remain in 2020. I hope the world is peaceful, I hope there is no suffering in the world, and I hope you will have a good life in another world.

It turned out that 2020 passed. Though I escaped the coronavirus pandemic, I was in the hospital one month before my 23rd birthday. I hope to get better and leave the hospital as soon as possible. I miss you!

Have the courage to be happy.

Mourning unites people despite their social and cultural differences. Against the state-engineered paternalistic care narrative and optimism, mourning reveals the vulnerability and precariousness of life (Butler 2006: 93). Anonymity makes the wailing wall a relatively safe space to disclose emotional experiences. It creates a vast emotion-display network among distant participants who relate to others through emotional outpouring. These strangers are brought together not only by their emotional attachment to Li but by their emotional disclosures. The emotional connection makes participants feel attached to the virtual wall and gives them a sense of belonging, encouraging intimate disclosure. Such emotional involvement configures an affective public that produces 'ambient, always-on feeds that further connect and pluralise expression' (Papacharissi 2015: 129). It brings together fluid, scattered, transient and emotionally resonant individuals driven partly by a quest for affective encounters. Their virtual encounters give visibility to personal feelings that feed into each other, blurring the distinction between private and public, individual and collective. These feelings include frustration, confusion, uneasiness, stress, anxiety and depression, signifying the vulnerability of life. They also contribute to shared sentiments of sympathy and empathy. When these feelings come together, the space infuses different personal styles with lived experiences to bear on the intersubjective construction of the affective public. The free circulation of personal affects fosters togetherness.

I was frustrated at the workplace today.

Dr Li, the college entrance examination is in 20 days. I am frustrated, but I must stick to it. I will try my best to stick to it. You also need to be fine over there. We all need to be fine.

I have been unemployed for nearly 100 days. What do you think?

Dr Li, I am a particularly unsuccessful person. I always know the value and effort only after the opportunity slips away. I always regret it. I don't know whether people have a destiny or not. This may be an excuse, but sometimes indirect hints in life really make me collapse. A few years ago, I went to the studio for the first time, and the last meal was in the restaurant. The hard plastic chopsticks I just took out broke. To tell the truth, I felt a little collapsed at that time.

Today, I was wronged at work. Though I worked overtime, I was criticised. I took a bus to the city centre to eat Japanese food without telling anyone at noon. I couldn't stop crying when I opened your microblog. Fortunately, I was wearing sunglasses.

Dr Li, I have recently lost my job, and my spouse has to shoulder the children's expenses and mortgage. I felt great pressure and I know that my spouse also feels the same. I have been looking for a job for nearly two months. I'm having a breakdown. I want to cry. Yesterday, my spouse sent our child back to our hometown temporarily. I wept while eating alone. Life is so difficult.

Dr Li, I'm so tired. I am an only child and my parents divorced. My mother, who has never cared about me, suffered from a sudden cerebral haemorrhage. She is not good to me. Since I was a child, she has restricted me from making friends. I dare not let my mother see me when I had a boyfriend. My mother was bad-tempered and I hated her from my heart. However, now, no one cares about her except me. I have no job. Relatives and friends have cut off contact with my mother and me. What should I do?

Sleepless, Dr Li. 18 days to pay the mortgage. Headache.

Dr Li, the article I submitted a month ago was rejected today. The reviewer was acute. I can't revise it. I changed the format at night and found another journal to resubmit it. I hope for good luck. Is there no SCI and fundraising pressure in heaven?

These posts harbour a wide range of emotional experiences that official narratives fail to capture: economic insecurity caused by unemployment or mortgage loans; frustrations in exams and careers; broken family relationships; political fear and depression. They register social realities facing ordinary people, such as unfair social distribution and fierce competition. They also reveal the deteriorating conditions of precariousness, marginalisation or exclusion during the outbreak. The emotion-display activities reveal the necessity of emotional dependence and support during the outbreak. In this sense, the wailing wall provides a place for frustrated, exhausted, depressed and dislocated individuals to seek emotional comfort and healing. This is why the space attracts a great deal of public expression of the self.

Dr Li, I just found that your comment section has become a secret base for so many people to share their secrets. I have had a quick look over everyone's comments and cried. I don't know why. I hope every kind person who lives in this society can live his or her life safely, healthily and happily. In the future, I will often come to this place to tell you what I think, and what others think, and then, continue to live bravely.

Whenever I have grievances, I will come to see your microblog. With you, I can swallow all grievances.

I always feel that this is the softest place in the heart.

This is a virtual place, but it is more real than reality. You can see the real words, sincere hearts and even the real self.

I feel that I may really have a life of nothing. People around me are struggling to move on. Only I am still doing nothing. It is the most terrible thing to watch myself sink soberly. If I have your courage and perseverance, maybe many things would be different.

Wenliang, you are the most familiar stranger. I often come here and find that life is still tough and there are so many optimistic people. I like to see what these people say. No one can save us except ourselves. Cheer up!

It has been raining all day here. Just want to stay with you for a while, look at everyone's messages.

Every time I come to see the message, I feel so warm.

Your blog has become the only place I am willing to talk. If I have the chance, I would like to go visit you.

I feel that everything I have done is wrong. I think of you when I feel helpless! Thank you for listening to me!

Dr Li is like a friend to me. When I am in a bad mood, I feel much better when I come here to talk to you.

I come and see you when I can't sleep.

Dr Li, there are many bad things this year, but life is still going on. Let's cheer together.

The wailing wall channels affective flows through which people can feel and share the sadness and pain of others. The display of personal experiences creates intensities of affective connectedness and stickiness. Vulnerability connects individuals and formulates their emotional subjectivity. Individuals stick to the virtual wall to seek emotional healing. As some scholars have described:

> Perhaps the significance of people's expression of sadness lies in the fact that such expression is linked to a collective desire, that is, for many people, to tell all kinds of sufferings experienced in daily life, such as disappointment, loss, downward destruction, etc., and these sufferings are often replaced by silence. However, at this moment when these pains are expressed, a temporary subject category emerges. (Harding and Pribram 2004: 420)

The wailing wall exposes the mourners' own sense of vulnerability and precariousness that the state fails to address. It enables individuals to pursue emotional fulfilment without appearing overtly political. Venting frustration, despair, injustice, unfairness and fear in a personalised way also helps avoid political risks.

> Hearing the songs written by my beloved rapper, I felt that this year was tough, but I finally got over it. I was so tired that I didn't even have the strength to be careful. I was pushed by bad luck.

What is the purpose of one's life? I don't look forward to the future at all. I wake up every day to face pain, no desire and no excitement. What is terrible is that this kind of life has lasted for 16 years and the suffering seems endless.

CONCLUSION

This chapter analyses how social media participation redistributes emotions and creates an affective space for popular memorialisation. It demonstrates that grief can inadvertently facilitate the emergence of an affective public with the potential to politicise popular sentiments in implicitly political ways. We examine the affective public's expressive forms and how their storytelling is activated and sustained by emotions. The affective public's distinct features include blurring the distinctions between private and public and between the personal and the political. This ambivalence enables netizens to evade censorship while bringing together strangers.

The 'wailing wall' is a rich repertoire of emotions. It is more than just an instrument for social connection: it triggers a moment of dissent that visibilises the emerging structure of feeling that the regime fails to capture. It reveals the broader logic of the culture and politics of mourning during the outbreak: spontaneous commemoration can entail unexpected outcomes; private concerns and personal stories can revive public contention with state accountability and censorship. The act of mourning enables individuals to renegotiate with state power. As a result, the affective object of grieving and remembering has multiplied and expanded to encompass a wide range of lifeworld situations. This tendency allows mourners to feel their way into a personal politics saturated with embodied, ephemeral sentiments. Their engagement formulates an online archive of feelings. With the tightening of social control, the complex emotions about the Covid experience refuse to disappear. In a tense political circumstance hostile to free expression, online engagement entails subversive emotional attachments that disturb the operation of state power in informal and indirect ways. Our analysis argues for the centrality of the personal in Chinese politics. The importance of exploring the wailing wall is the possibility of political agency arising from the intensity of grief. When the ungrieved are grieved, affective politics becomes possible.

NOTES

1. See Li Wenliang's Weibo: https://www.weibo.com/u/1139098205?nick =xiaolwl&is_all=1#1608002727514 (observed from 6 March 2020 to 20 December 2020).
2. We recognise the controversy over the recontextualisation and resignification of this term in relation to the Western Wall in Jerusalem, a place where individuals place written prayers within its cracks. The usage of this term could be seen as problematic in scope when compared to the mourning of Jews for the ancient temple's destruction and the anguish of exile. For a discussion of the scale of grief, see Pritzker (2023).

Bibliography

Abbas, Ackbar (1997) *Hong Kong: Culture and the politics of disappearance*. Hong Kong: Hong Kong University Press.

Ahmed, Sara (2004) *The cultural politics of emotion*. New York: Routledge.

Ahmed, Sara (2009) 'The organization of hate', in Jennifer Harding and E. Deidre Pribram (eds) *Emotions: A cultural studies reader*. London: Routledge, pp. 251–66.

Anderson, Benedict (1991) *Imagined communities: Reflections on the origin and spread of nationalism*. London: Verso.

Andrews, Julia F. (2010) 'The art of the Cultural Revolution', in Richard King (ed.) *Art in turmoil*. Vancouver: University of British Columbia Press, pp. 27–57.

Antonsich, Marco, and Michael Skey (2020) 'Introduction', *Environment and planning C: Politics and space*, 38(4), pp. 580–2.

Appadurai, Arjun (2009) 'Fear of small numbers', in J. Harding and E. Deidre Pribram (eds) *Emotions: A cultural studies reader*. London: Routledge, pp. 235–50.

Arendt, Hannah (1998) *The human condition*. Chicago: University of Chicago Press.

Badiou, Alain (2006) *Polemics*. London: Verso.

Bai, Xuefei 白雪霏 (2017) '"Zhanlang II": Yingxiong meng zhongguo meng' "战狼II"：英雄梦中国梦 ('"Wolf Warrior II": Hero dream, the "Chinese dream"'), *Chengde Daily*, 21 August, http://epaper.hehechengde.cn/cdrb/news/1197/13230/ 67752-1.shtml.

Baik, Yeongseo 白永瑞 (2016) 从核心现场重思 "新的普遍"：评论："新天下主义" ['Reconsidering "alternative universalism" from the standpoint of core location: A discussion on "new cosmopolitanism"'], 开放时代 [*Open Times*] (1), pp. 81–94.

Barbalet, Jack (1998) *Emotion, social theory, and social structure: A macrosociological approach*. Cambridge: Cambridge University Press.

Barbalet, Jack (2002) 'Introduction: Why emotions are crucial', in Jack Barbalet (ed.) *Emotions and sociology*. Oxford: Blackwell, pp. 1–9.

Barbalet, Jack, and Nicolas Demertzis (2013) 'Collective fear and social change', in Nicolas Demertzis (ed.) *Emotions in politics: The affect dimension in political tension*. London: Palgrave Macmillan, pp. 167–85.

Bargetz, Brigitte (2015) 'The distribution of emotions: Affective politics of emancipation', *Hypatia*, 30(3), pp. 580–96.

Barker, Colin (2001) 'Fear, laughter, and collective power: The making of solidarity at the Lenin Shipyard in Gdnask, Poland, August 1980', in Jeff Goodwin, James M. Jasper and Francesca Polletta (eds) *Passionate politics: Emotions and social movements*. Chicago: University of Chicago Press, pp. 175–94.

Becker, Jeffrey (2014) *Social ties, resources, and migrant labor contention in contemporary China*. Lanham: Lexington.

Bensky, Tova, and Eran Fisher (2014) *Internet and emotions*. New York: Routledge.

Berezin, Mabel (2002) 'Secure states: Towards a political sociology of emotion', in Jack Barbalet (ed.) *Emotions and sociology*. Oxford: Blackwell, pp. 33–52.

Berlant, Lauren (2015) 'Structures of unfeeling: Mysterious skin', *International Journal of Politics, Culture and Society*, 28, pp. 191–213.

Berry, Michael (2008) *A history of pain: Trauma in modern Chinese literature and film*. New York: Columbia University Press.

Bondes, Maria, and Günter Schucher (2014) 'Derailed emotions: The transformation of claims and targets during the Wenzhou online incident', *Information, Communication, and Society*, 17(1), pp. 45–65.

Britt, Lory, and David Heise (2000) 'From shame to pride in identity politics', in Sheldon Stryker, Timothy J. Owens and Robert W. White (eds) *Self, identity, and social movements*. Minneapolis: University of Minnesota Press, pp. 252–68.

Brown, Kerry (2018) *China's dream: The culture of Chinese communism and the secret sources of its power*. Cambridge: Polity Press.

Brown, Wendy (1995) *States of injury: Power and freedom in late modernity*. Princeton: Princeton University Press.

Buechler, Steven M. (2000) *Social movements in advanced capitalism: The political economy and cultural construction of social activism*. New York: Oxford University Press.

Burkitt, Ian (2002) 'Complex emotions', in Jack Barbalet, *Emotions and sociology*. Oxford: Blackwell, pp. 151–68.

Butler, Judith (2005) *Giving an account of oneself*. New York: Fordham University Press.

Butler, Judith (2006) *Precarious life: The powers of mourning and violence*. New York; London: Verso.

Butler, Judith (2013) *Dispossession: The performative in the political*. Cambridge; Malden, MA: Polity Press.

Butler, Judith (2015) *Notes toward a performative theory of assembly.* Cambridge, MA; London: Harvard University Press.

Callahan, William A. (2004) 'National insecurities: Humiliation, salvation, and Chinese nationalism', *Alternatives*, 29(2), pp. 199–218.

Callahan, William A. (2019) 'Surpass', in Christian Sorace, Ivan Franceschini and Nicholas Loubere (eds) *Afterlives of Chinese communism: political concepts from Mao to Xi.* Canberra: Australian National University Press, pp. 275–9.

CCTV News 央视新闻 (2020) '#Wuhan riji#:#Chiyuan Wuhan yisheng shahua riji#' #武汉日记#：#驰援武汉医生的沙画日记# ('#Wuhan Diary#: #The sand painting diary of a doctor in Wuhan #'). *Sina Weibo*, 25 February, https://weibo.com/2656274875/IvMAaC6h8?type=comment.

Chan, Jenny, and Mark Selden (2014) 'China's rural migrant workers, the state, and labor politics', *Critical Asian Studies*, 46(4), pp. 599–620.

Chan, Koon-Chung 陈冠中 (2012) *Zhongguo tianchao zhuyi yu xianggang* 中国天朝主义与香港 (*Chinese celestial empire and Hong Kong*). Niujin daxue chubanshe (zhongguo) 牛津大学出版社（中国）. Hong Kong: Oxford University Press.

Chan, Natalia Sui Hung (2000) 'Rewriting history: Hong Kong nostalgia cinema and its social practice', in Poshek Fu and David Desser (eds) *The cinema of Hong Kong: History, art, identity.* New York: Cambridge University Press, pp. 252–72.

Chang, Leslie T. (2009) *Factory girls: From village to city in changing China.* New York: Spiegel & Grau.

Chang, Ping 长平 (2020) 'Changping guancha: Li Wenliang weibo: "zhongguo kuqiang" xiade kangyi' 长平观察：李文亮微博——"中国哭墙" 下 的抗议 ('Changping Observation: Wen-Liang Li Weibo – Protests under "China's wailing wall"'), 20 March, *Deutsche Welle*, https://www.dw .com/zh/%E9%95%BF%E5%B9%B3%E8%A7%82%E5%AF%9F %E6%9D%8E%E6%96%87%E4%BA%AE%E5%BE%AE%E5 %8D%9A%E4%B8%AD%E5%9B%BD%E5%93%AD%E5%A2 %99%E4%B8%8B%E7%9A%84%E6%8A%97%E8%AE%AE/a-52 862102.

Che, Chang, and Amy Chang Chien (2022) 'Memes, puns and blank sheets of paper: China's creative acts of protest', *New York Times*, 28 November, https://www.nytimes.com/2022/11/28/world/asia/china -protests-blank-sheets.html.

Cheek, Timothy (2006) *Living with reform: China since 1989.* New York: Zed Books.

Chen, Cheng (2016) *The return of ideology: The search for regime identities in postcommunist Russia and China.* Ann Arbor: University of Michigan Press.

Chen, Chih-Jou Jay (2020) 'A protest society evaluated: popular protests in China, 2000–2019', *Mobilization: An International Quarterly*, 25, pp. 641–60.

Chen, Jianjia 陈健佳 (2016) 'Jinxiangjiang pingshen Bi Ming: Shinian yan-zhiyanwu, ju shidaixing' 金像奖评审毕明：《十年》言之有物，具时代性 ('Budming, jury member of the Hong Kong film awards: *Ten Years* is substantive and epochal'), *The HK01*, 4 April, www.hk01.com/港聞/14849.

Chen, Kuan-Hsing 陈光兴 (2001) 'Weishenme dahejie bu/keneng? Duosang yu Xiangjiao Tiantang zhimin/lengzhan xiaoying xia shengji wenti de qingxu jiegou' 为什么大和解不\可能？《多桑》与《香蕉天堂》殖民／冷战效应下省籍问题的情绪结构 ('Why is "Great Reconciliation" im/possible? De-Cold War/decolonization, or modernity and its tear'), Taiwan shehui yanjiu jikan 台湾社会研究季刊 *Taiwan: A Radical Quarterly in Social Studies*, 43, pp. 41–110.

Chen, Kuan-Hsing (2010) *Asia as method: Toward deimperialization.* Durham, NC: Duke University Press.

Chen, X. C., and N. W. Tu (2016) 'Shock by *Ten Years*! The film was banned from broadcasting in China'. [Radio podcast]. *PTSTalk*, 11 July, https://wwiiw.youtube.com/watch?v=yUa7PQn8ccE.

Chen, Xiangpeng 陈湘鹏 (2017) '"Zhanlang II" gudan de kuangre: Yipi meiyou lishi de lang' "战狼II"孤单的狂热：一匹没有历史的狼 ('"Wolf Warrior II" lonely fanaticism: A wolf without history'), *Zhihu*, 8 August, https://zhuanlan.zhihu.com/p/28395452.

Chen, Xiaochong 陈小冲 (2005) *Riben zhimin tongzhi Taiwan wushin-ian shi* 日本殖民统治台湾五十年史 (*Fifty-Year History of Japanese Colonization of Taiwan*), Shehui kexue wenxian chubanshe 社会科学文献出版社 Beijing: Social Sciences Academy Press.

Chen, Yingzhen 陈映真 (1998) 'Jingshen de huangfei: Zhang Liangze huangmin wenxuelun de piping' 精神的荒废——张亮则皇民文学论的批评 ('The despair of spirit: criticism of Zhang Liangze's theory of huangmin literature'), *Renjian sixiang yu chuangzuo congkan* 人间思想与创作丛刊 (*Renjian Series of Thoughts and Creative Work)*, 1998(4), pp. 97–105.

Cheng, Qingsong 程青松 and Huang Ou 黄鸥 (2002) *Wode sheyingji busa-huang: Xianfeng dianying rensheng dangan* 我的摄影机不撒谎：先锋电影人生档案——生于 1961–1970 (*My camera does not lie: Pioneer film-maker archives-born 1961–1970*), Zhonguo youyi chuban gongsi 中国友谊出版公司 Beijing: China Friendship Publishing Company.

Cheng, Tiejun, and Mark Selden (1994) 'The origins and social con-sequences of China's Hukou System', *China Quarterly*, 139, pp. 644–68.

Cheuk, Pak-tong 卓伯棠 (2003) *Xianggang xinlangchao dianying* 香港新浪

潮电影 (*Hong Kong New Wave Cinema*), Tiandi tushu 天地图书. Hong Kong: Cosmos Books.

China Media Group 中央广电总台中国之声 (2020) 'Zhansheng yiqing mogui, gaowei Li Wenliang yisheng' 战胜疫情魔鬼 告慰李文亮医生 ('Defeating the devil of the pandemic, comforting Dr Li Wenliang'), 7 February, *Sina*, https://tech.sina.com.cn/roll/2020-02-07/doc-iimxyqv z0932057.shtml.

Ching, Leo (2003) *Becoming 'Japanese': Colonial Taiwan and the politics of identity formation*. Berkeley: University of California Press.

Chiu, Melissa (2008) 'Introduction: The art of Mao's revolution', in Melissa Chiu and Zheng Shengtian (eds) *Art and China's revolution*. New Haven, CT: Yale University Press, pp. 1–17.

Cho, Alexander (2015) 'Queer reverb: Tumblr, affect, time', in Ken Hillis, Susanna Paasonen and Michael Petit (eds) *Networked affect*, Cambridge, MA: MIT Press, pp. 43–58.

Chow, Rey 周蕾 (1995a) *Xiezai jiaguo zhiwai* 写在家国之外 (*Alternative perspectives on Hong Kong culture*), Niujin daxue chubanshe (zhongguo) 牛津大学出版社（中国）. Hong Kong: Oxford University Press.

Chow, Rey (1995b) *Primitive passions: Visuality, sexuality, ethnography, and contemporary Chinese cinema*. New York: Columbia University Press.

Chow, Wing-Sun 周永新 (2015) *Xianggangren de shenfen rentong he jiazhiguan* 香港人的身份认同和价值观 (*Identity and values of Hong Kong people*), Zhonghua shuju 中华书局. Hong Kong: Chung Hwa Book Company.

Chu, Bailiang 储百亮 (2017) '"Zhanlang II" dianran zhongguo ren de yingpai aiguo zhuyi jiqing' 《战狼2》点燃中国人的鹰派爱国主义激情 ('"Wolf Warrior II" ignites the Chinese people's passion for war hawk patriotism'), *New York Times Chinese Edition*, 17 August, https:// d19mnbdbwa8nfg.cloudfront.net/china/20170817/china-wolf -warrior-2-film/.

Chun, Allen (2017) *Forget Chineseness*. New York: SUNY Press.

Clark, Paul (2008) *The Chinese cultural revolution*. Cambridge: Cambridge University Press.

Clarke, Simon, Paul Hoggett and Simon Thompson (2006a) 'Applying theory in practice: Politics and emotions in everyday life', in Simon Clarke, Paul Hoggett and Simon Thompson (eds) *Emotion, politics and society*. London: Palgrave Macmillan.

Clarke, Simon, Paul Hoggett and Simon Thompson (2006b) 'The study of emotion: An introduction', in Clarke, Simon, Paul Hoggett and Simon Thompson (eds) *Emotion, politics and society*. London: Palgrave Macmillan.

Cooper, Luke, and Wai-man Lam (2018) 'Introduction', in Wai-man Lam and Luke Cooper (eds) *Citizenship, identity and social movements in the new Hong Kong: Localism after the Umbrella Movement*. London and New York: Routledge, pp. 1–12.

Croizier, Ralph (2008) 'Politics in demand', in Melissa Chiu and Zheng Shengtian (eds) *Art and China's revolution*. New Haven, CT: Yale University Press, pp. 57–73.

Dahlberg, Lincoln (2001) 'The Internet and democratic discourse: Exploring the prospects of online deliberative forums extending the public sphere', *Information, Communication, and Society*, 4(4), pp. 615–33.

Dahlgren, Peter (2006) 'Doing citizenship: The cultural origins of civic agency in the public sphere', *European Journal of Cultural Studies*, 9(3), pp. 267–86.

Dai, Jinhua 戴锦华 (2000) *Wuzhong fengjing: Zhongguo dianying wenhua 1978–1998* 雾中风景：中国电影文化 1978–1998 (*Scenery in fog: Chinese film culture 1978–1998*), Beijing daxue chubanshe 北京大学出版社 Beijing: Peking University Press.

Dale, Gareth (2022) 'China's "white paper" protest movement echoes freedom struggles across Asia and the world', *The Conversation*, 30 November, https://theconversation.com/chinas-white-paper-protest-movement-echoes-freedom-struggles-across-asia-and-the-world-195487.

De Groot, Kristen (2022) 'Scholars look at ramifications from "zero COVID" protests in China', *Penn Today*, 8 December, https://penntoday.upenn.edu/news/scholars-look-ramifications-zero-covid-protests-china.

Demertzis, Nicolas (2013) *Emotions in politics: The affect dimension in political tension*. London: Palgrave Macmillan.

Deng, Iris (2022) 'Foxconn's largest iPhone factory confirms Covid-19 impact after central China campus restricted worker movement', *South China Morning Post*, 26 October, https://www.scmp.com/tech/tech-trends/article/3197287/foxconns-largest-iphone-factory-confirms-covid-19-impact-after-central-china-campus-restricted.

Dimitrov, Martin K. (2013) 'Understanding communist collapse and resilience', in Martin K. Dimitrov (ed.) *Why communism did not collapse: Understanding authoritarian regime resilience in Asia and Europe*. Cambridge: Cambridge University Press, pp. 3–39.

Dutton, Michael (2008) 'Passionately governmental: Maoism and the structured intensities of revolutionary governmentality', *Postcolonial Studies*, 11(1), pp. 99–112.

Economic Times Review 经济时评 *(2017)* 'Qiangda zhongguo chengqi "zhanlang" qiji' 强大中国撑起"战狼"奇迹 ('Powerful China holds up "Wolf Warrior" miracle'), *Economic Daily*, 10 August, http://finance.sina.com.cn/roll/2017-08-10/doc-ifyixcaw3761758.shtml.

Economist Intelligence (2022) 'Protests to push Chinese cities closer to living with virus', 28 November, https://country.eiu.com/article.aspx?ar ticleid=392610422&Country=China&topic=Politics&subtopic=Foreca st&subsubtopic=Political+stability.

Erickson, Britta (2010) 'The *Rent collection courtyard*, past and present', in Richard King (ed.) *Art in turmoil*. Vancouver: University of British Columbia Press, pp. 121–35.

Erni, John Nguyet (2001) 'Like a postcolonial culture: Hong Kong re-imagined', *Cultural Studies*, 15(3/4), pp. 389–418.

Evrigenis, Ioannis D. (2008) *Fear of enemies and collective action*. Cambridge: Cambridge University Press.

Fan, Cindy C. (2002) 'The elite, the natives, and the outsiders: Migration and labor market segmentation in urban China', *Annals of the Association of American Geographers*. 92(1), pp. 103–24.

Fang, Fang 方方 (2020) 'Fang Fang Wuhan riji quanji' 方方武汉日记全集 ('Complete Works of Fang Fang's Wuhan Diaries'), *Innovative Literature Network*, 28 February, http://www.zgcxwxw.com/html/sanwenzawen /sanwen/2020/0228/2968.html.

Fewsmith, Joseph (2008) *China since Tiananmen: From Deng Xiaoping to Hu Jintao*. Cambridge: Cambridge University Press.

Flam, Helena (2005) 'Emotion's map', in Helena Fram and Debra King (eds) *Emotions and social movement*. London: Routledge, pp. 19–40.

Foreign Languages Press (1968) *Rent collection courtyard*, Peking: Foreign Languages Press.

Fraser, Nancy (1997) 'Rethinking the public sphere: A contribution to the critique of actually existing democracy', in Nancy Fraser (ed.) *Justice interruptus*. London: Routledge, pp. 56–80.

Friedman, Eli (2014) 'Alienated politics: Labour insurgency and the paternalistic state in China', *Development and Change*, 45(5), pp. 1001–18.

Froissart, Chloé (2009) 'The rise of migrant workers' collective actions', in Khun Eng Kuah-Pearce and Gilles Guiheux (eds) *Social movements in China and Hong Kong*. Amsterdam: Amsterdam University Press, pp. 155–78.

Fu, Diana, and Greg Distelhorst (2018) 'Grassroots participation and repression under Hu Jintao and Xi Jinping', *China Journal*, 79(1), pp. 100–22.

Fujitani, Takashi, Geoffrey M. White and Lisa Yoneyama (2001) 'Introduction', in Takashi Fujitani, Geoffrey M. White and Lisa Yoneyama (eds) *Perilous memories: The Asia-Pacific War(s)*. Durham, NC: Duke University Press, pp. 1–30.

Galikowski, Maria (1998) *Art and politics in China 1949–1984*. Hong Kong: Chinese University Press.

Gan, Chen, Francis L. F. Lee and Ying Li (2017) 'Social media use, political affect, and participation among university students in urban China', *Telematics and Informatics*, 34(7), pp. 936–47.

Gan, Yang (2006) *Cultural awareness in the 1980s*. Shanghai: Shanghai People Publishing.

Gao, Yang 高扬 (2015) 'Jujiao wailai wugong renyuan yanglao baoxian: Tuibao beihou youwunai' 聚焦外来务工人员养老保险: 退保背后有无奈 ('Focus on the pension insurance of migrant workers: The helpless after insurance cancellation'). *Chinanews.com*, 4 March, http://www. chinan ews.com/gn/2015/03-04/7098136.shtml.

Garde-Hansen, Joanne, and Kristyn Gorton (2013) *Emotion online: Theorizing affect on the Internet*. New York: Springer.

Gharmaz, Kathy, and Melinda J. Milligan (2006) 'Grief', in Jan E. Stets and Jonathan H. Turner (eds) *Handbook of the sociology of emotions*. New York: Springer, pp. 516–43.

Glynos, Jason, and Yannis Stavrakakis (2010) 'Politics and the unconscious: An interview with Ernesto Laclau', *Subjectivity*, 3, pp. 231–44.

Goldman, Merle (2005) *From comrade to citizen*. Cambridge, MA: Harvard University Press.

Goodman, David S. (2014) *Class in contemporary China*. Cambridge: Polity.

Goodwin, Jeff, James M. Jasper and Francesca Polletta (2001) 'Introduction: Why emotions matter', in Jeff Goodwin, James M. Jasper and Francesca Polletta (eds) *Passionate politics: Emotions and social movements*. Chicago: University of Chicago Press, pp. 1–26.

Gould, Deborah B. (2016) 'Emotion', in Kathrin Fahlenbrach, Martin Klimke and Joachim Scharloth (eds) *Protest cultures*. New York: Berghahn, Kindle location 3453–61.

Greitens, Sheena Chestnut (2022) 'After a wave of protests, China's silent crackdown', *Journal of Democracy*, December, https://www.journalof democracy.org/after-a-wave-of-protests-chinas-silent-crackdown/.

Gries, Peter Hays (2004) *China's new nationalism*. Berkeley: University of California Press.

Grossberg, Lawrence (1988) 'Postmodernity and affect: All dressed up with no place to go', *Communication*, 10(3/4), pp. 271–93.

Grossberg, Lawrence (1992) *We gotta get out of this place: Popular conservatism and postmodern culture*. London and New York: Routledge.

Grossberg, Lawrence (1997a) *Dancing in spite of myself: Essays on popular culture*. Durham, NC: Duke University Press.

Grossberg, Lawrence (1997b) *Bringing it all back home: Essays on cultural studies*. Durham, NC: Duke University Press.

Grossberg, Lawrence (2007) 'Affect and postmodernity in the struggle over "American modernity"', in Pelagia Goulimari (ed.) *Postmodernism: What moment?* New York: Manchester University Press, pp. 176–201.

Guo, Ting (2020) 'Politics of love: Love as a religious and political discourse in modern China through the lens of political leaders', *Critical Research on Religion*, 8(1), pp. 39–52.

Guo, Yingjie (2004) *Cultural nationalism in contemporary China*. London and New York: Routledge.

Hackl, A. (2014) 'Democratise democracy! Interview with Chantal Mouffe', *transformations*, 16 April, http://transformations-blog.com/we-propose -democracy-interview-with-chantal-mouffe/.

Hall, Cheryl (2002) '"Passions and constraint": The marginalization of passion in liberal political theory', *Philosophy and Social Criticism*, 28(6), pp. 727–48.

Hall, Stuart (1996) 'The question of cultural identity', in Stuart Hall (ed.) *Modernity: An introduction to modern societies*. Oxford: Blackwell, pp. 595–634.

Hallward, Peter (2003) *Badiou*. Minneapolis: University of Minnesota Press.

Hansen, Mette Halskov, and Rune Svarverud (2010) *iChina: The rise of the individual in modern Chinese society*. Copenhagen: NIAS Press.

Harding, Jennifer, and E. Deidre Pribram (2002) 'The power of feeling: Locating emotions in culture', *European Journal of Cultural Studies*, 5(4), pp. 407–26.

Harding, Jennifer, and E. Deidre Pribram (2004) 'Losing our cool? Following Williams and Grossberg on emotions', *Cultural Studies*, 18(6), pp. 863–83.

Harding, Jennifer, and E. Deidre Pribram (2009) *Emotions: A cultural studies reader*. London: Routledge.

Hardt, Michael (2007) 'Foreword: What affects are good for', in Patricia Ticineto Clough and Jean Halley (eds) *The affective turn*. Durham, NC: Duke University Press, pp. ix–xiii.

Harper, Tom (2017) 'Seeing China's biggest blockbuster "Wolf Warriors 2" through the lens of its foreign policy', *Quartz*, 25 August, https://qz.com /1061787/wolf-warriors-2-reflects-chinas-changing-foreign-policy-and -growingmilitary/.

Hemmings, Clare (2005) 'Invoking affect: Cultural theory and the ontological turn', *Cultural Studies*, 19(5), pp. 548–67.

Hessler, Peter (2022) 'What Chinese people think of their government's "zero COVID" policy', *New Yorker*, 6 December, https://www.new yorker.com/news/news-desk/what-chinese-people-think-of-their-govern ments-zero-covid-policy.

Hjort, Mette, and Sue Laver (1997) 'Introduction', in Mette Hjort and Sue Laver (eds) *Emotion and the arts*. New York: Oxford University Press, pp. 3–19.

Ho, Denise Y. (2018) *Curating revolution*. Cambridge: Cambridge University Press.

Ho, Denise Y., and Li Jie (2016) 'From landlord manor to red memorabilia: Reincarnations of a Chinese museum town', *Modern China*, 42(1), pp. 3–37.

Ho, Haoyi 何豪毅 (2016) '"Shinian" Chow Kwun-Wai xiaocheng: Wo "zifen" le dianying shiye' 《十年》周冠威笑称：我"自焚"了电影事业 ('Chow Kwun-Wai from Ten Years laughed: I "SelfImmolate" the film business'), *PeopleNews*, 8 August, http://www.peop lenews.tw/news/d2823dc7-36b13411b-9347-\80b95612288b.

Hoggett, Paul (2009) *Politics, identity, and emotion*. Boulder: Paradigm.

Hsu, Kevin Fan (2017) 'China finally has its own Rambo', *Foreign Policy*, 1 September, https://foreignpolicy.com/2017/09/01/china-finally-has-its -own-rambo/.

Huang, Tsung-yi 黄宗仪 (2020) *Zhonggang xinanjue* 中港新感觉 (*The new sentiments in China and Hong Kong*), Lianjing chuban 联经出版. Taipei: Linking Publishing.

Hughes, Christopher R. (2006) *Chinese nationalism in the global era*. London and New York: Routledge.

Hung, Chang-tai (2011) *Mao's new world*. Ithaca, NY: Cornell University Press.

Hung, Ho-Fung 孔诰峰 (1997) 'Chutan beijin zhimin zhuyi: Cong Liangfengyi xianxiang kan xianggang jiafenglun' 初探北进殖民主义: 从梁凤仪现象看香港夹缝论 ('On northbound colonialism: Hong Kong's theory of edge from the phenomenon of Liang Fengyi'), in C. K. Chan 陈清桥 (ed.) *Wenhua xiangxiang yu yishi xingtai: dangdai xianggang wenhua zhengzhi lunping* 文化想象与意识形态: 当代香港文化政治论评 (*Cultural imagination and ideology: A review of contemporary Hong Kong cultural politics*), Niujin daxue chubanshe (zhongguo) 牛津大学出版社（中国）. Hong Kong: Oxford University Press, pp. 53–88.

Hutchinson, Emma (2016) *Affective communities in world politics*. Cambridge: Cambridge University Press.

Ignacio, Emily Noelle (2000) 'Ain't I a Filipino (woman)? An analysis of authorship/authority through the construction of "Filipina" on the net', *Sociological Quarterly*, 41(4), pp. 551–72.

Ip, Iam Chong 叶荫聪 (1997) 'Bianyuan yu hunza de youling: Tan wenhua pinglun zhongde "xianggang shenfen"' 边缘与混杂的幽灵：谈文化评论中的 "香港身份" ('Marginal and hybrid ghosts: On "Hong Kong identity" in cultural criticism'), in C. K. Chan 陈清桥 (ed.) *Wenhua xiangxiang yu yishi xingtai: dangdai xianggang wenhua zhengzhi lunping* 文化想象与意识形态: 当代香港文化政治论评 (*Cultural imagination and ideology: A review of contemporary Hong Kong cultural politics*), Niujin daxue chubanshe (zhongguo) 牛津大学出版社（中国）. Hong Kong: Oxford University Press, pp. 31–52.

Ip, Iam Chong (2017) 'Becoming a revanchist city: Reflections on Hong

Kong nativist affects', in Chih-Ming Wang and Daniel P. S. Goh (eds) *Precarious belongings: Affect and nationalism in Asia*. London: Rowman and Littlefield, pp. 169–94.

Jacka, Tamara, Andrew B. Kipnis and Sally Sargeson (2013) *Contemporary China society and social change*. Cambridge: Cambridge University Press.

Janssen, Davy, and Raphael Kies (2005) 'Online forums and deliberative democracy', *Acta Politica*, 40, pp. 317–35.

Jasper, James M. (2006) 'Emotions and microfoundations of politics: Rethinking ends and means', in Simon Clarke, Paul Hoggett and Simon Thompson (eds) *Emotion, politics and society*. London: Palgrave Macmillan, pp. 14–30.

Jasper, James M. (2014) *Protest: A cultural introduction to social movements*. Cambridge: Polity Press.

Javed, Jeffrey (2019) 'Speaking bitterness', in Christian Sorace, Ivan Franceschini and Nicholas Loubere (eds) *Afterlives of Chinese communism: Political concepts from Mao to Xi*. Canberra: Australian National University Press, pp. 257–62.

Ji, Pan (2016) 'Emotional criticism as public engagement: How Weibo users discuss "Peking University statues wear face-masks"', *Telematics and Informatics*, 33(2), pp. 514–24.

Jia, Zhangke 贾樟柯 (2002) 'Wobu shihua ziji de jingli' 我不诗化自己的经历 ('I don't poeticise my experiences'), in Cheng Qingsong 程青松 and Huang Ou 黄鸥 (eds) *Wode sheyingji busahuang: Xianfeng dianying rensheng dangan* 我的摄影机不撒谎：先锋电影人生档案——生于 1961–1970 (*My camera does not lie: Pioneer filmmaker archives-born 1961–1970*), Zhonguo youyi chuban gongsi 中国友谊出版公司. Beijing: China Friendship Publishing Company, pp. 365–71.

Joseph, May (1999) *Nomadic identities*. Minneapolis: University of Minnesota Press.

Jusdanis, Gregory (2001) *The necessary nation*. Princeton: Princeton University Press.

Kar, Law (2001) 'An overview of Hong Kong's new wave cinema', in Ching-Mei Esther Yau (ed.) *At full speed: Hong Kong cinema in a borderless world*. Minneapolis: University of Minnesota Press, pp. 31–52.

Karatzogianni, Athina, and Adi Kuntsman (2012) *Digital cultures and the politics of emotion: Feelings, affect and technological change*. London: Palgrave Macmillan.

Karl, Rebecca E. (2022) 'The social explosion of China's pent-up pain', *Nation*, 1 December, https://www.thenation.com/article/world/china-zero-covid-a4-protests/.

Kedourie, Elie (1993) *Nationalism*. Oxford: Blackwell.

Kemper, Theodore D. (2002) 'Predicting emotions in groups', in Jack Barbalet (ed.) *Emotions and sociology*. Oxford: Blackwell, pp. 53–68.

Kim, Seong-nae (2000) 'Mourning Korean modernity in the memory of the Cheju April third incident', *Inter-Asia Cultural Studies*, 1(3), pp. 461–7.

Kinnvall, Catarina (2013) 'Trauma and the politics of fear: Europe at the crossroads', in Nicolas Demertzis (ed.) *Emotions in politics: The affect dimension in political tension.* London: Palgrave Macmillan, pp. 143–66.

Kirby, Jen (2022) 'China's Covid narrative is backfiring', *Vox*, 1 December, https://www.vox.com/world/2022/12/1/23486439/china-covid-zero-protests.

Kleres, Jochen (2005) 'The entanglements of shame: An emotion perspective on social movements demobilization', in Helena Flam and Debra King (eds) *Emotions and social movements.* London and NY: Routledge, pp. 170–88.

Knudsen, Britta T., and Carsten Stage (2015) *Global media, biopolitics, and affect: Politicizing bodily vulnerability.* London: Routledge.

Koetse, Manya (2022) 'Long road home for Zhengzhou's Foxconn workers after Covid mismanagement', *What's on Weibo*, 30 October, https://www.whatsonweibo.com/long-road-home-for-zhengzhous-foxconn-workers-after-covid-mismanagement/.

Kong, Shuyu (2014) *Popular media, social emotion and public discourse in contemporary China.* London: Routledge.

Laclau, Ernesto (2005) *On populist reason.* London: Verso.

Lam, Willy Wo-Lap (2006) *Chinese politics in the Hu Jintao era.* New York: M. E. Sharpe.

Lang, Tian 朗天 (2003) *Hou97 yu xianggang dianying* 后 97 与香港电影 (*Post-1997 and Hong Kong cinema*), Xianggang dianying pinglun xuehui 香港电影评论学会. Hong Kong: Hong Kong Film Critics Society.

Law, Wing Sang 罗永生 (2007) 'Xianggang de zhimin zhuyi (qu)zhengzhi yu wenhua lengzhan' 香港的殖民主义 (去) 政治与文化冷战 ('Colonialist politics of (de)politicization and the cultural cold war in Hong Kong'), *Taiwan shehui yanjiu jikan* 台湾社会研究季刊 (*Taiwan: A Radical Quarterly in Social Studies*), 67, pp. 259–77.

Law, Wing Sang 罗永生 (2009) '(Wan)zhimin chengshi xiangxiang' (晚) 殖民城市政治想像 ['(Late) colonial political imagination of cities'], in C. H. Ng 吴俊雄, Eric K. W. Ma 马杰伟 and Tai-lok Lui 吕大乐 (eds) *Xianggang wenhua zhengzhi* 香港文化政治 (*Hong Kong cultural politics*), Xianggang daxue chubanshe 香港大学出版社. Hong Kong: Hong Kong University Press, pp. 33–51.

Law, Wing Sang (2018) 'Decolonisation deferred: Hong Kong identity in historical perspective', in Wai-man Lam and Luke Cooper (eds) *Citizenship, identity and social movements in the new Hong Kong: Localism after the Umbrella Movement.* London and New York: Routledge, pp. 13–33.

Lee, Ching-Kwan (2007a) *Against the law: Labor protests in China's rustbelt and sunbelt.* Berkeley: University of California Press.

Lee, Ching-Kwan (2007b) *Working in China: Ethnographies of labor and workplace transformation*. New York: Routledge.

Lee, Ching-Kwan (2010) 'Workers and quest for citizenship', in You-tien Hsing and Ching Kwan Lee Hsing (eds) *Reclaiming Chinese society: The new social activism*. New York: Routledge, pp. 42–63.

Lee, Ching-Kwan, and Eli Friedman (2009) 'China since Tiananmen: the labor movement', *Journal of Democracy*, 20(3), pp. 21–4.

Lee, Haiyan (2007) *Revolution of the heart*. Palo Alto, CA: Stanford University Press.

Lee, Haiyan (2014) *The stranger and the Chinese moral imagination*. Redwood City, CA: Stanford University Press.

Lee, Haiyan (2019) 'Class feeling', in Christian Sorace, Ivan Franceschini and Nicholas Loubere (eds) *Afterlives of Chinese communism: Political concepts from Mao to Xi*. Canberra: Australian National University Press, pp. 23–8.

Li, Na (2022) 'Foxconn Zhengzhou employee: Chaos gradually easing', *Yicai Global*, 1 November, https://www.yicaiglobal.com/news/exclusive -foxconn-zhengzhou-employee-chaos-gradually-easing.

Li, Qiang 李强 (2012) *Nongmingong yu zhongguo shehui fenceng* 农民工与中国社会分层 (*Peasant workers and Chinese social stratification*), Shehui kexue wenxian chubanshe 社会科学文献出版社. Beijing: Social Sciences Academic Press.

Li, Ying Xin 李映昕 (2016) 'Dianying shinian: xugou de wuge gushi, fei xugou de jiaolv' 电影《十年》：虚构的五个故事，非虚构的焦虑' ('The film *Ten Years*: Five fictional stories and non-fictional anxiety'), Tianxiazazhi 天下杂志 (*CommonWealth Magazine Group*), 2 August, http://www.cw.com.tw/article/article.action?id=5077681.

Liang, Wen-Dao 梁文道 (2020) Kan lixiang 看理想 (*Ideal*). https://mp.wei xin.qq.com/s/xYD0tK344DJa4FYjX6mPEQ.

Liao, Mei Xuan 廖梅璇 (2016) 'Shinian: Xianggang mori xiangxiang houde lishi zhenshi' 《十年》——香港末日想像后的历史真实 ('*Ten Years*: Imagining the doomsday of Hong Kong'), *MPlus*, 6 July, https://www .mplus.com.tw/article/1225.

Lin, Peter 林建岳 (2016) 'Lin Jianyue zhi shinian dejiang shi xianggang dianyingjie de buxing, cheng zhengzhi bangjia le zhuanye' 林建岳指《十年》得奖是香港电影界的不行，称政治绑架了专业 ('Peter Lin remarked that Ten Years' winning the award is the misfortune of the Hong Kong film industry, and that politics kidnaps professionalism'), *Mingpao News*, 4 April, https://news.mingpao.com/ins/instantnews/web _tc/article/20160404/s00001/1459705541641.

Lin, Xiaoping (2002) 'New Chinese cinema of the "sixth generation": A distant cry of forsaken children', *Third Text*, 16(3), pp. 261–84.

Lin, Yan 林燕 (2017) 'Zhanlang II weihe guonei zhengyi da haiwai piaofang candan' 《战狼2》为何国内争议大 海外票房惨淡 ('Why "Wolf Warrior II" has been controversial in the domestic and flopped overseas'), 13 August, http://www.epochtimes.com/gb/17/8/13/n9524822.htm.

Liu, Serena (2007) 'Social citizenship in China: Continuity and change', *Citizenship Studies*. 11(5), pp. 465–79.

Liu, Shih-Diing 刘世鼎 (2005) 'Jiang yazhou "qinmei" de zhutixing wentihua: Haixia liangan zuowei linglei de canzhao kuangjia' 将亚洲 "亲美" 的主体性问题化：海峡两岸作为另类的参照框架 ('Problematising the "pro-American" subjectivity in Asia: Cross Strait as an alternative frame of reference'), *Cultural Studies Association annual conference*. Taiwan Chiao Tung University, 8–9 January. Hsinchu, Taiwan.

Liu, Shih-Diing (2008) 'Undomesticated hostilities: The affective space of internet chatrooms across the Taiwan Strait', *Positions: Asia Critique*, 16(2), pp. 435–55.

Liu, Shih-Diing (2019) *The politics of people: Protest culture in China*. New York: State University of New York Press.

Liu, Yide (2017) '"Women and children first": The Great China discourse of "*Wolf Warrior II*," contradiction and the crisis of masculinity', *Router: A Journal of Cultural Studies*, 25, pp. 256–9.

Liu, Yu (2010) 'Maoist discourse and the mobilization of emotions in revolutionary China', *Modern China*, 36(3), pp. 329–62.

Lo, Kwai-Cheung (2005) *China face/off: The transnational popular culture of Hong Kong*. Urbana: University of Illinois Press.

Lo, Kwai-Cheung, and Laikwan Pang (2007) 'Hong Kong: Ten years after colonialism', *Postcolonial Studies*, 10(4), pp. 349–56.

Lu, Sheldon H. (1997) *Transnational Chinese cinemas: Identity, nationhood, gender*. Honolulu: University of Hawaii Press.

Lu, Zhi 鲁直 (2007) 'Shuishi yingxiong? Tan Zhang Yimou daoyan de dianying "yingxiong"' 谁是英雄？---谈张艺谋导演的电影：「英雄」 ('Who is the hero? On film "Hero" directed by Yimou Zhang'), 15 May, http://blog.udn.com/grotius6033/961003.

Lv, Bruce 吕炳权 (2016) 'Lv Bingquan: Kongju shinian? Shui zhizao beihou de kongju' 吕炳权：恐惧《十年》？谁制造背后的恐惧？ ('Bruce Lv: Fear *Ten Years*? Who Produces the Fear Behind?'), *Mingbao* 明报 *Mingpao News*, 6 April, https://news.mingpao.com/pns/dailynews/web_tc/article/20160406/s00012/1459878944760.

Lyon, Margot L. (1998) 'Missing emotion: The limitations of cultural constructionism in the study of emotion', *Cultural Anthropology*, 10(2), pp. 244–63.

Ma, Ngok (2018) 'Changing identity politics: The democracy movement in Hong Kong', in Wai-man Lam and Luke Cooper (eds) *Citizenship, identity and social movements in the new Hong Kong: Localism after the Umbrella Movement*. London and New York: Routledge, pp. 34–50.

Ma, Zijiao 马子骄 (2014) 'Cong shenmei lingyu shijiao kan "zhongguo haoshengyin" de minzhu jiazhi' 从审美公共领域视角看 "中国好声音" 的民主价值 ('On the Democratic Value of Sing! China from the Perspective of Aesthetic Public Sphere'). *Renmin wang* 人民网 *People's Network*, 31 March, http://media.people.com.cn/BIG5/n/2014/0331/c3 83103-24781419-2.html.

Mao, Zedong 毛泽东 (1991) 'Zai Yanan wenyi zuotan huishang de jianghua' 在延安文艺座谈会上的讲话 ('Speech at Yan'an Forum on literature and art'), in Renmin chubanshe 人民出版社 People's Publishing House (ed.) *Mao Zedong xuanji disanjuan* 毛泽东选集第三卷 *Selected works of Mao Zedong volume III*, Renmin chubanshe 人民出版社. Beijing: People's Publishing House, pp. 847–79.

Massumi, Brian (1996) 'The Autonomy of Affect', in Paul Patton (ed.) *Deleuze: A critical reader*. Oxford: Blackwell, pp. 217–39.

Massumi, Brian (2002) *Parables for the virtual: Movement, affect, sensation*. Durham, NC: Duke University Press.

Mathews, Gordon, Eric Ma and Tai-lok Lui (2008) *Hong Kong, China: Learning to belong to a nation*, London and New York: Routledge.

Meerjump 跳海大院 (2020) 'Meitian douyou chengqian shangwan renzai Li Wenliang weibo xiaxie riji' 每天都有成千上万人在李文亮微博下写日记 ('Every day thousands of people write diaries on Wen-Liang Li's micro blog'). *Financial Headlines*, 3 March, https://t.cj.sina.cn/artic les/view/5970362599/163dc80e701900qop0.

Mihai, Mihaela (2014) 'Theorizing agonistic emotions', *Parallax*, 20(2), pp. 31–48.

Militz, Elisabeth, and Carolin Schurr (2016) 'Affective nationalism: Banalities of belonging in Azerbaijan', *Political Geography*, 54, pp. 54–63.

Mitra, Ananda (2001) 'Marginal voices in cyberspace', *New Media and Society*, 3(1), pp. 29–48.

Mittler, Barbara (2012) *A continuous revolution: Making sense of Cultural Revolution culture*. Cambridge, MA: Harvard University Asia Center.

Mizoguchi, Yuzo (2001) 'Chuangzao rizhong zhishi de gongtong kongjian' 创造日中知识的共同空间 ('Creating the common space for Japan–China knowledge'), *Dushu* 读书 *(Reading)*, 266(3), pp. 1–11.

Mizoguchi, Yuzo (2003) 'Lishi renshi wenti shi shenme wenti?' 历史认识问题是什么问题？ ('What is at stake for the question of historical understanding?'), in Zhongguo shehui kexue yanjiuhui 中国社会科学研究会 Chinese Social Sciences Research Association (ed.) *Quanqiuhua xiade zhongguo yu riben: Haiwai xuezhe de duoyuan sikao* 全球化下的中国与日本：海内外学者的多元思考 *(China and Japan under globalization: Multiple thoughts of domestic and oversea scholars)*, Shehui kexue wenxian chubanshe 社会科学文献出版社. Beijing: Social Sciences Academic Press, pp. 1–16.

Moisi, Dominique (2009) *The geopolitics of emotion: How cultures of fear, humiliation, and hope are reshaping the world*. London: Bodley Head.

Morris-Suzuki, Tessa, and Peter Rimmer (2002) 'Virtual memories: Japanese history debates in manga and cyberspace', *Asian Studies Review*, 26(2), pp. 147–63.

Mouffe, Chantal (1993) *The return of the political*. London: Verso Books.

Mouffe, Chantal (2000) *The democratic paradox*. London: Verso.

Mouffe, Chantal (2002) *Politics and passions: The stakes of democracy*. London: Center for the Study of Democracy, University of Westminster.

Mouffe, Chantal (2005) *On the political*. London and New York: Routledge.

Mouffe, Chantal (2013) *Agonistics: Thinking the world politically*. London: Verso.

Mouffe, Chantal (2018) 'The affects of democracy', *Eurozine*, 23 November, https://www.eurozine.com/the-affects-of-democracy/.

Munt, Sally, and Cherry Smyth (1998) *Butch/femme: Inside lesbian gender*. London: Cassell.

NBS (National Bureau of Statistics of China) 国家统计局 (2015) *2014nian quanguo nongmingong jiance diaocha baogao* 2014 年全国农民工监测调查报告 (*The monitoring and investigation report of nationwide peasant workers in 2014*), National Bureau of Statistics, 29 April, http://www.stats.gov.cn/tjsj/zxfb/201504/t20150429_797821.html.

Ng, Janet (2009) *Paradigm city: Space, culture, and capitalism in Hong Kong*. New York: SUNY Press.

Nicholson, Linda (1999) 'Emotion in postmodern public sphere', in Linda Nicholson (ed.) *The play of reason: From the modern to the postmodern*. Ithaca, NY: Cornell University Press, pp. 145–62.

Nora, Pierre (1989) 'Between memory and history: Les lieux de mémoire', *Representations*, 26, pp. 7–25.

Nussbaum, Martha C. (2001) *Upheavals of thought: The intelligence of emotions*. Cambridge: Cambridge University Press.

Olick, Jeffrey K. (2003) 'Introduction', in Jeffrey K. Olick (ed.) *States of memory: Continuities, conflicts and transformations in national retrospection*. Durham, NC: Duke University Press, pp. 1–16.

Ost, David (2004) 'Politics as the mobilization of anger', *European Journal of Social Theory*, 7(2), pp. 229–44.

Ost, David (2005) *The defeat of solidarity: Anger and politics in postcommunist Europe*. Ithaca, NY: Cornell University Press.

Paasonen, Susanna, Ken Hillis and Michael Petit (2015) 'Introduction', in Ken Hillis, Susanna Paasonen and Michael Petit (eds) *Networked affect*. Cambridge, MA: MIT Press, pp. 1–26.

Pai, Hsiao-Hung (2012) *Scattered sands: The story of China's rural migrants*. New York: Verso.

Palacios, Margarita (2020) 'Becoming the people: A critique of populist aesthetics of homogeneity', *Theory and Event*, 23(3), pp. 787–809.

Pang, Laikwan 彭丽君 (2017) *Fuzhi de yishu: Wenge qijian de wenhua shengchan yu Shijian'* 复制的艺术：文革期间的文化生产与实践 (*The art of reproduction: Cultural production and practice during the Cultural Revolution*), Xianggang zhongwen daxue chubanshe 香港中文大学出版社. Hong Kong: Chinese University of Hong Kong.

Papacharissi, Zizi (2004) 'Democracy online: Civility, politeness, and the democratic potential of online political discussion groups', *New Media and Society*, 6(2), pp. 259–83.

Papacharissi, Zizi (2015) *Affective publics: Sentiment, technology, and politics*. Oxford: Oxford University Press.

Pei, Minxin (2010) 'Rights and resistance: The changing contexts of the dissident movement', in Elizabeth J. Perry and Mark Selden (eds) *Chinese society: Change, conflict and resistance*, third edition. London: Routledge, pp. 31–56.

Peng, Altman Yuzhu (2021) 'Neoliberal feminism, gender relations, and a feminized male ideal in China: a critical discourse analysis of Mimeng's WeChat posts', *Feminist Media Studies*, 21(1), pp. 115–31.

People's Daily 人民网 (2016) 'Cong "sange zixin" dao "sige zixin": Lun Xi Jinping zongshuji duiyu zhongguo tese shehui zhuyi de wenhua jiangou' 从"三个自信"到"四个自信"⸺论习近平总书记对于中国特色社会主义的文化建构 ('From "3 confidences" to "4 confidences": On the cultural construction of socialism with Chinese characteristics by General Secretary Jinping Xi'), *People.cn*, http://theory.people.com.cn/n1/2016/0707/c49150 28532466.html.

People's Daily 人民日报 (2020) 'Renmin ribao pinglunyuan: Wuhan sheng ze Hubei sheng, Hubei sheng ze quanguo sheng' 人民日报评论员：武汉胜则湖北胜 湖北胜则全国胜 ('*People's Daily* commentator: If Wuhan wins, Hubei wins, Hubei wins, and the whole country wins'), *People's Daily*, 5 March, http://opinion.people.com.cn/BIG5/n1/2020/0212/c1003-31582333.html.

Perry, Elizabeth J. (2002) 'Moving the masses: emotion work in the Chinese revolution', *Mobilization: An International Quarterly*, 7(2), pp. 111–28.

Perry, Elizabeth J. (2013) *Cultural governance in contemporary China: 'Re-orienting' party propaganda*, Harvard-Yenching Institute Working Papers, http://nrs.harvard.edu/urn-3:HUL.InstRepos:11386987.

Perry, Elizabeth J., and Mark Selden (2010) 'Introduction', in Elizabeth J. Perry and Mark Selden (eds) *Chinese society: Change, conflict and resistance*, third edition. London: Routledge, pp. 1–30.

Pritzker, Sonya E. (2023) '"What's going on with my China?": Political subjectivity, scalar inquiry, and the magical power of Li Wenliang',

American Anthropologist, 125(1), pp. 125–38, https://doi.org/10.1111/aman.13809.

Prokhovnik, Raia (2014) 'Introduction: The body as a site for politics: Citizenship and practices of contemporary slavery', *Citizenship Studies*, 18(5), pp. 465–84.

Pun, Ngai (2005) *Made in China: Women factory workers in a global workplace*. Durham, NC: Duke University Press.

Pun, Ngai (2016) *Migrant Labor in China: Post-Socialist Transformation*. Cambridge: Polity Press.

Pun, Ngai, and Lu Huilin (2010) 'Unfinished proletarianization: Self, anger, and class action among the second generation of peasant-workers in present-day China', *Modern China*, 36(5), pp. 493–519.

Pun, Ngai, Chris King-Chi Chan and Jenny Chan (2010) 'The role of the state, labour policy and migrant workers' struggles in globalized China', *Global Labour Journal*, 1(1), pp. 132–51.

Pun, Ngai 潘毅, Huilin Lu 卢晖临 and Huipeng Zhang 张慧鹏 (2010) *Dagong dishang: Zhongguo nongmingong zhige* 大工地上: 中国农民工之歌 (*On the big construction sites: The song of the migrant workers in China*), Shangwu yinshu guan 商务印书馆. Hong Kong: Commercial Press.

Pun, Ngai, and Jack Qiu (2020) '"Emotional authoritarianism": state, education and the mobile working-class subjects', *Mobilities*, 15(4), pp. 620–34.

Qian, Yijun 钱怡君 (2016) 'Xianggang rendui weilai de kongju, shinian chongman buan' 香港人对未来的恐惧, 《十年》充满不安 ('Hong Kong people's fear of the future: The film *Ten Years* is full of anxiety'), *TVBS News*, 4 April, http://news.tvbs.com.tw/china/647713.

Qiang, Shigong 强世功 (2008) *Zhongguo xianggang: Zhengzhi yu wenhua de shijiao* 中国香港: 政治与文化的视角 (*Hong Kong, China: A political and cultural perspective*), Niujin daxue chubanshe (zhongguo) 牛津大学出版社（中国）. Hong Kong: Oxford University Press.

Reed, Thomas Vernon (2005) *The art of protest: Culture and activism from the civil rights movement to the streets of Seattle*. Minnesota: University of Minnesota Press.

Ren, Hai (2010) *Neoliberalism and culture in China and Hong Kong: The countdown of time*. London and New York: Routledge.

Ren, Xuefei (2013) *Urban China*. Cambridge: Polity.

Robin, Corey (2004) *Fear: The history of a political idea*. Oxford: Oxford University Press.

Robinson, Jenefer (2005) *Deeper than reason*. Oxford: Clarendon Press.

Rofel, Lisa (2007) *Desiring China: Experiments in neoliberalism, sexuality, and public culture*. Durham, NC: Duke University Press.

Rosen, Stanley (2010) 'Chinese youth and state-society relations', in Dan

Lynch and Stanley Rosen (eds) *Chinese politics: State, society and the market*. London and New York: Routledge, pp. 160–78.

RTHK31 (2016) '*Ten Years* wins Best Film award, what are the implications for the industry?' *RTHK31*, 5 April, https://www.facebook.com/pg /rthk31thisweek/videos/.

Rucht, Dieter (2016) 'Protest cultures in social movements', in Kathrin Fahlenbrach, Martin Klimke and Joachim Scharloth (eds) *Protest Cultures*. New York: Berghahn, pp. 699–826.

Sabsay, Leticia (2020) 'Beyond populist borders: embodiment and the people in Laclau's Political Ontology', *Theory and Event*, 23(3), pp. 810–33.

Saich, A. (2004) *Governance and politics in China*, second edition. London: Palgrave Macmillan.

Sanjiaojun 三角君 (2020) 'Ganggang, Li Wenliang de weibo xiafang, fashengle guiyi yimu' 刚刚，李文亮的微博下方，发生了诡异一幕 ('Just now, a strange scene took place under Wen-Liang Li's microblog'), *Daily Headlines*, 20 June, https://kknews.cc/zh-sg/news/9v8nkbl.html.

Scheff, Thomas J. (1990) *Microsociology: Discourse, emotion and social structure*. Chicago: University of Chicago Press.

Scheff, Thomas J. (1994) *Bloody revenge*. Boulder, CO: Westview Press.

Scheff, Thomas J. (1997) *Emotions, the social bond, and human reality: Part/whole analysis*. Cambridge: Cambridge University Press.

Schell, Orville (2022) 'Xi's shattered illusion of control', *Foreign Affairs*, 5 December, https://www.foreignaffairs.com/china/xi-shattered-illusion -control-protests-revive-chinese-dissent.

Schmitt, Carl (1996) *The concept of the political*. Translated by George Schwab. Chicago: University of Chicago Press.

Schuman, Michael (2022) 'China's zero tolerance for Xi's COVID restrictions', *Atlantic*, 29 November, https://www.theatlantic.com/intern ational/archive/2022/11/china-zero-covid-protests-xi-jinping-shanghai -beijing/672278/.

Shalhoub-Kevorkian, Nadera (2015) *Security, theology, surveillance and the politics of fear*. Cambridge: Cambridge University Press.

Shenzhen Media Group 壹深圳 (2020) 'Meigeren de zhanzheng: Zhongzhi chengcheng kang"yi", women yizhi douzai' 《每个人的战争》 – 众志成城抗 "疫"，我们一直都在 ('Everyone's war – United efforts to fight the "pandemic", we have always been here') *Sina*, 14 February, http://sh enzhen.sina.com.cn/news/n/2020-02-14/detail-iimxyqvz2798918.shtml.

Shi, Jingnan 史竞男, Ying Bai 白瀛, Yang Wang 王阳 and Manzi Zhang 张漫子 (2017) 'Weishenme shi "zhanlang II"? Zhongguo dianying piaofang xingao de qishi' 为什么是"战狼II"⊠中国电影票房新高的启示 ('Why is *Wolf Warrior II*?: A revelation for the highest Chinese movie box office'), *Xinhuanet*, 15 August, http://news.xinhuanet.com/politics/2017-08/15 /c_1121485735htm.

Shi, Wei 史唯 (2007) 'Taiwan xindianying zhongde zhongguo xiangxiang' 台湾新电影中的中国想象' ('Imagination of China in Taiwan's new films'), in Hao Zhidong 郝志东 (ed.) *Guojia rentong yu liangan weilai* 国家认同与两岸未来 (*National identity and the future of cross-Strait relations*), Aomen daxue chubanshe 澳门大学出版社. Macau: Macau University Press, pp. 87–105.

Shi, Wei (2008) 'Undoing Chineseness in contemporary Chinese cinemas', PhD dissertation, Department of Communications, Goldsmiths College, University of London.

Shih, Sheng Mei (1999) 'Gender and a geopolitics of desire: The seduction of mainland women in Taiwan and Hong Kong media', in Mayfair Mei-hui Yang (ed.) *Spaces of their own: Women's public sphere in transnational China*. Minneapolis and London: University of Minnesota Press, pp. 278–307.

Shushangdemiaowu 树上的喵呜 (2022) 'Zhengzhou fushikang yiqing zhuangkuang daodi zenyang? Zaichang de yiwei yanjiusheng rushishuo' 郑州富士康疫情状况到底怎么样？在厂的一位研究生如是说 . . . ('What is the status of the Zhengzhou Foxconn epidemic situation? A graduate student at the factory said so . . .')[quoted from Bai Jiahao], *WeChat Public Platform*, 29 October, https://mp.weixin.qq.com/s/iEo_d2JS-b0O DWWBhVAjAQ?v_p=90&WBAPIAnalysisOriUICodes=10000011_10 000011&launchid=10000365--x&wm=3333_2001&aid=01A8mGVJi sVzLsSZ50UAuer9RTGGpOPf91Nm43GsEKVNIk5MQ.&from=10C A293010.

Sina.cn 新浪网 (2020) 'Wuhan geli: Yiqu, xinxi gudao yu yiliang e A che de piaoliu' 武汉隔离：疫区、信息孤岛与一辆鄂 A 车的漂流 ('Wuhan quarantine: Epidemic area, information island and the drift of a car from Wuhan'). *Sina.cn*, 28 January, https://k.sina.cn/article_5892736543_15f 3c061f0190015kb.html?from=news&subch=onews.

Skopeliti, Clea (2022) '"Now I see it's not just me who's angry": Readers in China on wave of protests', *Guardian*, 6 December, https:// www.theguardian.com/world/2022/dec/06/readers-in-china-on-wave-of-protests.

Smaill, Belinda (2010) *The documentary: Politics, emotion, culture.* London: Palgrave Macmillan.

Solinger, Dorothy J. (1995) 'The floating population in the cities: Chances for assimilation?' in Deborah S. Davis, Richard Kraus, Barry Naughton and Elizabeth J. Perry (eds) *Urban spaces in contemporary China: The potential for autonomy and community in post-Mao China*. Cambridge: Cambridge University Press, pp. 113–39.

Song, Lin, and Shih-Diing Liu (2022) 'Demobilising and reorienting online emotions: China's emotional governance during the COVID-19 outbreak', *Asian Studies Review*, DOI: 10.1080/10357823.2022.2098254.

Song, Xianlin, and Gary Sigley (2000) 'Middle Kingdom mentalities: Chinese visions of national characteristics in the 1990s', *Communal/Plural: Journal of Transnational and Cross-Cultural Studies*, 8(1), pp. 47–64.

Sorace, Christian (2019) 'Extracting affect: Televised cadre confessions in China', *Public Culture*, 31(1), pp. 145–71.

Standing, Guy (2017) 'The precariat in China: A comment on conceptual confusion', *Rural China*, 14(1), pp. 165–70.

Stavrakakis, Yannis (2007) *Lacanian left: Psychoanalysis, theory, politics*. Edinburgh: Edinburgh University Press.

Su, Ning 苏宁 (2017) 'Diyidai nongmingong laole, shuineng wei tamen yanglao?' 第一代农民工老了，谁能为他们养老？('The first generation of peasant workers, who can take care of them?'), *Sohu.com*, 4 June, http://www.sohu.com/a/146003294_507132.

Sun, Ge 孙歌 (2002) *Zhuti misan de kongjian: Yazhou lunshu zhi liangnan* 主体弥散的空间：亚洲论述之两难 (*Space of subject-dissipation: Dilemma of Asian discourse*), Jiangxi jiaoyu chubanshe 江西教育出版社. Nanchang: Jiangxi Education Publishing House.

Sun, Li 孙黎 and Ma Zhonghong 马中红 (2019) 'Xiaozhen qingnian de "kuaishou" shijie: Chengxiang guanxi de geti xushi yu qinggan biaoda' 小镇青年的 "快手" 世界：城乡关系的个体叙事与情感表达 ('The "kaishou" world of small town youth: Individual narrative and emotional expression of urban–rural relations'), *Zhongguo qingnian yanjiu* 中国青年研究 (*China Youth Study*), 11, pp. 29–36.

Sun, Wanning (2014) *Subaltern China: Rural migrants, media, and cultural practices*. London: Rowman and Littlefield.

Tang, Lijun (2009) 'Shaping feelings in cyberspace: The case of Chinese seafarer-partners', *Emotion, Space and Society*, 2(2), pp. 104–10.

Tanner, Eliza (2001) 'Chilean conversations: Internet forum participants debate Augusto Pinochet's detention', *Journal of Communication*, 51(2), pp. 383–403.

Teo, Stephen (1997) *Hong Kong: The extra dimensions*. London: British Film Institute.

Ter Haar, B. J. (1996) 'China's inner demons', *China Information*, 11(2/3), pp. 54–88.

The Economist (2023) 'China is still punishing those who protested against zero-covid', 12 January, https://www.economist.com/china/2023/01/12/china-is-still-punishing-those-who-protested-against-zero-covid.

Thompson, Simon (2006) 'Anger and the struggle for justice', in Simon Clarke, Paul Hoggett and Simon Thompson (eds) *Emotion, politics and society*. London: Palgrave Macmillan, pp. 123–44.

Thompson, Simon, and Paul Hoggett (2012) 'Introduction', in Paul

Hoggett and Simon Thompson (eds) *Politics and the emotions: The affective turn in contemporary political studies*. New York: Continuum, pp. 1–19.

Tismaneanu, Vladimir (2013) 'Ideological erosion and the breakdown of communist regimes', in Martin K. Dimitrov (ed.) *Why communism did not collapse: Understanding authoritarian regime resilience in asia and europe*. Cambridge: Cambridge University Press, pp. 67–98.

Tong, Jingrong (2015) 'The formation of an agonistic public sphere: Emotions, the Internet, and news media in China', *China Information*, 29(3), pp. 333–51.

True Exploration of Jellyfish 水母真探 (2020) 'Nanyi zhixin! Li Wenliang de weibo xiafang, dansheng le hulianwang qiji' 难以置信！李文亮的微博下方，诞生了互联网的奇迹 ('Unbelievable! Miracle of the Internet under Wen-Liang Li's microblog'). *True Exploration of Jellyfish*, 12 March, https://mp.weixin.qq.com/s/QTh3ExvxEgyg0EB-Apk5qg.

Wang, Chih-Ming (2017) 'Introduction', in Chih-Ming Wang and Daniel P. S. Goh (eds) *Precarious belongings: Affect and nationalism in Asia*. London: Rowman and Littlefield, pp. vii–xxi.

Wang, Xiaojuan 王小娟 (2017) *Dianshi zongyi jiemu zhongde gonggong lingyu jianshe yanjiu* 电视综艺节目中的公共领域建设研究：以当代中国电视真人秀为例 (*Research on public sphere construction in TV variety show: Taking contemporary Chinese TV reality show as an example*), Kexue chubanshe 科学出版社. Beijing: China Science Publishing and Media.

Wang, Hui (2003) *China's new order: Society, politics, and economy in transition*. Cambridge, MA: Harvard University Press.

Wang, Rui 王蕊 (2016) Huanqiu shibao: Shinian xiahu xianggang shehui, neidi guanbuliao 环球时报：《十年》吓唬香港社会，内地管不了 ('Global Times: *Ten Years* scares the Hong Kong community, for which the Mainland cannot control'), *Sohu News*, 22 January, http: //star.news.sohu.com/20160122/n435441719.shtml.

Wang, Vivian (2022) 'A protest? A vigil? In Beijing, anxious crowds are unsure how far to go', *Japanese Times*, 29 November, https://www.japantimes.co.jp/news/2022/11/29/asia-pacific/china-protests-how-far/.

Wang, Xiaoming 王晓明 (2003) *Banzhang lian: Zhongguo de xinyishi xingtai* 半张脸：中国的新意识形态 (*Half a face: China's new ideology*), Niujin daxue chubanshe (zhongguo) 牛津大学出版社（中国）. Hong Kong: Oxford University Press.

Wang, Zheng (2012) *Never forget national humiliation: Historical memory in Chinese politics and foreign relations*. New York: Columbia University Press.

Watkins, Megan (2010) 'Desiring recognition, accumulating affect', in

Melissa Gregg and Gregory J. Seigworth (eds) *The affect theory reader*. Durham, NC: Duke University Press, pp. 269–85.

Williams, Raymond (1975) *The long revolution*. Westport, CT: Greenwood Press.

Williams, Raymond (1979) *Politics and letters: Interviews with New Left Review*. London: New Left Books.

Wong, John, and Yongnian Zheng (2000) 'Nationalism and its dilemma: Chinese responses to embassy bombing', in Wang Gungwu and Zheng Yongnian (eds) *Reform, legitimacy and dilemmas: China's politics and society*, Singapore: Singapore University Press and World Scientific, pp. 321–43.

Wu, Guo (2013) 'The social construction and deconstruction of evil landlords in contemporary Chinese fiction, art, and collective memory', *Modern Chinese Literature and Culture*, 25(1), pp. 131–64.

Wu, Haiyun (2017) 'How blockbuster war movies capture China's changing nationalism', *Sixth Tone*, 15 August, https://chinafilminsider.com/how-blockbuster-war-movies-capture-chinas-changing-nationalism/.

Wu, Qingqing 吴青青 (2017) 'Leixing dingwei, zhongguo xiangxiang he wenhua dingwei' 类型定位, 中国想象和文化定位 ('Type orientation, Chinese imagination and cultural orientation'), *Dianying pingjie* 电影评介 (*Movie Review*), 13, pp. 11–14.

Xiang, Zairong (2017) 'Toxic masculinity with Chinese characteristics', *Cultural Studies*, 25, pp. 260–1.

Xiao, Zibang (2022) 'Chinese public shows mixed emotions about Covid zero ending', *Bloomberg*, 27 December, https://www.bloomberg.com/news/articles/2022-12-27/chinese-public-shows-mixed-emotions-about-covid-zero-ending.

Xilisheng 犀利声 (2020) 'Yiwei gaozhongsheng gei "Fangfang ayi" de xin 一位高中生给 "方方阿姨" 的信 ('Letter from a senior high school student to "Aunt Fang Fang"'), 17 March, https://mp.weixin.qq.com/s/EMvF9P930L_9eiqyIZbG0w.

Xu, Jilin (2018) *Homeland: Individual, state and world identity in modern China*. Hong Kong: Joint Publishing.

Yang, Guobin (2000) 'Achieving emotions in collective action: Emotional processes and movement mobilization in the 1989 Chinese student movement', *Sociological Quarterly*, 41(4), pp. 593–614.

Yang, Guobin (2005) 'Emotional events and the transformation of collective action: The Chinese student movement', in Helena Fram and Debra King (eds) *Emotions and social movement*. London: Routledge, pp. 79–98.

Yang, Guobin (2009) *The power of the Internet in China: Citizen activism online*. New York: Columbia University Press.

Yang, Guobin (2018) 'Demobilizing the emotions of online activism in

China: A civilizing process', *International Journal of Communication*, 12, pp. 1945–65.

Yang, Guobin (2022) *The Wuhan lockdown*. New York: Columbia University Press.

Yang, Guobin, and Shiwen Wu (2018) 'Remembering disappeared websites in China: Passion, community, and youth', *New Media and Society*, 20(6), pp. 2107–24.

Yang, Jie (2014) *The political economy of affect and emotion in East Asia*. London and New York: Routledge.

Yang, Jisheng 杨继绳 (2013) *Zhongguo dangdai shehui jieceng fenxi* 中国当代社会阶层分析 (*Chinese contemporary social strata analysis*). Jiangxi gaoxiao chubanshe 江西高校出版社. Jiangxi: Jiangxi Universities and Colleges Press.

Yang, Kai (2023) 'Beyond parochial activism: Cross-regional protests and the changing landscape of popular contention in China', *Journal of Contemporary China*, 32(140), pp. 280–95.

Yau, Esther (1994) 'Border crossing: Mainland China's presence in Hong Kong cinema', in Nick Browne, Paul G. Pickowicz, Vivian Sobchack and Esther Yau (eds) *New Chinese cinemas: Forms, identities, politics*. Cambridge: Cambridge University, pp. 180–201.

Yin, Hong (2017) '"Wolf Warrior II' ignites the Chinese people's passion for war hawk patriotism" [Quoted from Bailiang Chu], *New York Times Chinese Edition*, 17 August, https://cn.nytimes.com/china/20170817/china-wolf-warrior-2-film/zh-hant/.

Yin, Hong 尹鸿 (1998) 'Zai jiafeng zhong zhangda: Zhongguo dalu xinshengdai de dianying shijie' 在夹缝中长大：中国大陆新生代的电影世界 ('Growing up in the cracks: The new generation of movie world in mainland China'), *Ershiyi shiji* 二十一世纪 (*The Twenty-First Century*), 49, pp. 88–93.

Yong, Xiong, Hande Atay Alam and Nectar Gan (2020) 'Wuhan hospital announces death of whistleblower doctor Li Wenliang', *CNN*, 7 July, https://edition.cnn.com/2020/02/06/asia/li-wenliang-coronavirus-whistleblower-doctor-dies-intl/index.html.

Young, Iris Marion (1990) *Justice and the politics of difference*. Princeton, NJ: Princeton University Press.

Yuan, Guangfeng (2021) 'Towards a theoretical path of "practice": Understanding the expression of emotion in public opinion', *Chinese Journal of Journalism and Communication*, 6, pp. 55–72.

Yuan, Li 袁莉 (2020) 'Dang Li Wenliang de weibo chengwei zhongguo de kuqiang' 当李文亮的微博成为中国的哭墙 ('When Wen-Liang Li's Weibo became China's Wailing Wall'), *New York Times*, 14 April, https://cn.nytimes.com/china/20200414/coronavirus-doctor-whistleblower-weibo/zh-hant/.

Zeng, Yuli 曾于里 (2017) '"Zhanlang II" de juli yu "jianjun daye" de juxing' "战狼II"的聚力与"建军大业"的聚星 ('Cohesive forces of "Wolf Warrior II" and gathering of stars in "The Founding of an Army"'), *Jiefang Daily: People's Net*, 3 August, http://media.people.com.cn/BIG5/n1/2017/0803/c40606-29445952.html.

Zhang, Ding 张定 (2016) 'Xianggang shinian kongju deshi shenme?' 香港《十年》恐惧的是什么？ ('What is the fear of *Ten Years* of Hong Kong?'), *The Udnnews*, 13 May, https://udn.com/news/story/6846/1692024.

Zhang, Huiyu (2014) *Contemporary China's cultural imagination and social reconstruction*, Guangzhou: Sun Yat-Sen University Press.

Zhang, Huiyu 张慧瑜 (2017) 'Zhanlang II de "qiji" beihou' 《战狼2》的"奇迹"背后 ('Behind the "miracle" of "Wolf Warrior II"'), *Sohu.com*, 17 September, http://www.sohu.com/a/192408526_550962.

Zhang, Li (2001) *Strangers in the city: Reconfigurations of space, power, and social networks within China's floating population*. Palo Alto, CA: Stanford University Press.

Zhang, Meiyue 张美悦, Ruiyang Li 李瑞洋 and Ruowa Zhang 张若洼 (2020) 'Zhongguo "kuqiang": Li Wenliang weibo xiade 90 wantiao liuyan' 中国"哭墙"：李文亮微博下的 90 万条留言 ('China "wailing wall": 900,000 messages on Wen-Liang Li's Weibo'), *Initium Media*, 5 May, https://nei.st/medium/initium/coronavirus-liwenliang-weibo-wailing-wall.

Zhang, Xudong (2001) 'Nationalism, mass culture, and intellectual strategies in post-Tiananmen China', in Xudong Zhang (ed.) *Whither China? Intellectual politics in contemporary China*. Durham, NC: Duke University Press.

Zhang, Yulin 张玉林 (2012) *Liudong yu wajie: Zhongguo nongcun de yanbian jiqi dongli* 流动与瓦解：中国农村的演变及其动力 (*Flow and disintegration: The evolution and dynamics of rural China*), Zhongguo shehui kexue chubanshe 中国社会科学出版社 Beijing: China Social Sciences Press.

Zhang, Zhen (2007) *Urban generation: Chinese cinema and society at the turn of the twenty-first century*. London: Duke University Press.

Zheng, Changren 郑昶人 (2020) 'Bierang putongren Li Wenliang, jinjin chengwei tizhi benghuai de zhujiao' 别让普通人李文亮，仅仅成为体制崩坏的注脚 ('Don't let ordinary person Wen-Liang Li just become a footnote to the collapse of the system'), *Initium Media*, 7 February, https://theinitium.com/article/20200207-in-memory-of-li-wen-yuan/?from=singlemessage&isappinstalled=0.

Zheng, Shengtian (2008) 'Art and revolution', in Melissa Chiu and Zheng Shengtian (eds) *Art and China's revolution*. New Haven, CT: Yale University Press, pp. 19–39.

Zheng, Wang (2003) 'Gender, employment and women's resistance', in Elizabeth J. Perry and Mark Selden (eds) *Chinese society: Change, conflict, and resistance*, second edition. London and New York: Routledge, pp. 162–86.

Zheng, Yongnian 郑永年 (2001) 'Zhongguo xinyibo minzu zhuyi: Genyuan, guocheng he qianjing' 中国新一波民族主义——根源、过程和前景 ('China's new wave of nationalism: Origin, process and prospect'), in Lin Jialong 林佳龙 and Zheng Yongnian 郑永年 (eds) *Minzu zhuyi yu liangan guanxi* 民族主义与两岸关系 (*Nationalism and Cross-Strait Relations*), Xin Ziran Zhuyi 新自然主义 Taipei: Green Futures Publishing Company, pp. 35.

Zheng, Yongnian (2012) 'China in 2011: Anger, political consciousness, anxiety, and uncertainty', *Asian Survey*, 52(1), pp. 28–41.

Zhou, Baohua 周葆华 and Yuan Zhong 钟媛 (2021) '"Chuntian de huakai qiutian de feng": Shejiao meiti, jiti daonian yu yanzhanxing qinggan kongjian: Yi Li Wenliang de weibo pinglun (2020–2021) weili de jisuan chuanbo fenxi' "春天的花开秋天的风"：社交媒体、集体悼念与延展性情感空间——以李文亮微博评论（2020–2021）为例的计算传播分析', ['Social media, collective mourning and extended affective space: A computational communication analysis of Li Wenliang's Weibo comments (2020–2021)']. *Guoji xinwen jie* 国际新闻界 (*Chinese Journal of Journalism and Communication*), 43(3), pp. 79–106.

Zhou, Haiyan 周海燕 (2020) 'Qinlizhe koushu: Cong geti xushi dao shehui xingdong' 亲历者口述：从个体叙事到社会行动 ('Experiencer's oral narration: From individual narrative to social action'), *Tansuo yu zhengming* 探索与争鸣 (*Exploration and free views*), 2020(4), pp. 244–51.

Zhou, Li, Lu Cai and Yinjiao Ye (2019) 'Online emotional expression in response to an emergency: A sentiment analysis of public discourse on micro-blogs in response to a heavy rainfall in Wuhan, China', *China Media Research*, 15(1), pp. 52–66.

Zhou, Xing 周星 (2017) 'Zhanlang II weihe ruci chenggong?' 《战狼2》为何如此成功? ('Why is Wolf Warrior II so successful?'), *Financial Street Online*, 10 August, https://kknews.cc/entertainment/l6vg25e.html.

Žižek, Slavoj (1994) *Mapping ideology*. London: Verso.

Žižek, Slavoj (2007) 'Introduction', in Mao Zedong (ed.) *On practice and contradiction*. London: Verso.

Zou, Songhua 邹颂华 (2016) 'Xianggang guancha: Dianying shinian xiaoying' 香港观察：电影《十年》效应' ('Hong Kong watch: The effect of the film *Ten Years*'), *BBC Chinese Web*, 12 April, http://www.bbc.com/zhongwen/trad/hong_kong_review/2016/04/160412_hkreview_hk-film_ten_years.

Index

A page number in *italics* shows a figure.

217

EU representative:
Easy Access System Europe
Mustamäe tee 50, 10621 Tallinn, Estonia
Gpsr.requests@easproject.com

www.ingramcontent.com/pod-product-compliance
Lightning Source LLC
Chambersburg PA
CBHW050648270326
41927CB00012B/2930